▲▲▲

THE HIGH VALLEY

THE HIGH VALLEY

▲▲

KENNETH E. READ

Illustrated with Photographs and Maps

COLUMBIA UNIVERSITY PRESS

New York

Columbia University Press
New York   Guildford, Surrey

Columbia University Press Morningside Edition 1980
This edition reprinted by arrangement with Charles Scribner's Sons
Preface to the Morningside Edition Copyright © Columbia University
Press 1980

Printed in the United States of America
10 9

For Michael, with love

PREFACE TO THE MORNINGSIDE EDITION

It is fourteen years since the first edition of *The High Valley* was published and twenty-nine years since I began the field work on which the book is based. This new edition gives me the opportunity to add some thoughts about the work and a little more information about the people who appear in it.

I have not been back to the Gahuku-Gama or to the village of Susuroka since I left New Guinea at the end of 1952, but I have not lost all contact with people whom I knew there. Goroka, the nearest government station, had no more than fifteen permanent white residents when I arrived to begin my work. It is now a flourishing town of considerable size with hotels and other amenities that could only be imagined in 1950. It is possible to visit Goroka on packaged tours from the United States; and over the years, strangers who have made the journey have helped me keep in touch with people whom I knew more than a generation ago. Some of these tourists have written to me telling me that they took my book with them and, using its maps, managed to find their way to the village where I lived with Makis, and that they spoke to people who appear in its pages as well as others who were only toddlers when I was there. They have also told me that the book is *there*—in the village. It has been brought out, carefully wrapped, and still probably unread, for them to see; and it has given me a particularly warm feeling to know it is where it belongs and that young people may read it in the future and may, perhaps, learn some things they did not know about the past from which they came.

The messages transmitted by these tourists from the distance of half a world and more than half a lifetime have been either personal notes dictated to them in pidjin English or tape-recorded casettes on which my Gahuku friends speak to me in their own language. Unfortunately, I have lost all the Gahuku I knew, and I cannot recognize more than a few honorific phrases of address. But the living voices are there, as they will always be, until I have no memory; for the time I lived with them is still close to me, still so sharp and vividly recalled that I can dissolve the walls of my present house in a flash and place myself again in the center of the bare village street among the cloudscapes casting their moving sea-shadows on the mountains; among the early morning mists rising from the gardens; and among the clamor of voices and the pride of stamping feet that carried me away—beyond and outside myself—on the great occasions of the life I was privileged to observe and, in some sense, share. The villagers of Susuroka, Gehamo, and Ekuhakuka do not know what they gave me; for the last and most difficult lesson was one you do not flaunt like a banner and cannot express in the conventions of academic prose.

My friend and mentor, my Gahuku "elder brother," Makis is dead. He was killed most uselessly and most ironically by a truck as he was returning to his village one evening along the Highland Highway—the "main road," mentioned in the book, where I often walked with him when it was little more than a track. His death, according to a report I received at the time, caused a great and potentially dangerous commotion at Goroka, for the driver of the truck and its other occupants were not Gahuku, and old enmities complicated reaching agreement on the amount of the indemnity owing to his group for the loss of such an important man. Makis is buried at Susuroka, and people who never knew him go there to view his grave which, I am told, is honored with a fenced enclosure and a commorative plaque, surely the first of this kind to be erected for the dead among the Gahuku. I am glad he is remembered in this way. In his time, and with far fewer charts than many of us possess, he had ventured toward the future: a voyager sailing close to the eye of a hurricane that would sweep over his people with changes that others have had centuries rather than a mere decade to assimilate. I keep the hope that I will be able to make my own pilgrimage to the place where he lies, but it does not matter if this never comes to pass. He is not forgotten as long as I live and as long as his people remember him.

Asemo, Hunehune, Zaho, and Tarova are still among us. Perhaps I should not say anything more about them, for they have gone on to make lives on which I have no right to comment—if, indeed, I had that right in the beginning. But perhaps I can say that Zaho is presently an elected official in the government structure of Papua-New Guinea, and that Tarova's first marriage did not last.

She quickly returned to the warmth and affection of her extended family who had not wanted her to go but who were constrained to acquiesce by rules and obligations built into the structure of intergroup relationships.

I am not sure that I ever had the right to mention living people by name and to attribute to them characteristics that are based mainly on intuition or are extrapolated from the frames of reference developed for such matters in our own culture. I have not resolved this question, but I would rather err on the side of a common humanity than strip away the flesh and examine only the bones and the precise ways in which they are articulated.

All readers of *The High Valley* should be advised that it is not and never was meant to be a conventional ethnography. It is essentially a journey toward some inconclusive state of knowing: the record of a dialectic between one kind of person and other kinds of persons as, with good will and certainly different motivations, they try to reach a reasonable accommodation.

Before putting the first words of *The High Valley* on paper, I had decided that it would be an experiment in ethnography, faithful to what I had been able to learn about the formal properties of Gahuku life but also including many of my subjective reactions to it. I did not want to intrude too much, but I wanted to convey something of the interior processes that are inextricably involved in producing good ethnographies. It was the latter dimension that caused me the most uncertainty (delaying the completion of the book for at least seven years) and that often led me to apologize for what I was doing when colleagues asked me about my work in progress, for I had ample reasons to believe that if I told them the truth they would have dismissed the enterprise as unscientific—as popularization. Some other anthropologists before me had faced the same accusation, and a few of them tried to avoid it either by publishing under pseudonyms or presenting their material in the guise of fiction. I rejected both these alternatives because I felt it was time to say something about the essence of the anthropological experience, an experience that is like no other and that has a human value transcending the generation of theories and the development and testing of hypotheses. The essence of the experience is being able to find your way between and to live with different systems of the human imagination, the one you bring to the field as a creature of your own culture and the one your subjects bring to bear on the same basic phenomena. All cultures, without a single exception, are systems of the imagination that we are nevertheless taught to accept as real; and the multitude of their differences testifies to the fertility of one of the few qualities that distinguish men from other animals. Though they often seem to be unaware of it, all the social sciences depend on data that are products or expressions of the human imagination, and all the theories associated with them are imaginative abstractions.

Since the first publication of my book (1965), it has become a little more acceptable in anthropology to address some of the personal epistemological questions it raises indirectly (and be sure I do not suggest any causal connection). Among the most recent of the genre, I recommend Jean-Paul Dumont's *The Headman and I* (University of Texas Press, 1979). I have found it to be a marvelous book and one that gives a greater scholarly attention to the processes of "knowing" I tried to convey in my work.

Lastly, I must say that I had another goal in writing this book, one that it may seem pretentious even to mention: in the final analysis, I wanted it to stand on its own as a work of literary art, hoping that readers who had no connection with anthropology might find that it touched some shared emotional and aesthetic chords. I shall say no more about this dimension except to thank reviewers who recognized my intention and found some merit in it on the precise grounds I had hoped it might be judged.

Kenneth E. Read
Seattle, Washington
1979

PREFACE

▲▲▲▲▲

This book is a personal record of almost two years of field work among the Gahuku tribes of the Australian Trust Territory of New Guinea. I went to the Gahuku as a social anthropologist. Yet what is set down here is not contained easily within the customary boundaries of that discipline. For this is frankly a subjective work rather than a scientific treatise. Any similarly situated anthropologist, alone in an exotic culture for a considerable length of time, could undoubtedly write a comparable record; yet it is seldom done, and, to my mind, this is a loss. The field-working anthropologist undergoes a unique experience; no one else knows quite so personally what it is like to live in an entirely alien culture. Missionaries do not know; government officials do not know; traders and explorers do not know. Only the anthropologist wants nothing from the people with whom he lives—nothing, that is, but information, nothing but an understanding of and an appreciation for the texture of their lives. And this comes from a kind of training, requires a closeness of contact, that are both his objective and his special possession.

Why, then, is so much anthropological writing so antiseptic, so devoid of anything that brings a people to life? There they are, pinned like butterflies in a glass case, with the difference, however, that we often cannot tell what color these specimens are; and we are never shown them in flight, never see them soar or die except in generalities. The reason for this lies in the aims of anthropology, whose concern with the particular is incidental to an understanding of the general.

This is the way in which all systems of knowledge are built. But it is only one part of the process of knowing; the other is personal. A particular individual—of some particular background, of this or that quality of temperament, formed by some specific circumstances—meets and interacts with another individual whose eyes and mind have been differently formed, where, superficially, objectively, all that the two possess in common is that they are both "forked creatures." What this confrontation means is seldom told, lost in the pursuit of ends that transcend it; yet it is with the anthropologist in the field each day. It is the basic datum of his experience, and some cannot accommodate to

xi

the terms it imposes. This is the experience I have tried to record here, an expression of my personal imperative, that which led me into anthropology.

The volume owes a great deal to many people. The field work was carried out when I was a Research Fellow of the School of Pacific Studies of the Australian National University, and of all those at that institution I am particularly indebted to the late Professor S. F. Nadel. He was the intellectual mentor of my years as a graduate student. Dr. H. Ian Hogbin, Reader in Anthropology at the University of Sydney, was my first teacher in anthropology. He introduced me to the peoples of Melanesia and New Guinea, and no one could have done it better. No other person has reported so sensitively and so graciously on an area of the world that became my own abiding interest. He taught me to appreciate its people as individuals.

Many other friends and colleagues have read the manuscript and have given me encouragement. I am particularly grateful to Professor Melford E. Spiro and to his wife Audrey Spiro, to Isabel S. Caro, Dr. Luyse Kollnhofer, Dr. Walter Fairservis, Jr., Dr. Lewis L. Langness, Mr. E. Hollis Mentzer and Mr. Toby Oldfield. I am indebted to Mr. Kerry J. Pataki for the maps; to Mrs. Virginia Lewis, Mrs. Aline Carlson, and Mrs. Margaret Cook for typing and proofreading the manuscript; to many of my students at the University of Washington, the University of British Columbia, and the University of Hawaii who wanted to know more about the Gahuku. I hope that the book repays them all, in some measure, for their interest.

Among those I knew in New Guinea, I owe a special debt to the late Dudley Young-Whitforde who took me to Susuroka, the village of Makis. I received many kindnesses from the District Commissioner at Goroka, Mr. George Greathead, from Mr. James Leahy, and, during my illness, from Dr. Talis Rubins and Dr. Ken Meehan. But the greatest debt of all is owed to the Gahuku, the people of Susuroka, Gohajaka, Gehamo, and Meniharove—those who appear in the pages of the book and many others who are not mentioned by name. I shall never forget them.

None of my work, however, would have been possible without the encouragement and support of my parents. It is too late to thank them; I cannot return to them what they gave to me so willingly.

Honolulu, Hawaii KENNETH E. READ

CONTENTS
▲▲▲▲▲

LIST OF ILLUSTRATIONS
(following page 142)

A NOTE ON PEOPLE AND PLACES
▲▲▲▲▲

Pronunciation

In pronouncing the names of both places and people the following values should be given to vowels:

a	as in *father*	*o*	as in *cold*
e	like the "ay" of *may*	*u*	as in *rude*
i	like the "ee" of *heel*		

Thus, Makis is pronounced approximately "Ma'kees."

Tribes, Clans, and Villages

The name GAHUKU is used inclusively for a number of separate tribes in the Asaro Valley in the Eastern Highlands of the Australian Trust Territory of New Guinea. The Gahuku tribes mentioned in the book are:

ASARODZUHA	GEHAMO	NOTOHANA
GAMA	NAGAMIDZUHA	UHETO

Each of these tribes contains a number of named, patrilineal clans, a clan being a group of men and women who believe in their common descent through males from some common ancestor in the distant past. In the Nagamidzuha tribe there are two such clans:

OZAHADZUHA   MENIHAROVE

The members of these clans live in villages named:

SUSUROKA	EKUHAKUKA
GOHAJAKA	MENIHAROVE

In the Gehamo tribe there are two clans:

GOROHADZUHA   ANUPADZUHA

Gorohadzuha is also a village of the Gehamo tribe.

ASARODZUHA is a village (and also a clan) of the Asarodzuha tribe.

HUMELEVEKA is the site of an early government patrol post in the valley. It was replaced by the present town of GOROKA.

TOFMORA is a village in the Markham Valley, where the author lived in 1944–45.

People

Most of the people who are mentioned by name are members of the Nagamidzuha and Gehamo tribes. They are:

Members of the Nagamidzuha tribe

MAKIS (or URUGUSIE), a man of the Ozahadzuha clan,
　　the luluai (official headman) of Nagamidzuha
GOTOME, the senior wife of Makis
TOHO, the daughter of Makis and Gotome
MOHORASARO, the second wife of Makis
ALIMA, daughter of Makis and Mohorasaro
GUMA'E, third wife of Makis
LUSI, daughter of Makis and Guma'e
SUSURO, adopted son of Makis

MANIHA, a man of the Ozahadzuha clan,
　　an elder half-brother of Makis
ASEMO, son of Maniha

GIHIGUTE, an elder of the Ozahadzuha clan
TAROVA, daughter of Gihigute
HUTORNO, son of Gihigute

GESEKUNIMO, a man of the Ozahadzuha clan,
　　a younger half-brother of Makis

SESEKUME, an elder of the Ozahadzuha clan
HASU, a son of Sesekume

GUMILA, a girl betrothed to Hasu

NAMURI, a man of the Ozahadzuha clan
IZAZU, wife of Namuri
GIZA, son of Namuri and Izazu

BIHORE, a man of the Ozahadzuha clan,
a younger brother of Namuri

GASIETO, the luluai of the Meniharove clan
LOTUWA, son of Gasieto
KAMAHOE, wife of Lotuwa

HUNEHUNE, a young man of the Ozahadzuha clan

HELEKOHE, a man of the Ozahadzuha clan

HELEKAZU, a man of the Ozahadzuha clan

GAPIRIHA, a man of the Ozahadzuha clan

ALUM, an old woman of the Ozahadzuha clan

Members of the Gehamo tribe

ZAHO, a man of the Gorohadzuha clan
ILATO, the wife of Zaho, a member of the Ozahadzuha clan

HELAZU, mother of Ilato

GOLUWAIZO, a man of the Gorohadzuha clan,
the tul-tul (official assistant) to Makis

IHANIZO, a man of the Gorohadzuha clan

▲▲

THE HIGH VALLEY

INTRODUCTION

▲▲▲▲▲

In 1944 I was living in a village called Tofmora in the Upper Markham Valley in New Guinea. I was a member of the Australian armed forces but was engaged in work that is also my civilian occupation, social anthropology. The combination was not unusual during the war; yet it was largely by accident that I was in New Guinea at that time. Several months before I had completed two years of service in the north of Australia, and like many others who had been rushed there when the Japanese advance threatened the mainland, I had seen the war move farther and farther away while we seemed to have been forgotten. Then by chance I came across a newspaper report mentioning one of my former teachers in connection with military research in the islands of the Malay Archipelago. I wrote to him, asking if he had a place for me. Shortly afterward, I was recalled to Melbourne and within another month was at Lae, waiting to proceed up the Markham Valley.

I lived at Tofmora nearly ten months. Though nominally attached to the Australian New Guinea Administrative Unit, I saw less than a dozen other Europeans during the entire period. The research involved gathering information on native reactions to the war and the Japanese occupation, a charge that necessitated a thorough enquiry into most aspects of the people's lives. Few members of my profession have been so poorly equipped for field research. Only the barest minimum of supplies necessary to support me and to further my work was available: writing materials, the normal issue of army clothing, two cases of canned corned beef, some flour, hard biscuits, and a small chest, or caddy, of trade tobacco. Apart from ten Australian pounds, which I took with me in cash, I had only my corporal's pay, and was unable to draw on this until I returned to the coast. When I ran out of food, I existed for three months on whatever the villagers were willing to give me, for by then there was no money to buy the things I needed. Yet this was one of the happiest periods of my life.

3

In retrospect it is possible to distinguish many reasons why the experience was so rewarding, though when living through it there was no time to examine my reactions, nor to ask myself why I seemed to move so effortlessly with the rhythm of the days rather than against them. I was fortunate in the physical location of the place where I had chosen to live. The valley of the Markham River runs inland from the Huon Gulf in a northwesterly direction; it is a broad expanse of open country flanked on either side by uninterrupted ranges, whose uppermost heights are veiled perpetually in clouds. Because of the gentle slope to the sea—the highest extremity of the valley is less than a thousand feet in elevation—the course of the river is a maze of shifting channels that in the dry season usually are shallow and easily crossed. However, during the months of heavy rain, when it is overburdened by the volume of water fed to it by tributary streams, the river becomes a furious destructive force that inundates vast stretches of country. To try crossing it then is extremely hazardous. When events in other settlements compelled people to attempt it, they held their belongings above their heads and ran diagonally across the current, landing several hundred feet below their point of entry. Unable to swim, their survival depended upon an ability to remain upright in water that swirled around their necks. Even the most hardy refused to face the crossing at the peak of the wet season, when its dangers were compounded by boulders torn loose from the bed of the stream. Waking at night to hear the loud crack of these stones through the pouring rain, I had no doubt that they could crush the legs of anyone who was foolhardy enough to venture into the river.

Like most of the settlements in this area, Tofmora lay on the north side of the valley; it was the center of a chain of five villages spaced along a narrow strip of fertile territory where the Finisterre Mountains rose from the grasslands. The paths connecting inhabited sites ran through dense plantings of coconut palms whose fronds met overhead to form a vaulted ceiling thirty to fifty feet above the ground. Light penetrated only fitfully through this gently moving screen; even at midday the village was cool and shadowed, filled with a silence that seemed to ignore the crushing intensity of the sun vibrating in the open valley. Beyond the palms, groves of banana trees, a lighter more translucent green, encroached upon ochre-colored hills patched with scattered gardens of sweet potatoes, yams, and taro. These in turn gave way to tier upon receding tier of jungle covered heights. The stream Burubward rose inside this mass of tangled vegetation, and, slipping through the folds of the hills, approached within two hundred yards of the village. Its deep pools were my bathroom, overhung with leaves and bottomed with sand in which specks of mica shone like gold. Whenever I left the house with my towel, some small boy came with me to warn away the women at work in the nearby gardens, and while I swam he sat on the bank several feet from my clothes, studiously looking in the opposite direction.

The main route to the prewar government post of Kaiapit crossed the stream where I bathed. From there it mounted the bare hills for several miles until it reached a point where the Yafats River, a major tributary of the Markham, debouched out of its formidable gorge. This was a desolate, stony spot completely without shade or vegetation. Everything had been destroyed by the river, which, in flood, cascaded over the mountainside in a score of torrents. But the heights afforded an unexampled view of the whole valley. Returning from a day's walk in the ranges, tired, my skin inflamed and stiff from the sun, I often paused here to bathe my feet in the water. Gradually, my mind and body began to relax; and with the tension gone, the landscape rose toward me with the heart-catching loveliness of a distant cry. I was reminded of childhood times at the seaside when, standing on a bare reef, I had looked down into a pool and marveled at the gradations of color, the shades of jade, emerald, and cobalt; the miniature forests, lifting to the ocean's pulse; and the valleys of sand held in nets of suffused light. When I rose to continue my journey home the mood would not leave me. The day closed over my head as I began the descent, and thereafter I progressed through an unreal world where the ochre colors of grasslands and the varying greens of jungle and plantations flowed past me in gentle succession, completing the illusion that had commenced when I stood on the heights.

The day-to-day exhilaration informing this period of my life was due to something more than the beauty of my surroundings, however. I was continually aware of a sense of accomplishment; not only in my work, but also at a deeper, personal level the rewards were more than I had expected. Though I enjoy the company of others, I am not gregarious and do not find it easy to interact in the polite and superficial fashion that is generally expected of us. I had imagined that this reserve, which has prevented me from having large numbers of friends, would prove to be a severe handicap in a situation where success depended upon the personal rapport I was able to establish with the villagers. This fear was compounded because I had no idea what they might expect from me or how I ought to treat them. I knew not a word of their language, and their life was as different from anything with which I was familiar as the stone age is removed from us in time.

The first few days in Tofmora were among the most difficult I have faced, and even after several months I was often filled with despair. But gradually I began to respond to the villagers as individuals. It is not possible to say when this first occurred (perhaps when I found myself sitting with a man in the evening and realized that I had sought him simply for companionship and not because I wanted information), but the discovery has remained one of the most rewarding in my life.

I realize now that it is one of the benefits of my profession to experience this response to persons whose outlook and background could hardly be more dissimilar from my own. I can remember many of the villagers better than friends of only a short time ago; it is not necessary to try to recall their names. I was as much at ease with some of them as I have been with only a few other people. Yet I was not, and never could be one of them. Even in their midst, my life was entirely different from theirs, and I could not expect them to appreciate many of the things that concerned me deeply. Looking down on the village from one of the gardens, I visualized it in an aesthetic convention wholly foreign to the man who stood beside me with his arm around my shoulders; and though I might learn to see with his eyes, it was unlikely that he would ever see with mine. Yet this did not make the weight of his arm any less companionable; we did not have to have been born in the same environment to like each other. Indeed, their custom did not require that such emotions should be controlled and people held at a distance.

Looking back now, I believe I was permanently elated most of the time I was there. At least this is the only name I can give to a state of mind in which certainty in my own abilities and discovery of myself joined with a compassion for others and a gratitude for the lessons in acceptance that they taught me.

Yet my mind was not always on my work and the people around me. Sometimes in the afternoon, wanting to be alone for a while, I left my house to walk a short distance into the grasslands. As I passed from the palm grove to the open country, the light struck my face a visible blow, forcing me to close my eyes. Brought to a sudden stop, I was overcome by a spinning darkness. When I was again able to look, the great valley seemed to billow into the distance like a russet sea breaking against the escarpment of the southern chain of mountains. It was the most dramatic part of the territory, more even than the green silence of the jungle, where the infrequent cry of a bird exploded like an arrow in the stillness. In that bowl of pulsing light I was more keenly aware of the whole country, second in size only to Greenland among the world's islands, and of the character of the life within it. The multiplicity of peoples, divided by language, belief, and custom, are fastened in remote regions whose only entrance passes through the clouds, or they spend their days in houses built above the sea, where the air is heavy with the smell of kelp and where a child's first sight of the world is the moving brightness of watery reflections on thatched roof and plaited walls. The valley also recalled the enmities and suspicions that further separated these groups from one another; for it was here, not so very long ago, that men from Tofmora and its sister settlements set out to raid and kill, moving downwind through tall grasses that concealed their approach from their victim.

More and more often I thought of the people living nearby whose existence was patterned after a way of life that only the old men in Tofmora remembered. Occasionally some of them appeared from the mountains in the north to trade with us: men of Ibiaga, naked except for a G-string, whose presence set the dogs barking and brought my more sophisticated friends running from their gardens to gather patronizingly around the uneasy visitors.

But it was not the forests of these people that intrigued me. As I looked across the valley my eyes inevitably stopped at the escarpment forming its southern wall. Beyond that wall the country gathered into serried ranges, twisting and turning upon each other as though giant fingers had dabbled in sculptor's clay. A little more than a decade earlier, no European had penetrated to the other side of the mountains. Reports I had read told of the startling discovery made by a group of white prospectors in the early 1930's. Gold took them up the Ramu River, and climbing to its source, they came out in an upland region, five to six thousand feet above the sea, where fertile valleys preceded one another in an immense chain across the center of the island. Almost overnight, estimates of the country's population had to be doubled. Even in 1944, relatively few Europeans had been there, and the greater part of the area remained unknown, its peoples uncontrolled.

I may have decided at that time that I would go beyond the source of the Ramu. If I continued in my present occupation after the war, I would certainly return to New Guinea, and I was sure that then I wanted to be among people who had had less contact with Europeans than the Markham villagers. But at most it was only a vague promise that could not be fulfilled for several years. In any case, the prospect of my departure from Tofmora put an end to any plans for the future.

It has always been difficult for me to leave a place where I have been settled for some time, and it was not easy to walk away from Tofmora knowing that I was unlikely to see it again. I would not have wanted to remain indefinitely, but it was as if in this place I had tested myself and had discovered some personal resources that I had doubted I possessed. I knew now that I was capable of being alone, without others of my own kind, for a considerable length of time; that it was not some personal inadequacy, some failure to make the right response, that prevented me from experiencing the enthusiasms of most of my acquaintances. While I had not found the answers to the questions I asked, I had discovered that there were questions for which answers might be sought and felt myself better equipped to seek them. Some abiding friendships had also been made; they affected me the more deeply because there had seemed to be such little common ground on which to base a personal relationship. Though it was necessary to leave these friends I would never forget them. They were a part of my life from this time onward, and there have been few others to whom I owe so much of my inner development.

"When you go," Maiamuta, the headman of Tofmora, said to me once, "it will be as if you died. I will cut off my finger and cover my head with dirt. Then I will burn your house so I do not have to see it every day." Though he spoke figuratively, I will not believe that he chose his words only for effect. He was ill on the day of my departure, and I said good-by to him in his house, kneeling to look at him where he lay on the ground in the semidarkness. As I walked away, someone told me that he had pulled himself to the door of the hut and called to me. I did not want to look back, and I have not seen him since.

I returned to Lae and to the routine of army life. Here, back among my own countrymen, I found we had little to say to one another. Tofmora was deliberately put out of my mind. All I wanted now was to leave, and I chafed at the delays and the aimless waiting before my name appeared on the list to be transferred to the mainland.

From the time my transfer came through until the end of 1945, I was an instructor in the army School of Civil Affairs at Canberra and Sydney. Then after two years in London I returned home to teach at the Australian School of Pacific Administration and later at the newly created Australian National University. In 1950 I was appointed a Research Fellow of the University and found myself again in Lae, stopping over on my way to the Asaro Valley in the Central Highlands, the area that had beckoned me six years before, when I looked across the grasslands from Tofmora.

Lae, like the other coastal towns of New Guinea, was a generally unattractive place. These towns are pieces of outback Australia grafted to an alien setting; the iron roofs of the bungalows are either brightly new or splotched with rust, never weathering softly like the thatch and walls of native houses. I think of them only as stopping places on the way to somewhere else and have always been glad to leave them.

In 1950 the only hotel in Lae consisted of a group of disused army barracks several miles from the rebuilding township. The accommodations were no better than the decaying structures permitted: rooms were divided from one another by partitions that came to shoulder height; the bath was a partially roofed tin shed containing a row of cold-water showers. The linen on the iron beds, the mosquito nets, and the towels bore the broad arrow of Defense Department stores. Everything smelled of dampness from the rain, which began regularly in the early afternoon and continued through most of the night.

Nothing is more confining, nothing gives me a more intense feeling of isolation than this coastal rain. For two days it cascaded in leaden sheets from the eaves and drummed incessantly on the roof at night. The storms of my country childhood were a dramatic event, building up in the western plains and descending upon us in a rush of cold air that seemed to renew the world. But this rain brought no refreshment; even the surfeited leaves turned away from it in rejection.

A chartered plane was to take me the last part of the journey. Since early morning is the best time to fly in New Guinea, I had arranged to leave Lae at eight o'clock, and by six-thirty had left the hotel and was on my way to the airport. Everything appeared quite different at that hour. The rain, as usual, had stopped during the night; the air was still, and for once the world was fresh and young. Edging the sea, the main street formed an empty tunnel under its rows of arched flamboyants pointing out to mountain slopes behind the town where banners of mist swung gently in the inland currents of air. The unusual poignancy of the hour was heightened by the knowledge that its innocence was so short-lived.

When we were airborne, we circled over a dull sea lapping around dejected, rusting hulks. As we leveled off and turned inland to follow the Markham River, I had a last glimpse of the township, a view from several hundred feet up of the lines of new bungalows distributed with a suburban economy of space on the top of a small hill overlooking the forlorn beach.

As we flew inland, with the Markham River below us, six years of my life seemed to fall away. This was the route to Tofmora, and I looked for the airstrip from which, after landing that time, I had walked out to the villages. I recalled my uncertainty on my first night there and the cool reception I had received—so very different from the kind of welcome that, had I known it, waited for me now. The names of the villagers kept running through my mind as I passed probably as close to them as I would ever find myself again. Familiar landmarks appeared, slopes I had climbed and settlements I had visited; but our route took us toward the southern side of the valley, and Tofmora was only a distant spot of green at the edge of the brown expanse beneath us, detached and remote from my present circumstances like the seaweed a high tide has abandoned to dry on a beach. It had hardly appeared through the window on my right when we turned to the west and, gaining height, entered the clouds above the Kratke Ranges.

For half an hour or so we were flying blind. Above my gear, secured by a net in the body of the plane, the pilot scanned the swirling, white vapors that had engulfed us when we left the valley. Knowing that we must be nearing the point where he expected to descend, I had almost reconciled myself to turning back when he signaled to me that an opening lay ahead. The nose of the plane dropped sharply. For less than a minute perhaps—though it seemed much longer—the clouds rushed over us. Then all at once we were through them, flying level in the open air.

We were above the center of a valley about twenty miles in width. The mountains on either side curved toward each other in two broad arcs that met in the distance to form a solid blue wall closing off the rest of the country. From the forested northern slopes the land fell away in a sweeping trough, drawn toward the precipitous, treeless foothills to the south, which hung against the sky like a translucent wave, every fold and small depression veined with violet shadow. Farther out, as far as the eye could see, ranges churned and tossed against each other, cobalt and dark sea green like the deepest water and plumed with white clouds that concealed the highest peaks. The floor of the valley appeared to be as level as a well-tended lawn and was ornamented with scattered groves of trees and shrubs that rose from the soil in feathery heraldic clusters. I recognized the airy formality of bamboo; but the trees were unfamiliar to me. They were soft in color and lightly foliaged, delicately spired in the manner of pines in temperate northern latitudes. Momentarily it seemed to be some European valley, but there were no houses in the green depression beneath me, not even a sign of habitation.

Then the curve of our descent carried us farther down between the mountains until the trees on a nearby spur were suddenly higher than the plane. When I found myself looking at shadows penciled on the reddish soil, the astonishing intimacy of the valley struck me for the first time. The northern slopes were broken by a series of parallel streams, radial veils of a bright leaf, flowing southward to join the silver curve of the Asaro River. Between the streams, elevated ridges fell away from the mountains like flying buttresses, steeply angled at their point of attachment but gradually widening and flattening as their arches met the floor of the valley. A threadlike line wound through tall grasses until it entered a clump of trees where the light, slanting from almost over-head, pushed aside the shadows and showed thatched houses clustered like beehives at the edge of a patch of open ground. After this I had no trouble in locating the dwellings. Every grove had its complement of houses, and time and again whole new settlements, where the trees had not yet grown tall enough to top the conical roofs of the huts, were plainly visible.

But the quality of the light was the most remarkable ingredient of all. It was difficult to tell where it came from. Every feature of the landscape seemed to be its own source of brightness, possessed of such dazzling clarity that I could not trust my judgment to the usual yard-stick of reality. How far was it to the summit of the mountains in the south, where each tree was precisely etched against the sky? The gardens clinging to slopes below looked close enough to dip my hands into the shadows under their vines; and where a stream flowed between adjacent ridges, I could see the water shedding itself in pewter-colored fragments on the dry stones that rose above its surface.

I was reminded of a sixteenth-century painting in which every element of a landscape is rendered with careful attention to detail and perspective, where the eye follows a road through wayside flowers, past fields of harvesters and peaks crowned with castles, across a ford where travelers rest in the shade, through all of fifty miles to mountain slopes where armies battle and pennants toss like flocks of enameled birds in the forests. In the compass of a small canvas a whole world is displayed so completely that as it transcends reality it also endows the viewer with abilities he does not ordinarily possess, making of him an omnipotent observer who encompasses in a single glance the whole design of a way of life.

The plane's descent ended on a long green airstrip cut from the tall grasses on the floor of the valley. Clumps of bamboo and vivid marbled croton shrubs rushed past the windows as we taxied along the runway. Minutes later I stepped out into the brightness and breathed the thin, high air sharp with the freshness of morning, which perfectly matched my mood of exhilaration.

I was met at the airstrip by Dudley Young-Whitforde, the Assistant District Officer, and taken by jeep to his house on the summit of a hill that the local people called Humeleveka and that the whites called Goroka. I walked the same two miles many times later on, but the journey never again seemed quite as unreal as on this occasion. We passed the entrances to two villages where rows of round thatched houses hid in the shadows. Then the road ran downhill, crossed a covered bridge above white water, rose to the light in careless but wholly enchanting abandon, and brought us out to a green plateau at the edge of the valley.

I went to bed that night pleasantly relaxed, but unusually tired from the unaccustomed altitude. The plaited walls of the room were similar to my house in Tofmora, but otherwise there was nothing to remind me of the New Guinea I had known then. Cold air blew over my face. The sound of the wind in the thin needles of the casuarina trees was unlike any of my memories of the tropics.

I inevitably measured everything against that earlier background. The intervening years had increased my desire to experience the quality of primitive life before it had been altered appreciably by contact with the West. It had become a personal need that was quite as important to me as any contribution to knowledge coming from my work. I did not discount the seriousness of my professional ends, but I was also aware that this was an effort to rediscover something learned on that previous occasion, to reassure myself that it had the meaning my memory assigned to it.

There were some initial disappointments. It was apparent that I had arrived at a time when the life of the valley was changing rapidly, fulfilling the expectations of every past visitor to these high and temperate regions. New bungalows, replicas of the boxy homesteads on Australian farms, each sensibly and unimaginatively placed in what could be a suburban square of lawn, were rising near the airstrip where I landed. Eventually they replaced the decorative but insubstantial houses of native materials that stood so unobtrusively among the trees of Humeleveka. The neat streets of a settlement were marked out in surveyor's pegs, and the town plan in the District Office properly stipulated the sections for future residential and commercial development. It was an idiom I disliked even on its home ground; here it seemed completely misplaced, so insensitively imposed upon alien elements that even the flamboyant crotons, crouching like plumed warriors against the neutral background of the tall kunai grass, were reduced to stiff and brassy vulgarity in the rectangular beds and borders.

But there were compensations. The visual properties of the valley seemed to suspend belief, and even after two years they still had the power to surprise me suddenly, breaking through to my mind like an unexpected personal discovery. Time and again I felt that I had entered a world whose inherently dramatic character required as its natural complement the sweep and flair of an older way of life that I had glimpsed occasionally at Tofmora.

On advice I had received in Australia I planned to work with the Gahuku, a tribal group of about seven thousand people occupying the area between Humeleveka and the Asaro River. Knowing little else about them, I had written to the District Office explaining my plans and asking for assistance in locating a suitable settlement. The letter was passed to Young-Whitforde, who happened to have it on his desk when Makis of the Nagamidzuha tribe, one of the Gahuku headmen, came to see him.

I can imagine Makis entering the office with his flair for coloring everything he did with drama, appearing first of all in the rectangle of sunlight beyond the doorway, a dark silhouette set within a nimbus of brightness that momentarily extinguished the shadows as he stepped across the threshhold and came to attention in the approved manner, the movement of his arm, lifted in a smart salute, causing his ornaments of shell to clash and jingle bravely. In later months he often appeared before me in this manner when I was working alone at night, materializing suddenly in the hissing glare of my kerosene, or tilley, lamp and filling the whole room with his presence. Other objects lost their color and substance in the lamp's blatant illumination, but Makis transformed it. His skin absorbed the uncompromising harshness, and as he came toward me an iridescent sheen accentuated the planes of his face, the volume of his naked chest and thighs. He might have sat for the portrait of a king who lived in the fierce yet innocent centuries of man's beginning, a prince of Sumer whose pride and swagger inform a terra-cotta figure or a stone image. He was short by Western standards of masculine perfection, but all his movements exhibited a self-awareness that overcame the inadequacies of stature. Dark brown eyes looked out from curving lids that complemented the upward tilt of his lips when he smiled. His cheek bones and the bridge of his nose rose strongly from shadows that changed position with every movement of his head. A mane of tightly braided hair swung to the level of his shoulders.

When Young-Whitforde asked him his business Makis quickly assured him that none of his people were in trouble. He had come alone and on his own initiative, he said, to ask the government for a white man. At first Young-Whitforde thought he referred to one of the several Europeans who were looking for land in the valley; but Makis answered that this was not the kind of man he wanted. Further questioning was unable to elicit a more definite statement of his wishes. He became embarrassed and said that the government ought to know the kind of man to give him. At that point Young-Whitforde remembered my letter. He read it through and explained to Makis that it spoke of a white man arriving in Humeleveka in few days' time who wanted to live in one of the local villages. Makis was elated and asked Young-Whitforde to take me out to his settlement.

Learning of the interview when I arrived, I was doubtful of the wisdom of calling on him. Though I believed his request had been faithfully reported, I did not know his motives and was anxious to avoid placing myself in a false position, assigned from the outset to a role that might be neither to my liking nor useful to my work. But since his purpose could be quite innocuous I agreed to see him.

There were times in the next two years when I credited him with nothing but cupidity, knowing, even when I thought it, that this was unjust to him, that there was much more to his wanting me than the very moderate material benefits I was able to provide. The noticeable difference between myself and other Europeans lent his group and himself, as my mentor, a useful prestige, and it soon became apparent that I had to be wary of attempts to enlist the influence I was presumed, quite wrongly, to have at the District Office. It was necessary to refuse the flattering requests to write letters explaining the merits of a pending court case because, as he put it, I knew the local customs. Yet this, too, was only incidental to something else he hoped to gain. I did not expect him to be able to express it (he belongs to a people who are not given to introspection or abstract thought), but I began to feel that his request had been his commitment to the future, a reaching out for one among many possible untried guide lines to tomorrow. He was certainly the last of his people who would achieve eminence and influence solely by traditional means, and the skills and abilities that had earned him followers and reputation were even then losing their efficacy to sustain authority. I believe he knew, or understood, that there was only one road open, that it led directly toward the world of Humeleveka, and that in the continual competition facing men of his position, the advantage lay with those who turned to the horizon.

If this was the case, I was more closely tied to Makis than if he had wanted me simply for material gain. Youths and young men in their twenties could sample the character of the new world by hiring out as laborers and domestic servants to Europeans, they could take the limited opportunities to acquire new skills and perhaps discover the secret of the white man's power and affluence. But there were fewer opportunities and choices for a man of thirty-six. His decision had been beautifully direct, but it also caused an underlying tension in our relationship—on his part a hope or expectation that he could not phrase but that I was supposed to understand, and on my part the knowledge that I could not provide him with an answer, that I had to fail him.

This problem was not apparent, however, when Young-Whitforde and I climbed into the jeep in the late afternoon and set out for Makis' village. Leaving the heights of Humeleveka we plunged into the blue and golden air, now descending steeply into a ravine, then turning upward in a series of magic curves to where the light struck the western faces of the outcroppings with a dazzling brightness. The road had a charm completely lacking in the swathes of concrete that dissect our own countryside with such faultless mechanical precision, a personal quality that was communicated by the people whom we passed: the men with long hair carrying their bows proudly in their hands, the files of women bearing the assorted fruits of the day's gardening in bilums, open-mesh bags, delicately balanced on their heads, the children who scrambled behind the safety of a fence to watch us with open mouths and startled eyes. It was reminiscent of an earlier time, when roads were avenues of excitement, friendly yet spiced with possible danger, where the sequence of passing events provided the traveler with endless gossip when he reached his home.

About three miles from Humeleveka we turned sharply toward the center of the valley. I pressed my feet against the floor to retain my seat, as we bumped along an unsurfaced track hardly wider than the jeep. The crest of the ridge remained just above our heads to the right, obscured by the tall kunai grass that brushed against my face and arms, completely hiding the view. For the first time since arriving I felt a sense of confinement. I had tried to avoid traveling through this grass during my stay in Tofmora, hating its stifling corridors where for hours on end there was nothing to see except the sweat running down the back of the man walking immediately ahead. I burn extremely easily, and the heat and the intensity of the light stabbing at the tassels of the grass caused me such utter misery that my mind was tense as a closed fist, drawn as tight as the muscles of my face as I breathed painfully through smarting lips. Then, without any warning, the kunai parted, and gathering speed we bounced down a small incline and came to a lurching stop in the village.

It might have been the effect of the rough ride or the completely unexpected sensation of height, but when we broke through the grass into the open the sky and distant mountains appeared to swing around my head. As I got out of the jeep the ground seemed to lift to meet my feet, as though I had stepped on some insubstantial construction of vine and cane bridging empty space. The crest of the ridge in front of me had been cleared to provide an open area about sixty yards long by twenty wide. The land fell away sharply on each side toward the valley floor that, at this late hour, was already becoming indistinct, its contours hidden under a wash of blue threaded with burnished streaks where the setting sun fired the higher terraces above a river. There were no trees to block the view, but a line of fifteen to twenty round houses stood to one side in dark relief against the evening sky. A long staff projected from the point of each conical roof with such theatrical effect that I almost expected to hear the welcoming sound of trumpets and to see a mass of gaily colored banners unfurl and toss in the wind.

We had arrived when most of the villagers were outside their houses taking the evening meal. I have a confused impression of people stumbling to their feet while squealing pigs scattered away from the ovens, strewing steaming refuse over the ground. Naked children swarmed around us, ignoring the angry shouts of men who began to push their way toward us from the edge of the crowd. In the excitement I did not hear Young-Whitforde ask for Makis, but I guessed who it was when I found myself confronted by his dark, smiling face. He spoke a few rapid words then took me into his arms and held me against him in the customary full embrace of greeting.

We stayed no longer than ten minutes that first afternoon. Speaking through an interpreter, Young-Whitforde told Makis that I would need a house if I agreed to live with him. He nodded vigorously, and placing his hand on my shoulder indicated the summit of a small rise some distance from the entrance to the village. He listened while I explained that I preferred to live inside the settlement; then, picking up a stick, he led me to the edge of the ridge opposite the row of huts, bent down and drew a circle on the ground. It was the simple blueprint for the thatched house that eventually became my home.

Returning to Humeleveka through the dusk, I felt it had been a propitious beginning, particularly when it was compared to the welcome I had received ten years before at Tofmora. I remembered the confusion of that first evening and the doubts, the feeling of inadequacy and the weary sense of failure when I realized that I was not wanted in the village. The villagers had been polite and quite unabashed in their curiosity, crowding into the small room where I unpacked my gear, sitting around me on the floor, watching and commenting on everything I did, and refusing to leave until far into the night. After several hours of this forced intimacy I was tired from smiling and nauseated by their incessant spitting. That night in Tofmora was my first experience at close quarters of the filth, the sheer squalor, that is an unavoidable part of primitive life, and when I noticed a woman clean her child's streaming nose with her hand, rubbing off the heavy yellow mucus on her bare thigh, I wondered if I would ever find them attractive. Besides, I wanted to be alone to consider the virtual ultimatum that had been delivered shortly after my arrival. One of the first questions asked of me was how long I intended to stay, and I had answered possibly nine months. I thought no more about it, but my reply had evidently become the subject of considerable discussion, for after a while one of the younger men, speaking in pidgin English, informed me that the elders had decided to allow me to remain for "two moons," after which they thought I ought to transfer to another village farther up the valley. In fact, they preferred that I leave the following day, but since it was the wet season and the river was in flood, they were unable to take me to the opposite side.

I did not leave at the end of two months and the subject was never mentioned again. By then I had also learned to appreciate and to sympathize with their initial attitude. Their previous experience had given them no cause to welcome Europeans, and there was nothing to indicate that I would treat them any differently. In time most of them accepted me in good faith; but until the very end of my stay there were some who steadfastly refused to help me in my study and who tried to discourage others from confiding in me.

The contrast in the Gahuku's attitude toward me could hardly have been more marked; yet I cannot say that my time among them was as happy as the months I spent at Tofmora. Perhaps the circumstances might have been reversed if they had been the first people I had known in New Guinea. Certainly life was presented to me in Tofmora with a newness and a vividness that probably I could not expect to experience again. I was also younger, and if my uncertainty created problems the satisfactions were greater when difficulties were solved. When I went to the Gahuku there were some things that I could take for granted, that I would never have to rediscover. I expected to make friends and to find both order and purpose in the unfamiliar life around me. I also knew that given time and patience, the widest differences in thought and interests were not sufficient to conceal a common and far older heritage.

However, the more clinical and objective attitude of this second field trip was not the only reason for my different reaction. Though I did not romanticize the life of Tofmora, it never distressed me or left me with the feeling of inner exhaustion and mental protest that became my common lot among the Gahuku. The causes were not physical, though village living had more than its fair share of squalor. The round houses, so dramatic when the last light of day slanting low across the valley set them in a lambent frieze against the evening sky, were noisome places, dark and redolent with the smell of pigs and unwashed bodies. It always required an act of will to go down on my knees to enter the houses through their narrow openings, and more than once, crushed into the tiny interior with thirty other people, my resolution was threatened by a mounting, suffocating panic, an unreasoning but desperate urge to escape into the night air. The panic was only intensified by the alien singing, alternately shrill and deep, reverberating in the confined space, until I felt myself dissolving into it as though my mind had become a sounding board for the massed voices. But I am not intolerant of physical discomfort, and I became accustomed to the total absence of any standards of personal cleanliness—to the crust of dirt adhering to skins that had been lovingly anointed with rancid pig's fat and to the sight of a woman who had draped her hair in a snood made from the bloody lining of an animal's stomach. So, I must look elsewhere to explain the tension that was never far removed from the level of consciousness, finding the reason in the fact that Gahuku life, its collective interests and its dominant values, emphasized everything that was antithetical to my own temperament.

It was not long before I realized that this was a highly demonstrative, extroverted, and aggressive people. The lack of any privacy had existed in Tofmora as it did here. It is an inevitable accompaniment of a small society where life is more intensely personal, characterized by a more tangible physical and spiritual closeness than anything to which urban living has accustomed us. But with the Gahuku this particular hardship was so magnified that it often felt as though I were smothering under the presence of my fellow men. It was not only that they came and went as they pleased in my house, rousing me at night when they had an impulse to talk, nor simply that it was virtually impossible for me to withdraw from them, since wherever I went people seemed to materialize to accompany me. It was rather the strain of continual exposure to the physical possessiveness that characterized their relationships, for they appeared to need direct contact with other people. Their customary greeting, a standing embrace in which both men and women handled each other's genitals, was an unfailing source of sniggering amusement to Europeans; but even in the villages, among people who saw one another every day, hands were continually reaching out to caress a thigh, arms to encircle a waist, and open, searching mouths hung over a child's lips, nuzzled a baby's penis, or closed with a smack on rounded buttocks.

This demonstrativeness set the constant tone of both public and domestic life. Men were admired most of all for a quality of "strength." Though it had a necessary connection with stamina, it implied much more than physical prowess. It described the warrior, his nakedness transformed into a bizarre totem by red and yellow pigments when he stood up to shout his boastful challenge at the enemy; but it was equally the quality displayed by the man who killed by stealth, waiting near a path to strike down an unsuspecting traveler or appearing suddenly at a garden fence to massacre a group of women and children. Strength showed in every muscle of the clan orators as they stood alone in a circle of their fellows declaiming their set speeches with sweeping, florid gestures punctuated with moments of studied immobility when a taut leg or outflung arm lent emphasis to words resting on the air like the sound of a vibrating string. It was expressed in pride and a quickness of temper, in violence unleashed at a moment's notice; it involved a strong awareness of self and a readiness to take offense at a suspected or intended slight or injury. Material rewards and reputation went to the "strong," and most transactions were competitive, reflecting the twin aims of anyone who wished to be considered more than ineffectual: a continuing effort to achieve equality and to surpass others.

There was a preposterous, overweening swagger to much of the life I observed. Understandably, it reached its peak at times of celebration, when indeed there was much to be said for the heightened emotional tone that set such events apart from the routine aspects of existence. No matter how often I accompanied them on ceremonial visits to other settlements, the studied theatricality of the occasion never failed to suborn my objectivity. As we entered the village in a slow procession, the waiting throngs became an undifferentiated, critical presence that had to be won. Fixing my eyes on my companions, seeing only the rhythmic swing of their hair, I felt the pride that lifted their heads and the arrogance of their carriage, absorbing it through the measured tread of fifty pairs of feet. When the silence erupted into a mass of shouting figures who charged to within a yard or two of our ranks, I could not conceive of a more fitting way for men to express their accomplishments.

Yet if this sense of drama was entirely appropriate for great occasions, carried over into the routines of daily living it could be as exhausting as an interminable assault on the emotions by actors who had never learned the virtues of understatement. Its effects caught up with me almost two years to the day after my plane set down in the valley, and during the weeks of my illness and convalescence I began to understand why these experiences were set so sharply against the earlier period when I had lived at Tofmora.

I remember waking one night in the house Makis had built for me, overcome by extreme nausea. I was barely able to find my way outside before I began to vomit uncontrollably. In the morning I was weak and my back ached as though I had been beaten. I had no idea that anything was seriously wrong, and I went out as usual, walking four or five miles to a village where a girl was celebrating her first menstruation.

On the following night I woke again with the same symptoms, but this time the pain was intense when I returned to bed, and several hours later, following a second attack, I began to shiver with cold although my body was drenched with perspiration. I eventually slept, or fainted, for the next thing I recall is realizing that it was midmorning. The light patterns on the bamboo walls indicated that the sun was already high, and through the open door I could see a narrow stretch of dusty street. The silence told me that the village was probably deserted by now, everyone having left for the day's work in the gardens. I knew that my boys were sure to be playing one of their interminable games of cards while they waited for me in the kitchen, a smaller hut built some distance from the house in order to minimize the risk of fire, and thinking to call them, I sat up on the edge of the bed. I felt tired, but the pain had left me; it did not occur to me that I was ill until I put my feet to the ground and tried to stand. Then, unaccountably, the bright strip beyond the doorway began to lift like a wave. The points of sunlight seemed to leap from the walls, and as they whirled together, extinguishing everything else in a single vivid flash, I realized I was losing consciousness.

I knew nothing else until I found myself lying on the bed where my boys had lifted me. By then I was aware that I needed help, and in the intervals when the vertigo left me I was able to write a note to the European medical assistant and to order one of the boys to deliver it at the government station. The medical assistant arrived several hours later, and after a brief questioning and examination informed me that I had a hemorrhaging ulcer.

There was no European hospital nearer than the coast, and the only qualified doctor was two days' walk from the station on one of his tours of inspection. The medical assistant decided to move me to his own house. He told one of my boys to dress me and to put together the things I would need while he returned to the station. Within the hour he was back in the village in a borrowed jeep. I was wrapped in a blanket and lifted into the front seat where I had almost my last view of the settlement where I had first seen Makis.

I was in bed for nearly two months. When the doctor arrived he told me that I could be flown to Lae where there were adequate medical facilities, but there was some risk that the bleeding, which seemed to have stopped, might start again under the conditions of the flight (and considering the blood I had lost already, I might not survive another attack). Alternatively, I could remain where I was, which seemed to him the more sensible course provided there were no further complications. Trusting his judgment, I chose to stay, and I have never regretted my decision.

The following weeks were a period when I knew a feeling of peace and self-contained completeness such as I have rarely found. It did not occur to me that I might die. The calmness that had come over me from the moment of my final attack was like a sudden releasing of the spirit, as though all my defenses had fallen before this weakness, leaving only the central citadel of self to which I had thankfully retired, realizing that it was the refuge I had always sought yet somehow missed in fussing over the perimeters of my existence.

Nothing could have been more appropriate for this state of mind than the physical conditions of my convalescence. The medical assistant's house was several years old and already showing signs of disrepair, but it had a charm and a feeling of airy openness, a closeness to the world outside that the newer frame bungalows entirely lacked. Built on a spur above the valley, it was almost completely isolated from the rest of the government station, commanding its approaches with the windy impregnability of a fortress. An unglazed window had been opened in the plaited wall beside my bed, its height such that there was no need to sit up in order to enjoy the view. I slept a great deal at first, and whenever I woke the valley was my bridge to returning consciousness. In the early morning when opalescent light stippled its shadowed gullies and ravines, it lay beneath me like an inland sea whose buoyant swells, rolling toward the mountains, seemed to lift the spur and the quiet house as tenderly as a prow responds to the movement of the ocean. Later in the day clouds chased their blue reflections on its surface and the heat rose in smoking veils, building toward that point where the mind hopes for any patch of shade, however small, to provide relief and reference in the colorless void. But the rarest hours were those in which I was called from sleep into a full awareness of the white night. The brilliance falling across my bed dissolved the walls as though they were gauzy curtains in a transformation scene, and high above the valley I felt myself possessed by the silence, filled with an inward wonder that sought completion in the far reaches of the sky behind the swinging net of stars.

A week or so after the onset of my illness my first visitor from the village came. When he arrived I was neither asleep nor properly awake but lying with closed eyes in the state of half-awareness in which I spent most of my time. I realized someone had entered the room when I felt the bamboo floor receive his weight; and listening to its crackling protest as he sat down, I knew beyond any question that it was Makis.

He stayed for perhaps half an hour. I did not look at him until he was about to leave, but his face and his mannerisms were so familiar that I saw him clearly against my eyelids, sitting with crossed legs a few yards from my bed, his loin cloth folded modestly between his thighs, and his hands resting loosely on his knees. Finely plaited bands at his wrist made a faint metallic scraping against his shell pendant as he reached behind him for the string bag where he kept his belongings, bringing it round and rummaging inside it for the makings for a cigarette—a six-inch strip of newspaper and shredded black trade tobacco, which he preferred to the wad of raw native leaf inserted into a bamboo tube. I heard a spurt of flame as he drew a match across the serrated surface of a tin box, then he inhaled deeply, holding the smoke in his lungs and releasing it slowly while he studied me.

Matching what must have been his movements to these familiar sounds, I may have dozed for a while. At all events, I came fully awake as he began to rise. He smiled when our eyes met, showing his filed teeth; and gesturing in the customary manner of someone taking his leave (a patting motion of the hand away from the body), he crossed the springy floor with an easy but slightly crouching gait, as though instinctively accommodating to the low-pitched roof of his own house. In the sunlight outside he straightened up and, adjusting the string bag on his shoulder, moved out of my line of vision.

After this he came to see me at least once a week, sometimes alone but more often accompanied by several other villagers. For some reason I did not want to see them, and in other circumstances I might have shut myself in another room, hoping they would leave when they failed to find me. But a closed door would not have been enough to deflect them from their purpose, and since even this was denied me I tried to discourage them by turning my face to the window. I had not thought of the village since leaving it. All my notebooks, the result of two years' work, were in my house and I had made no effort to have them brought to me. Having temporarily given up the past, I was not ready to move into the future and wanted to prevent the intrusion of anything that threatened to take me out of the suspended present.

Listening to their voices as they sat on the floor a few feet from my bed, I tried to excuse my attitude by telling myself that they came only because they expected something from me, and I felt a perverse satisfaction whenever they asked for trade tobacco or a cigarette. They constantly made the same demands of each other, but I reminded myself that I was different, that standing outside their system altered the quality of the asking. For since they had nothing I needed, our relationship was entirely one-sided; it simply meant that they knew I was fair game. Yet as soon as they had gone I blamed myself for maligning them. Even if they did regard me as an easy source of charity, in their position I would have done the same, and they had been generous with what they had to give, not only in material things but more importantly in granting me their confidence and in encouraging me to know at first hand the texture of their lives.

As I realized that their openness went far beyond anything that I had a right to expect, I also understood that this very willingness, this insistence to involve me was partly responsible for my attitude toward them. For though I ought to be willing to take what is offered and to give myself in return, I can do so only after some time and with considerable pain. My Gahuku friends had this distressing quality of openness to an exaggerated degree. From the beginning they pressed themselves on me, expecting an involvement in their lives that I was not prepared to give. At Tofmora it had been very different. There the general suspicion of my motives acted to my advantage in two ways. My relationship with those who remained antagonistic had precise, if implicit limits that helped to cushion the impact of their thoroughly alien way of life. At the same time, I was more deeply indebted to those who chose to ignore the limits and in going against the opinion of their own people offered me something more than the usual relationship between outsider and informants. Meeting them at a deeper, personal level quickened my appreciation of the individuality concealed beneath the screen of unfamiliar customs and ideas.

The complete lack of reserve I met in the Asaro Valley was not only a new experience, it also left me more exposed to things I found distasteful and distressing. It required a conscious effort to separate the person of the villagers from those aspects of their lives to which I could not give my inner assent, and there was little time or energy for the attempt when every day made so many other demands of me.

Yet as I lay in bed I knew there had been times when understanding suddenly cast all this confusion aside, and I felt that sharp elation that is the tender, painful cry of flesh recognizing its own across the immense distance of two separate lives. I looked at Makis sitting near me on the floor and wanted to find the words before leaving to tell him what I had seen one late afternoon about six months after our first meeting.

It was the perfect hour of day when the sky assumed the color of a milky emerald and the thatched houses, rising from a bar of shadows, were a boy's dream of some barbaric encampment. All along the village street families were gathered near the steaming ovens, and strident voices screamed imprecations at pigs whose greed drove them to anticipate their share of the evening meal. Sitting near the door of his house, I was watching Makis distributing the food from his oven, taking out the bundles of grubby sweet potatoes and yams, and the corn wrapped in its tender green husks. When all had been removed, he placed a portion of each variety on the sections of banana leaf that served as plates, naming the completed piles for individual members of his household. This duty done, he did not follow his usual practice of joining the rest of his family, but picking up his bow and arrows he turned abruptly and walked down the path leading away from the settlement. Something in his manner held my attention, and I rose to follow him.

Catching up with him at a point where the path seemed to turn in the air above the valley, I called his name and asked him where he was going. Though I was no more than a pace or two behind, he gave no sign of recognition. I was vaguely disturbed, wondering if I had offended him, and I kept the short distance between us as he turned aside from the path and stood among the tall grasses. His profile was silhouetted against the green question of the sky as he fitted an arrow to his bow, drew the string with slow deliberation, and released it into the gathering dusk. Then his body relaxed, and when he turned to me his eyes held a quietness I had not seen before.

Walking back with him, I was aware of the sudden freedom, the effortless release that arrives so unexpectedly at certain turning points on the path to understanding others. There was no need for an explanation, and it would have been difficult for him to try. But he seemed to want to talk, and somehow he made me know that there are times when a man is oppressed by such a heaviness of spirit that it is good for him to be alone and to shoot his arrows at the air. He, too, was familiar with the disenchantment that settles on us unawares in a crowded existence, with the untutored pause the mind seems to take while it lets the world recede and shows us to ourselves poised on the edge of the abyss.

As my body healed, a gradual change took place in my attitude toward the villagers. Instead of resenting them, I hoped they would come. I learned to expect them in the afternoon and spent the morning hours waiting for them at the window. Five miles across the valley I could see the house where I had lived. In another six months or so the casuarina seedlings I had planted would have grown tall enough to hide it behind a grey-blue screen, and in a year, unless its frail materials were properly maintained, it would no longer be habitable. As usual when I face the termination of any period in my life, I began to think of the things left undone. It was not my work that concerned me; in that respect I knew I had done my best; extra time would not be a remedy if it fell short of success. Rather, my thoughts were all of the people who had helped me.

As I looked into the morning sunlight, I often found myself back in the village. I again listened to the sounds as it woke, or left my house to enter its midday silence when there was not another soul in sight except old Sesekume, lying asleep beside the smoldering fire that eased the cold ache in his bones. I saw the street crowded with people on the day they gave Tarova to her new husband, and I felt my heart cry when we took our leave of her, each of us showing her our duty as we left a gift where she sat among strangers. I also relived the night when Makis sat with me while his young third wife was in labor and, with no word for love in his language, tried to tell me what it would mean to him if she died.

By the time my visitors arrived I was ready to keep them there indefinitely. Though it was useless to try, I wanted to tell them that I did not regret any part of the last two years. Even the ending was fitting, for nothing had been as I expected it when I set out for the valley. I had been exposed to much that I had to reject. And I wanted to remember this as well as the times when I had been deeply moved, for the brassy dissonances could not be omitted without subtracting from the stature and identity of the people who had let me know them. It was to them that I felt my greatest debt and my responsibility, and I promised that some day I would take the time to discharge it in the only way I knew.

CHAPTER ONE

▲▲

THE VILLAGE

Perhaps if I went back now I would not recognize Makis' village of
Susuroka, for it was a new settlement when I went to live there, not
much over a year old. There was nothing around it except the russet
kunai and a single clump of ancient bamboo that shaded a turning in
the pathway leading down to the principal garden areas. Half a mile
farther along the ridge its mother settlement Gohajaka stood in the deep
shadows of a casuarina grove. Like the seedlings behind each house at
Susuroka these trees had been planted by hand, for apart from foliaged
strips beside the numerous streams there is no natural timber in the
valley.

The casuarina grows rapidly, and it is not long before it tops the
roofs of the round village houses, extending its branches to cover the sky
and shutting out the surrounding landscape. The wooded air of the older
settlements has the beguiling charm, the remoteness and romantic isolation of a forest clearing. They are places where sounds die slowly,
hanging in suspension without the space to escape into the larger world;
so at any period of the day, even when there is no one about, the ghost
of a busy life is present.

At times the rawness of Susuroka was bound to compare unfavorably
with these qualities. Wide open to the sun, its street was churned into
dust during the dry season, and whenever there was an event of special
importance flimsy lean-tos were erected in front of the houses to provide
a patch of weak shade that was no more than a smoky blur across the
light. There the villagers waited through the interminable afternoons
watching the ovens emitting their thin plumes of steam like a row of
miniature quiescent volcanoes. The glare was often intolerable; yet even
when I longed for the soft relief of trees I realized that this absence
lent the village a distinctive character that absolved it of any faults. It
was the first thing I noticed on setting foot to its soil, a sensation of
stepping into the heart of a crystal and floating in refracted light, much

as the small islands of the Pacific—attached to the earth's crust by some
invisible pinnacle of rock or coral—float in a jewelled world of sky and
water.

Probably more often than I realized the view from Susuroka helped
to sustain me. It was more than a background to the events I witnessed.
They owed at least some part of their impact to their surroundings,
receiving from their setting the kind of assistance in establishing a mood,
in creating an aesthetically satisfying whole, that expert lighting and
scenery provide in the theater. Almost everything I recall is touched
with the transforming effects of this dimension of experience: my picture
of a procession of dancers seen from a distance as they approached the
village, only their plumes visible like fantastic flowers above the grasses;
or again, my recollection of men carrying the sacred flutes along the
crest of the ridge with the valley spread beneath them like a supplicant
and the unfamiliar music shrilling in counterpoint to the singing color
of the sky. Even the gesture of an orator's hand is not the same unless
I add the mountain slopes behind him and the glitter of the sun on the
pearl-shell pendent hanging against his naked chest.

Yet unlike the scenery for a play, which requires the action for which
it is created, the setting of Susuroka had an integrity and completeness
of its own. If it added its alchemy to the human events occurring within
it, it needed nothing from those to whom it gave, and when I wanted
some relief from the pressures of village life I found I could forget them
in its independent existence.

Mornings here began with a unique magic. In my country childhood,
the working day had an early start; the same was true in Susuroka.
And although I was often too tired to manage it, I liked to be outside
before the villagers were about. Wearing a sweater against the chilly air,
I walked to the fence Makis had built around my house to protect my
plot of garden from the village pigs. A stile gave access to the empty
street where refuse from the previous evening's meal made an untidy
litter in front of the row of round huts. They were peculiarly affecting
at that hour, looking larger than usual, due to the absence of any living
thing to provide a measure of comparison. They seemed asleep—their
narrow doorways fastened with planks, and the shadows beneath their
neatly trimmed eaves suggesting the curve of dark lashes against a
cheek. I felt like an intruder in the presence of the silent monuments
more impressive civilizations have left behind.

Contributing to the atmosphere of unreality and isolation, rivers of mist coursed along the ravines below the level of the houses. Only the narrow ridge remained above the white flood that grew in width and volume until far out in the valley, meeting the morning air, it was deflected upward. Then, curving back upon itself, it threatened to engulf the village from above as well as below. As the sun rose, the mass of vapor glowed with light, pulsed with a hundred hues of lavender and rosy pink, of lambent gold and the liquid, fiery red that streaks the heart of opals.

Though there were days when they lingered until a late hour, the mists usually left the village by nine o'clock. Even in the wet season the mornings were mostly clear, the overburdened clouds building their strength in the higher reaches of the mountains until the midafternoon rains. Little by little, as the mists withdrew, the environs of Susuroka were revealed, beginning with the clustered spires of the casuarinas at Gohajaka, where wisps of vapor hung on the upper branches, adding a touch of the solitude of high places. Farther to the south, concealed by the height of the grove but known to me from many visits, the hamlet of Ekuhakuka clung to the extremity of the ridge, its five or six dilapidated houses threatening to slide into the floor of the valley thirty feet below. From here it was no more than fifteen minutes' walk to Meniharove, a larger settlement than any of those on the ridge but lacking the feeling their elevation gave of commanding everything in sight, for there was only a gradual slope from here to the Asaro River and then another gentle rise, a broad green swell, sweeping out to the distant mountains.

If I left the center of the street and walked to either side of Susuroka I looked down upon similar scenery. The gardens began immediately below the crest of the ridge, neat rectangles quilting the precipitous slopes and the narrow terraces overhanging the tributary streams of the Asaro River. It was the custom to separate the rows of produce by shallow ditches that followed the gradient of the land. This practice led the eye into the landscape, down the hills, and up the opposite side of the ravine much as the conventions of perspective serve the same end in draftsmanship. Morning shadows accentuated the feeling of three-dimensional solidity. The fences enclosing each plot were firmly erect, each bright leaf in the rows of sweet-potato vines nestled on its own bed of darkness; the stalks of corn and the motionless fans of the banana trees were edged with lines of golden light.

Scattered garden houses were visible on the terrace flats, single dwellings isolated from one another by the tall grasses or casuarinas that concealed them when approached from below. Several narrow tracks passed through the trees and down the face of the cliffs, entering the denser vegetation clothing the banks of the stream. When one entered this strip of territory it was as if a door closed on the rest of the valley. The open ridge tracing a wavy line against the sky and the sun burning on the bare cliffs slipped out of view to become no more than a memory, a mental image that lies in the recesses of the mind waiting for the moment of recall. Instead of the airy spaciousness of the village, this was a world filled with sounds reluctant to impose themselves on the stillness: the almost inaudible movement of the thin needles of the trees, no more than the evocation of the restless, living air; the cushioning response of damp earth to the intruder's foot; the ruminative purling of the water, silvered with the solitude of its mountain source, as it divided around smooth stones and slid into the silence of viridian pools. Even the light was hushed, a soft effusion slanting in transverse beams through the clerestory of the trees with the promise of an infinite progression. Leaves of giant taro plants, higher than an average man, were delicate vaults fashioned from the thinnest jade, their ribs and· veins indicated as precisely as the details in an architectural drawing; the unfamiliar forms of croton and dracaena shrubs clustered in motionless hieratic groups like naïve symbols of some primitive nature cult.

As the valley opened up behind the retreating mists other settlements came into view—Gorohadzuha, lying across the stream on the western side of the ridge, and Asarodzuha sited on a bluff to the east. The former was nearer than Gohajaka, only a short walk from Susuroka, and since there were many ties between the two villages I knew it well. The people of Susuroka did not have much to do with Asarodzuha's inhabitants—they were traditional enemies—but it lay across a route to the government station that saved me at least a two mile walk, so I often passed through it when I went to buy my stores.

The track began near my house and, skirting the gardens of a man named Zaho, ran east down the hillside for several hundred yards toward a stream. At the bottom of the slope there was a section of swampy ground that made it advisable to take the longer route after heavy rain; but even then I sometimes chose to cope with the mud in order to enjoy the remainder of the journey.

My pleasure began on reaching the stream, which was wide and quite shallow at a point where I crossed, wonderfully clear and racing in a green and white flurry over a stony bottom. On the opposite side a shaded grove led to the base of a series of stepped cliffs that mounted to the village, standing perhaps a hundred feet above it.

Asarodzuha was three times as large as Susuroka and obviously much older, its double row of houses shaded by dense clumps of bambo and casuarinas. Perhaps because it abutted on the main road and therefore came under the constant scrutiny of government officers, it was unusually clean, and its approaches were landscaped in reasonable imitation of the garden style most popular with Europeans: a grass walk flanked by an avenue of trees and edged with the ubiquitous, brightly colored shrubs whose vivid markings were oddly at variance with the stiff, suburban attempts at achieving formal values. It also possessed two unique features. One was pointed out to me on my first visit: an orange tree, grown from a seed that its owner, suspecting he had come across a valuable prize, had salvaged from the refuse of one of the station houses. Its poor sour fruits failed to ripen and turn to gold, but I bought them when he offered them to me, not wishing to spoil his enterprise or to make him question his assumption that white men thought them highly desirable. The other feature was not drawn to my attention and might have escaped my notice if I had not trained my eye to look for variations in the plan and furnishings of different villages. It stood a little apart from the houses, surrounded by a circular fence that may have called it to my attention, for otherwise the object could have been mistaken for a clump of shrubs. But a closer look showed that it was man-made, a small platform four feet high whose vertical supports had taken root in the soil and begun to put out leaves that hid the bleached jawbones of pigs suspended from the corners of the horizontal timbers. When I first asked about its purpose, it was described in a noncommital, off-hand manner as a "table"; not until several months later after piecing together many other clues, did I discover its significance.

The platform had been built for a fertility rite that occurred throughout the valley in various local forms. In Gahuku the rite was called *ozaha neta*, "the old men's thing," possibly because the ritual was performed only once in a generation, so that its details were seldom known to anyone who was not advanced in years. However, the infrequency of its occurrence bore no relationship to its importance. It was second only to the great pig festivals, which were so essential to tribal prestige, in its significance, and during the several days required to complete it a whole community came under severe proscriptions—fasting and prohibitions against lighting fires or engaging in sexual activity. The whole welfare of the group depended on the rite. It assured the fertility of men and animals, promised strength to repel the attacks of enemies, governed the physical development of the young, and fortified the congregation with the hope and expectation that the world of man and nature would continue on its appointed course, that everything necessary for life for yet another span of time would be provided: food, people to take the place of those who died, wealth, and both a reason for and an opportunity to demonstrate one's pride, to indulge in one's love of self-display.

There was no logical reason why it should have been so, but the orange tree and the ozaha neta came to symbolize the life of the valley as I knew it. They were the future and the past, the new and the old, a basic commentary on the situation of a people who had been thrust into the modern world with the abruptness of the apocalypse.

Always, as I watched the retreating clouds of white vapor the northern tier of mountains was the last section of the valley to emerge. Villages too numerous to mention by name appeared singly and in clusters, standing in isolation on a ridge or scattered across the green troughs of the minor hanging valleys that extended farther and farther back into the ranges becoming ever narrower and steeper between the converging lines of forest. Looking toward the heights I felt as if the entire landscape was poised above me, held in momentary suspension as the ranks of the invisible mountains stayed their pressure from the rear or gathered strength for the appropriate time to resume the forward rush that would send the rest of the world cascading past me into the valley. The flickering splashes of light penetrating the clouds completed the illusion of instability conveyed by these upper regions, and the ridge of Susuroka, separated from them by a dark bar of shadow lying across the approaches to the village, became a tiny island, a poignant speck of earth standing with absurd confidence behind its shielding reef.

For weeks after my arrival I knew the valley only as a visitor knows a strange city. Such a person becomes familiar with the names of streets and the style of architecture. He notices the character of different quarters and begins to appreciate the tone or feeling of the whole, but he cannot know the place with the intimacy of its native citizens, whose perception of its suburbs and its buildings is colored by the events of their own lives. Yet it was this kind of knowledge I hoped to obtain as I sought to identify the complex strands of the valley's social fabric. The task occupied me for the duration of my stay, for even gross relationships were not easy to discover, and my attempt to locate the village in this larger context underwent repeated revisions.

The central portion of the valley, roughly the area between the government station and the Asaro River, held about five thousand people who spoke the same language and observed the same customs. Though they shared many traits with bordering peoples, there were differences noticeable to even a casual traveler—styles of dress, speech, and ornamentation—as well as others, mainly of a ritual character, that required a more extensive knowledge of the region to perceive them. The groups in the center of the valley emphasized the differences rather than the things they shared with their neighbors; yet among themselves there was no readily identifiable or definable unity. They had no common name nor any centralized authority, and they raided and fought each other constantly.

There were twelve named tribes in this population, groups whose members had a rather vague belief in a common origin and recognized rights within delimited territories. These tribes had no central organization, no hierarchy of chiefs or other officials, nor anything easily recognized as a system of government. Each contained a number of smaller named units, clans and sub clans in which membership was reckoned through descent in the male line of an individual's ancestry. Within a tribe there was a normal expectation of peace. If any of its clans opposed one another in a dispute, moral ideals required them to settle their differences amicably without resorting to force; they were "as brothers" and therefore should not fight each other.

The external affairs of each tribe were conducted principally on the basis of traditional friendship or enmity with other groups. Each recognized certain others as its friends, ties that were traditional in the sense of "always háving been." Friends intermarried and exchanged wealth and gave each other sanctuary in time of need. When involved in a dispute they sometimes came to blows, but a peaceful settlement of their differences was expected. The fighting was not regarded as warfare, an activity engaged in only with enemy tribes. Enmity was also traditional; enemy tribes were in a state of permanent hostility with one another; they needed no excuse to fight. Though a battle was often triggered by a particular event such as homicide, sorcery, the theft of livestock, or in retaliation for a previous attack, it was enough that another tribe was an enemy, the appropriate group against which to demonstrate strength in its most explicit and unequivocal form.

While it was not considered possible for friends to become full-fledged enemies, embassies often negotiated alliances with a hostile tribe when it seemed expedient to enlist assistance against a common foe. Quantities of livestock and shell valuables were offered to those whose help was sought, and if they were accepted the enemies feasted together to signify the change effected in their relationship. Yet these pacts were never joined with any idea of permanence. For a time the allies kept the peace. They visited each other and sometimes celebrated festivals together, but they seldom intermarried, their reluctance to exchange women testifying to the essential instability of the alliances. It was customary and prudent to marry only where there were long-standing ties of friendship. As a general rule this did not include women of one's own clan, who were classed as "sisters." Men therefore sought their wives in other clans of their tribe or among the women of a friendly tribe who, though not born members of their husband's group and in native thought bound more closely by sentiment and loyalty to their own kinsmen, posed less of a threat to a man's safety. The danger lay in a wife's opportunity to procure her husband's semen at the request of a sorcerer who wished to harm him, and she was more likely to receive the request if her kinsmen were among his traditional enemies. Some men chose to ignore the risk, but the characteristic fate of the alliances suggested it could be a foolhardy action, for they were usually dissolved by treachery.

This pattern of unceasing hostility crisscrossed the valley from end to end, and, not surprisingly, every group had experienced striking vicissitudes in the course of its recent history. When its enemies prevailed its members were often forced to abandon their gardens and settlements and to flee, seeking sanctuary with friends and allies, sometimes scattering as far afield as the mountains to the south and west of the Asaro River. Men who married in exile occasionally remained permanently with their wives' people, but the majority of them regarded their sojourn as a temporary plight, a period in which they not only sought to recoup their losses and to regain their strength but also, through the manipulation of alliances, to enlist the help that would enable them to return to their own territory. Permanent conquest was not the principal end of warfare, so in most cases victors did not take over the lands of a defeated foe; indeed, after some time had elapsed, it was not unusual for them to invite the exiles to return to their homes. But such apparent magnanimity did not betoken a radical change of heart, for even though a period of uneasy peace or an alliance followed the invitation, the two groups were almost certain to resume their hostile relationship in the long run. Enemies seem to have been as necessary as friends for the satisfactions generally sought by the Gahuku. One obtained women from one's friends and also needed them for the prestigious, largely competitive activity of exchanging livestock and valuables. But one required enemies too, for warfare epitomized the highly prized qualities of strength and aggressiveness that brought most renown to groups and individuals alike. It is not fortuitous that the borders of each tribe adjoined those of at least one friend and one traditional enemy.

The history of Susuroka exemplified this pattern of events and relationships. The men of the village were members of the Nagamidzuha tribe, one of the smaller of the central valley groups. It contained two principal clans—Ozahadzuha and Meniharove. Most of the Ozahadzuha lived in the settlements on the crest of the ridge and the Meniharove on the floor of the valley. Leaving Meniharove it was only a short distance to the territory of the Gama, a tribe about three times as large as the Nagamidzuha and linked to it by traditional friendship. To the southwest, across the stream Galamuka, the area as far as the Asaro River was occupied by the enemy Uheto, whose nearest settlement was only half an hour's walk from Susuroka. Even so, it was farther away than Gorohadzuha, whose people belonged to the Gehamo tribe and were currently friendly with Nagamidzuha, though until quite recently they had been enemies.

Though the Nagamidzuha considered themselves the equal of all these neighboring groups, they admitted that they were less fortunately placed than some. They stood "in the middle," with enemies on every side but one, a strategic disadvantage they held responsible for a series of defeats in which their strength had been seriously depleted. Their most recent reverse had occurred some years before white men entered the valley. It had been brought about by the repeated attacks of the Gehamo and Uheto who, though enemies, had joined forces to crush their common foe. Under this concerted pressure the Nagamidzuha abandoned most of their villages retaining only one, which was well to the southeast of Meniharove and close to the border of Gama. The defeat fell most heavily on the Ozahadzuha clan, whose section of the tribal territory was closer to Gehamo and Uheto. Breaking into small groups, its members sought refuge with friends in widely separated parts of the valley, some crossing to the southern side of the Asaro River and others finding a haven with the Kotuni, a tribe situated in the upper reaches of the northern foothills.

It is impossible to estimate the duration of their exile, but Europeans had not yet appeared when the Gehamo invited them back to the ridge. Makis had been directly involved in this change in the fortunes of his people. His maternal grandmother had been a Gehamo woman of Gorohadzuha, married by his grandfather during a previous period of friendship between her tribe and the Nagamidzuha. The Gorohadzuha were therefore his mother's closest maternal relatives, which entitled her to the affection and consideration given to a daughter. She must have visited them often in her childhood, and when she married Uwaizo, the father of Makis, the Gorohadzuha received a portion of her bride price, a customary entitlement that recognized their residual claims to her as a child born to one of their women.

The connection with Gorohadzuha lent protection to Makis and his mother in the event of hostilities between Gehamo and Nagamidzuha, but during the latter group's period of eclipse the family fled to the borders of Gama where, soon afterward, Uwaizo was killed by the Uheto.

The chronicle of the family's fortunes entered another phase when the widow's Gorohadzuha kinsmen, mindful of their obligations and sorry for her plight, persuaded her to leave her husband's people and live with them. She took her child with her, and Makis grew to youth and young manhood among the Gehamo. By the time he was sixteen and a fully initiated member of the men's organization, he already possessed qualities promising a reputation that would be the equal of a famous father and an even more renowned grandfather. His ties with Nagamidzuha had not lapsed during his time away from them, and it is virtually certain that Makis would have returned to live permanently in the group where his rights were conferred by birth. But he did not have to choose, for the Gehamo, turning against their allies the Uheto, sent embassies to the Nagamidzuha and invited them to return to the ridge. The settlement of Gohajaka apparently dated from this event, when the clans of Nagamidzuha in concert with the Gehamo began to take reprisals against the Uheto, engaging them in a long series of raids that, still in progress, had lifted them to virtual supremacy when

white men entered the valley. The pendulum would probably have
swung in the opposite direction once again, but the European interdic-
tion on intertribal fighting prevented the Uheto from seeking the customary form of vindication, and though they had returned to full
occupancy of their territory by 1950 they continued to smart under the
boasts and arrogance of the Nagamidzuha. Susuroka was established by
Makis at the peak of his career, when his talents were not only recognized among his own people but had also obtained him the support of
government officials at Humeleveka. By then the older settlement had
became overcrowded, and was admittedly rather dank, owing to the
thick growth of trees, and somewhat inconveniently situated for those of
its inhabitants whose principal garden areas lay toward the northern
end of the ridge. Apart from such practical considerations the founding
of Susuroka exemplified a common development in the careers of influential men for whom establishing a new village stood as evidence of
their ability to attract and to hold followers.

Susuroka was not a large settlement, only thirteen round houses
faced my own across the street; some of these were not occupied permanently, for although most of the men were of Ozahadzuha, the clan
to which Makis belonged, a few who had joined him from Meniharove
also maintained houses in that village. The dwellings housed forty-five
people including children, a number often increased by visitors staying
overnight or for longer periods and by the constant flow of men and
women moving about their everyday business along the paths that
brought them past my door.

I had chosen to place my house in the center of the village because
of the obvious advantage of observing the day-to-day activities of the
people. My personal life would have been much easier had I done as
Makis suggested and built on the rising ground outside the settlement.
At least I would have been spared some of the physical and emotional
strain of the constant lack of privacy; but then I would have missed a
great deal that was revealing—not only the routine details of domestic
life, but also the sudden events that broke the normal rhythm like
jagged peaks in a recording of the earth's pulse, and I would not have
known the feeling of a whole day, from its quiet beginning to its close
in the suspended silence of the night.

On those mist-filled mornings when I was about early, the village
came to life in a gradually unfolding sequence that hardly varied from
one occasion to another. The day began with a clatter of wooden planks

as here and there along the street invisible hands unfastened the sealed
entry to a house and, grunting impatiently, the pigs emerged with a
rush, making for the piles of refuse with the greedy singleness of purpose
that directed them through all their waking hours. Shortly afterward
the dark-skinned figures began to appear like shadows in the half-light
and the rising vapors. Sometimes the first was Namuri, whose house stood
directly opposite my own. He was almost five feet eleven, taller by several inches than the average Gahuku, and built proportionately. He came
through his doorway on his knees holding a smoldering brand in one
hand. Squatting at the edge of the street he raked together some
scattered leaves and charred sticks, drawing them into the space between
his knees and building a small fire. Moments later, as smoke stroked
his chest with its promise of warmth, he was joined by his wife and
his son Giza, about nine years old, who stood against his father's thigh
and looked into the fire with the lost concentration of children just
aroused from sleep, his chin cradled on his crossed forearms and his
hands clasped behind his neck. The woman, also withdrawn, sat several paces to the rear, her legs extended and her face foreshortened and
partly hidden by the greased ringlets that fell forward from under the
bilum she had piled loosely on her head.

I did not speak to them. The closeness of the house from which they
had appeared—its personal and confining darkness, its familiar warmth
and mingled odors—held them together like a cloak in which they
sheltered from the rest of world, and it seemed an unwarranted breach
of their privacy to intrude on them. Nor did they take any notice of me
or of other people in the street, for each house in the row soon had its
complement of figures seated in similar attitudes on the dusty ground.
Even sounds seemed to be confined behind the intangible barrier separating the groups from one another. Owing perhaps to some quality of the
thin morning air, voices did not mingle into the undifferentiated background characteristic of crowded places. Each was distinct and identifiable: the querulous tones of Hore that, because she was old (her breasts
were little more than flaps of dry and wrinkled skin) might have been
mistaken for a complaining child (her own small granddaughter, Aliho,
with whom she shared her house at the far end of the village); Makis'
wife Guma'e solicitously chiding Lusi (the daughter whose birth had
almost ended my work in the valley), who arched her back and
screamed with frustration when she lost her hold on her mother's nipple;
gentle Bihore, whom no one took seriously when he pretended anger,
dividing a piece of cold cooked taro with a bamboo knife and talking

quietly to two of his young sons who knelt in front of him, watching him so intently that their heads jerked round with a start when their mother suddenly laughed at one of his remarks. Each scene was as sharply etched as the brightly lit vignettes framed in the uncurtained windows of a suburban street at night. Like a solitary passer-by I felt a sudden emptying of the heart, which was partly a longing for the comfort and assurance of my own kind and partly doubt that the invisible barriers would ever lift sufficiently to allow me to cross to the other side of the street.

As a rule it was Makis who broke in upon my isolation. Because I was in the village at his invitation he seemed to hold himself responsible for me. During the first weeks of my stay he came to my house every night and sat cross-legged on the floor beside my camp stool, his eyes glinting like light reflected from a mirrored surface as he followed my movements or studied my possessions. Though I was pleased to see him I always found his visits a strain. He had only a slight command of pidjin English, and I knew none of his language, so we quickly exhausted our few topics of conversation and sat, for my part, in an awkward silence in which the normally gentle hiss of my lamp built to a loud and insistent hum. Later on, as I began to need the nights to organize the data I had collected during the day, I became impatient for him to leave. Yet when he failed to come for several nights in a row I found I missed him and hoped his absence did not mean that he sensed my irritation. He set my mind at rest on his next visit. Drawing on the cigarette I had offered him, he remarked that he had not come these past few nights because from his house across the street he had seen that my room was filled with other people. It pleased him, he said, because it showed I was not "new" any longer. At once I realized that he had been coming for my sake as much as anything else, to put me at ease in my strange surroundings and to help me over the loneliness of having no one with whom to talk. It was the first of those moments of illumination in which I responded to him with the quickening concern and gratitude that is still with me whenever I think of him.

Perhaps this sense of duty moved him to call me by the name he had given me, Goroha Gipo, or red-colored son, asking me to join him outside his house. It was mostly from this vantage point, sitting on a door plank Guma'e drew to the edge of the fire, that I continued to observe the quickening pageant of the morning.

The villagers ate very little at this hour—some cold leftovers from the main meal of the previous afternoon, a cob of tough unappetizing corn, or a piece of taro rolled briefly in the ashes of the fire. I looked past Makis, who was using his long fingernails to scrape the dirt from a sweet potato, and noticed the woman Alum entering the street from the direction of Gohajaka. She was as old as Hore, and her legs were hardly any thicker than the staff in her left hand, yet she was often the first to leave for work and the last to return. Sometimes she came to my house to exchange some produce for salt or a spoonful of beads for her daughter's son, who lived with his mother in a Gehamo village. I invariably took whatever she offered, as much to lighten her load as from any need for her goods, adding more than they were worth for the sake of her thin arms and the hollows in her back, large enough to contain my fists, which were the stigmata of her lifetime of carrying. As she passed us Makis gave her a ribald greeting, and her obscene reply, thrown back without so much as a glance in his direction, sent a wave of gusty laughter down the street. He bore the joke with the good-humored patience proper to the liberties permitted to the aged.

Like an awaited signal, the laughter rolled back the last barriers of the night. Voices met and mingled; the static groups began to break apart, spilling over the intervals between houses and flowing back and forth along the whole length of the street. Two girls went by, hips and shoulders touching, arms encircling one another's waist in giggling companionship. One was Sesue, whose tongue seemed absurdly pink as she laughingly turned her head for a quick glance in my direction. She had recently arrived at her father's house and announced that she had no intention of returning to the village of the young man to whom she had been betrothed. In time her prospective relatives-in-law would come to claim her, and watching her pass I thought that the swinging arcs of her string apron, which exposed the full length of her legs, showed little concern for the angry debates and the wrangling that were bound to follow.

I heard someone speak to Makis and, turning, found that Namuri and his family had joined us at the fire. They were on their way to work; Giza evidently went with some reluctance, holding his father's hand and kicking fretfully at the dust with his bare foot in the universal manner of children under adult duress. Where children are strictly disciplined Giza would have been considered spoiled, but so would any Gahuku boy of his age; for until the painful trials of initiation they were lauded, indulged, and given virtually complete freedom. Indeed,

at that moment his mother Izazu was treating Lusi to a typical display
of lavish affection. Sitting on the ground, she extended her arms in a
customary gesture of concern, palms upwards, her fingers opening and
closing, eagerly squeezing, a graphic accompaniment to the rush of
uninhibited endearments with which she accepted the baby, taking it
into her lap and attempting to force her nipple into its mouth. Meeting
with no success she lifted the child like a platter, one hand under its
buttocks, the other supporting its neck, and bending down rained resounding kisses between its legs, stopping only when Namuri called
her to follow him.

By this time the street was virtually empty. The usual crowd of
naked children and youths filled the shelter that served as my kitchen,
but most of the houses stared blindly at the scattered refuse and the
black stains on the dusty ground, which were all that remained of the
morning fires. Makis was also preparing to leave, raking the embers
with a calloused foot, stirring them momentarily into a cloud of yellow-
ish smoke while Guma'e readied the baby for the journey to their
gardens. First she placed a bilum on her lap and lined it with a mat of
bleached pandanus leaves. She completed the bed with an assortment
of dirty and malodorous rags, then placing Lusi on it she transferred
her hands to the mouth of the bag and swung it up to the top of her
head. As she rose easily under the weight Makis directed her to fasten
the door of the house, then turning to where I had also risen he took
his leave with the explicit if somewhat peremptory statement "You
stay, we go!"

On days when there was nothing to keep me at home I left the
house after I had eaten the unappetizing breakfast my cook-boy Hunehune served at the folding table where I worked. I was not long behind
the villagers, and although the sun had taken the chill from the morning the air was buoyant, water bright, and fresh as I set out along the
ridge. The narrow and uneven path, wide enough for only one person,
began immediately beyond the last house in the street, a furrow in the
black soil, several inches deep and unpleasantly slippery after rain,
which ran between a luxuriant growth of kunai and fences of living
pit-pit (a variety of cane) used to enclose the older gardens. Both
the tassels of the grass and the swordlike leaves of the cane were taller
than my head, and since the path twisted and turned with the contours of the ridge it was often possible to see only a few yards ahead.
Rounding a bend I was likely to come face to face with a startled

woman, bent under the weight of her load of sweet potatoes, who stepped into the grass to allow me passage, or perhaps with a man carrying his bow who stopped me to feel my thighs in greeting and to ask the inevitable questions concerning the place and purpose of my visit. Much as I preferred the more open parts of the route, even this tunneled section seemed to enhance my awareness, to sharpen and increase my capacity to perceive and to contain everything in my immediate environment, so that even as my eyes studied my footing I could see the bright gold flowers of crotalaria foaming against the blue sky and, invisible behind the fences, the rows of dark green vines pricked with metallic light.

Emerging on the open sections of the ridge was like the sudden, lifting freedom with which a swimmer breaks the surface of the sea in a shower of flashing drops. On these exposed heights I often felt alone at the pinnacle of the world. The warmth of the sun released scents not discernible at other times, and the air seemed to have been lightly brushed with the volatile oils of grass and honied crotolaria. The silence was as wide, as limitless as the valley; yet layered beneath it, audible to some more finely tuned interior ear, was a broad current of sound, the intangible evocation of all the life contained between the mountains, an invisible stream fed by my memory of everything I had heard and seen within the landscape.

At those moments, though it seemed that I had traveled as far as it was possible from my beginnings, I felt a sudden gratitude for the circumstances of my childhood. I was brought up on the land, in a region of plains where in winter the bright nights crackled with frost and the summer days were pitilessly hot and as dry as the dust that covered the sky with a yellow haze. After my ninth birthday I was away at boarding school for most of the year, but my home life was still a country life, its tenor governed by the seasons and the requirements of stock and crops. My most vivid recollections of it are the summer sound of pumps lifting green river water to the lucerne flats, the smell of tar and the oily texture of the raw-wool fleeces covering the sorting tables in the shearing shed, the acrid dust of stockyards, dogs barking on the flanks of a mob of sheep, sweaty saddles, and the thin blue shadows of eucalyptus leaves flicking over my horse's neck.

I could no more hope to share these details with the villagers of Susuroka than I could expect to explain to their satisfaction my purpose among them. Yet my past unexpectedly brought dividends that helped

me to appreciate the daily pattern of their lives. For their livelihood also
came from the land. When they talked about their gardens and their
pigs (and at times the conversation seemed to consist of nothing else)
only the phrasing of their thoughts and the ends they hoped to achieve
distinguished them from a group of men gathered in a hotel bar, leaning over a fence, or sitting in canvas chairs in the exhausted summer
evenings at home. There were forgotten echoes in the things they saw
in the landscape, in the appraising glance that measured a man's good
fortune, his industry, perhaps his morals, by the condition of his crops.
They discussed the points of their pigs with the tireless interests of
the crowds I used to see moving slowly among the pens where the
bloodstock were displayed at the local agricultural show, and on their
journeys their eyes reported on the poverty or richness of the soil from
the height of the natural grasses and subtle changes in the vegetation.

Surrounded by so much that was alien, I responded unexpectedly
to these familiar attitudes that reached into my past. In the beginning
I may have forced myself to acquire an interest in this side of the
villagers' lives, seeking for any means to pierce the barriers of my
isolation and to overcome the desperate feeling that my time would
expire with nothing accomplished, but this soon passed with the discovery that I could draw upon a neglected range of experience to
increase my appreciation of essentially unspectacular, everyday routines. Often on those mornings as I walked along the ridge, listening
below the silence for the welling sounds that were like the pulse of the
valley, I felt that I stood outside myself discovering the unity of my
life for the first time.

When I left the village for my walks I was seldom alone, for as soon
as I stepped outside the house several naked children with thin legs
and round, protruding stomachs left the group gathered around my
kitchen fire, running after me and jostling one another as they com-
peted shrilly for the job of carrying my camera. They were eager to
act as my guides, and as they conducted me around their company gave
my walks a picnic air. I enjoyed listening to their chatter, yet their
presence was often an unwanted and irritating intrusion. They could
not know that when I sat down after a stiff climb I not only needed
the rest to quiet the heartbeats pounding in my throat but also wanted
to renew my accord with the valley in silence. Then, when it returned
I would gladly have them with me for the remainder of the way. Learning that I was interested in knowing my surroundings, they took it upon

themselves not only to be my guide but also to teach me the names of trees and plants and vines, and they darted into the grass to bring me berries and colored beetles, or they told me to halt and urged me to listen for a rat scurrying through the undergrowth.

Even when my novelty had worn off and I knew my way around the environs of Susuroka, I seldom managed to be alone for long. No matter how empty the landscape seemed to be, the grass was almost sure to part beside the track and a troop of boys would surround me, their grimy hands clutching the toy bows with which they menaced small girls. Or, with complete indifference to the pain they caused, they grasped the end of a pliant strip of bamboo attached to the bedraggled neck of a captured bird or a large green beetle, prodding it to flutter and to describe erratic, iridescent circles. From early morning till mid-afternoon (and until a much later hour on moonlit nights) they roamed the valley, and as I came upon them in deserted villages, in the jade shadows of taro gardens where their shouts and laughter were carried away on the water, on paths inching across the face of light-soaked cliffs, I gradually became familiar with the pattern of their childhood.

This world of children recalled the busyness of water insects darting to the broad surface of a stream and whirling back toward the sun on gauzy wings. It was as crowded as the summer air above a pool, and there was no place for the solitary child or the uncompetitive nature, for though its lines were loosely drawn they managed to suggest the bolder, more uncompromising strokes that laid out the pattern of adult existence. The toy bows with their arrows fashioned from the stiff stalks of kunai grass were fired more frequently, and with more effect, at naked legs and arms than at the small animals and birds that invariably escaped unharmed. A familiar rowdiness during rough-and-tumble games concealed the seriousness with which supremacy was sought and defeat revenged. There were always scores to settle, for no blow or tackle was accepted with good grace—and so much the better if equality was restored or advantage gained by trickery and stealth.

It was a free republic, but already its ranks were forming after the manner of the larger world. Boys in their early teens were its senior citizens, still thin and immature but standing with narrow hips and flat stomachs at the threshhold of the shattering experience of initiation that would end their official childhood. They were easily distinguished by their *gene* headdresses, narrow strips of bark cloth that were white, tipped with red dye, but that after a matter of days became the color of the dark hair to which they were attached like artificial braids. Thrown back from the shoulders, the long streamers fell below the knees and at moments of rest touched the slight figures with a theatrical dignity, a prefiguring of taut arrogance and manly pride that was strangely moving in contrast to the flying tangles accompanying a scuffle or the bizarre complement to grinning faces suspended by the ankles from the branches of a tree. These children lorded it over the age group immediately below them, demanding of their juniors services that it would be their lot to provide until, many years later, free of most of the debts incurred on their behalf, they had acquired their own households. The new independence this step announced was often marked by a move away from the vicinity of an elder brother's dwelling, the physical separation expressing a rankling hostility that it was improper for close kinsmen to display in open antagonism but that showed itself in childhood in sullen anger or crumpled, injured cries following a sharp blow and in the contrasting look of satisfaction on the young male exercising his right to discipline.

Very little escaped the notice of the bands of children. Their curiosity was boundless and their bodies, filled with a restless energy, were seldom still. I seldom took them by surprise, but sometimes in the noon heat, when the clouds seemed bruised and swollen with pain and the valley stretched beneath them in exhausted torpor, unnoticed I came upon them at a garden homestead. Six or seven figures were crouched on the ground before a boarded house, their heads bent forward in a circle that complemented the motionless walls of kunai, the long streamers of their artificial hair parted by the curve of their backs. I thought that my rubber soles made no sound on the dusty ground, but as a rule I advanced no more than a few paces toward them before a head in the circle lifted and a pair of startled eyes, white in the dark face, searched the clearing for the source of the intrusion. Once my familiar figure was found, the alert uncertainty vanished in a wide look of recognition and a rush of words that brought the whole band to its feet, roused into action like the flocks of pink and grey birds who scatter from the bare branches of a gum tree at the warning cry of a sentinel.

When I met them alone they treated me with a familiarity that was restrained at other times by the watchfulness of their elders (whose solicitousness came from a concern lest they offend the white man rather than any special consideration for my own person). As I complied with the children's demands for tobacco and cigarettes I often wondered what useful information might be concealed behind their grinning faces. For as they filled the hours along the ridge they reminded me of self-appointed scouts patroling the unattended perimeters of village life. It was they who discovered Ragaso hanged at Ekuhakuka. She had threatened to kill herself in retaliation for harsh treatment by her husband (whom she accused of wanting to take a second wife because she was childless). When they entered her boarded house in search of some pork she had recently received (a misdemeanor forgotten in the ensuing confusion) she was already dead. When Kamahoe did not appear to help her sister-in-law with the evening meal, they reported that they had seen her on the track to Gama, leading two pigs and carrying all her possessions, behavior confirming the longstanding suspicion that she was dissatisfied with Lotuwa, the youth who had been chosen as her husband. They knew that Ipaha of Gehamo had been alone with Ilia, wife of Mihore, in her taro garden and that Hasu had stolen a march on his age mates by having intercourse with Gumila before the elders had given their official dispensation. Most of the things they saw eventually reached the adults, and when Mihore beat his wife it was highly probable that the gossip that aroused his suspicions had started the morning some children had seen her meet Ipaha in the garden.

The character of my own day on the ridge did not vary greatly. If there was some special activity I tried to be present at it, but because the villagers failed to inform me I often missed events I had been hoping to see. In the long run it did not matter very much, since the opportunity usually came again, but when I was new and anxious such disappointments added to the general load of frustration. Otherwise the time was spent in mapping the village lands and observing the everyday routines of gardening.

Looking back on them, I find it difficult to believe that I was not bored by the long stretches of uneventful days; yet often they did not seem monotonous. Though I did not consciously plan it, most of my time was spent in the gardens of a small number of men—Makis, Zaho, Ihanizo, Gesekunimo, and later Goluwaizo, whose acquaintance with me began with a heated argument and mutual distrust but whom I recognized eventually as possibly the most complex of my friends. At first, as at night, I saw more of Makis during the day than any of the others. It seemed the obvious thing to seek him out, to capitalize on our special relationship. He clearly expected me to do so, and I was often grateful that I had entered Susuroka under his auspices, for the other villagers also accepted the fact that I was there at his invitation and it made it easier for me to force myself on their company, something more necessary, but no less difficult for me to do than among my own people. Yet Makis showed no sign of slight or injury if I preferred to be with others. My guilt when I had neglected him for several days reflected a deeper uneasiness that I did not want to face, the knowledge that even if there was nothing I could do to alter it I was misleading him. I knew the unexpressed hopes he had centered on me, and my mere presence in the village was enough to encourage them. At these moments, I was often moved to drop whatever I had in hand to look for him and to let him know that I was grateful, not in words, for nothing is more difficult for me even in my own language, but simply in being near him. And sometimes when I found him, after searching and inquiring for him on the ridge, I felt that he understood. At least the openness of his greeting helped to quiet my own distress.

If I was not bored by days when nothing in particular happened, it was precisely because it was then that I established my closest relationships with some of the villagers. There was no privacy in the village street, and I was never comfortable in the round houses, which were nothing more than a divided circular room, the rear portion raised a foot or so above the ground, the front half hardly large enough to accommodate the full number of human beings and animals. The doorway was the only opening in the walls, and when it was closed the houses were abysmally dark, for the thatch was impervious to both light and rain. A circle of stones inside the entry served as a hearth where a fire burned at night and on afternoons when it was too wet to cook outside. The timbers of the roof were grimed with dirt and smoke; the air was always stale, and there were often fleas to add to the list of disadvantages. Expressing a basic opposition in Gahuku life, only women, girls, and uninitiated boys formerly slept in these dwellings, the adult men retiring at night to a clubhouse. The custom was dying throughout the valley, but it was revived at Susuroka during my stay, when Makis built himself a house in my compound and allowed the village youths and some of the married men to use it.

It suited me that the houses were used infrequently, since it meant that there were few occasions when it was absolutely necessary to enter them; but the public character of the street was not helpful in fostering intimate relations. It was as crowded as the strips of beach where I used to be taken on Sundays, places I always disliked intensely; and though the street gave me unrivaled opportunities for observation, there were also continual distractions and interruptions. These were not present in the gardens, which I often found to be more private than my own house, and I began to look on them as the places best suited to the delicate task of trying to reach the individuality of the men who I thought were willing to respond. In this I was being no different from the villagers who found the living fences of cane an ideal protection for the exchange of confidences.

My first appearances in the gardens were met with a tolerant amusement and, often, a little embarrassment. It was odd behavior for a white man (to judge from the explanations that those who knew me best were called upon continually to provide), and because the people were ill at ease their welcome was often overdone, a solicitiousness that threatened to defeat the very ends I hoped to achieve. Zaho's attitude was typical of the others. He was younger than Makis, about thirty, and taller than the average Gahuku, his body displayed to advantage in bark-cloth vees, which covered the genitals and had a narrow fringe that parted on his thighs. He had come to see me even before I moved to Susuroka, appearing one morning at Young-Whitforde's house at Humeleveka and waiting at a respectful distance from the front verandah until I spoke to him. Because he said he came from Nagamidzuha I sat with him in the shade of the casuarinas for an hour or so, hoping to start an acquaintance that might be useful during the first difficult days in the village. But he was neither physically attractive nor a sympathetic personality. For one thing he was unbelievably dirty. The traditional hair style of the Gahuku—the long ringlets greased with fat—is highly unsanitary, yet it adds a quality of drama to an arrogant face as the hair moves in rhythmic complement to expressive bodies, but Zaho lacked even this. He had an abundance of hair, so much that his face seemed unnaturally small, and he wore it in an unkempt, tangled cloud coated with dust. Small pieces of rubbish clung to his eyebrows and the fine, almost invisible hairs of his chest and legs, giving him the appearance of having recently rolled in chaff. Even the circular bone ornament in his nose was discolored.

Seeing so many ill-favored features, I failed to notice the sensitive curve of his lips or the inquiring softness in his eyes. When he spoke he simply confirmed my initial repulsion. It was clear that he had an axe to grind. Zaho was not a Nagamidzuha man. He had close connections with Makis, but he belonged to the Gehamo tribal group and lived at Gorohadzuha. Almost at once he tried to involve me in the political rivalries of Gehamo and Nagamidzuha. The details were not clear until much later, but the point at issue seemed to be that the white administration recognized Makis as the official representative of some of the Gehamo villages. The Gehamo resented this, for he was not of their tribe. To compound the injury they had been clearly in the ascendancy at the time the whites arrived in the valley. Zaho wanted me to use my influence to end this situation. He said the Gehamo hoped to obtain an official spokesman of their own, and he mentioned the man whom I knew later as Goluwaizo.

I wanted to avoid identification with any local factions, and though he pressed me to visit Gehamo to talk to other people I had no immediate intentions of accepting the offer. Besides, I thought that I recognized his type and had summed him up as typical "grease man," the appropriate and highly evocative pidjin-English phrase for a man who seeks to further his self-interest through flattery and ingratiation. I decided to avoid him.

I saw him again soon after moving to Susuroka, and it was then I learned that he worked the relatively new garden that I could see from the rear of my house. Since it was convenient, and also because he was not a complete stranger, it was among the first I visited when I began to tour the ridge. I went back often in the following months to the garden itself and also to the clearing at the brow of the hill where Zaho had a house shaded by a clump of castor-oil tree. Thinking of him now, I picture him either there, squatting on his heels beside me with the indented leaves and the vermillion fruits of the trees patterning the sky above our heads, or coming to meet me on the first morning when I went to see him at work.

He was in the garden with his wife Ilato and his mother-in-law Helazu when I arrived unannounced at the stile. Ilato, who was closer than the others, was the first to see me, looking up from the furrow where she sat on her heels weeding between the young vines and calling out a phrase I already recognized as "white man." Some distance behind her, partly concealed by the curve of the ground, Zaho rose to his feet with the quickness I always admired in the Gahuku men. He dropped the strips of cane he had been using to repair the fence, stepped rapidly across the rows of sweet potatoes, and met me several yards from the women, folding his arms around my waist and pressing me to his body. Releasing me, he spoke rapidly to Ilato who had stopped her work and was watching us with a wide smile. She replied in the slightly injured, querelous voice I heard so often that I began to expect it as a woman's natural form of expression. The tone barely recognized a man's right to command and thus asserted the woman's own will even while complying with his demands, just as Ilato did now, reaching behind her and handing Zaho an empty bilum, which he laid in a furrow to make a seat for me.

I did not want this kind of attention, but not knowing how to tell him so I sat down where he indicated and brought out my cigarettes. They were corktipped, and I had to show him which end to light, burning my fingers with the match while he handled the cigarette uncertainly before he put it in his mouth. (Such mistakes, showing a lack of sophistication, always convulsed the teen-age boys who watched carefully, waiting to laugh, whenever I offered my cigarettes to an older man.) With the cigarette lit at last, Zaho sat back on his heels and inhaled so noisily that I thought I ought to warn him not to swallow it. He held the smoke for an intolerable time, then, smiling broadly, expelled it with such gusto in my face that it threatened to make me choke. The women, who had been watching intently, immediately extended their hands toward me in the squeezing gesture of appreciation, accompanying the movement of their fingers with a rattle of polite phrases indicating what they would like to do with various parts of my body, all of them calculated to shock anyone brought up to avoid public references to the genitalia or bodily excretions.

Zaho knew enough pidjin English to communicate with me at more than a minimal level, but it was hardly sufficient to sustain a conversation. There was also my inability to be at ease with strangers, compounded in these situations not only by the vastly different background of the people with me but also by the fact that at first I did not really like them. I had to make an effort to know them, but doubted if I would ever care for them enough to make the effort worthwhile. They were not a pleasing trio; indeed, no Gahuku women seemed attractive to me. Taken singly their features sometimes recalled the conventions of beauty to which I was accustomed, but the total effect was completely undesirable. From their cracked and calloused feet to their thighs, their bare legs were grained with dirt and streaked with dust. A coating of grease and soot frequently decorated their faces, accentuating broad cheeks and a wide flat nose pierced in the fleshy parts of the nostrils, where they stuck a jaunty array of small objects, from used matches to colored feathers. Even their ringlets lacked the body and bravura of the men's hair, hanging around their ears in listless strands, indistinguishable in color from the worn string bags they piled loosely on top of their heads. And while some of the men bathed occasionally, the women almost never washed. They carried an odor of smoke, stale sweat and rancid fat that became intolerable when I walked behind them in the heat through the narrow, breathless corridors of grass.

Ilato's comparative youth was the only quality that redeemed her a little, for there were a thousand extra folds and wrinkles in Helazu to collect the dirt and dust, and like the older women generally she was more garrulous, less likely to affect an embarrassed coyness, and more prone to demonstrate the privileges of her status by an embrace or by stroking my legs and arms, attentions borne in a manner that I trusted did not show distaste. Zaho squatted beside me watching, smoking his cigarette, and sometimes translating her remarks. There were compensations in these exhibitions of interest, for while they lasted nothing was asked of me but passive acquiescence, whereas when the ministrations stopped I had to think of something to say. It would have been easier if the women had returned to their work, but apparently they were not to be deprived of this unaccustomed treat. Being the object of their undivided interest was uncomfortable enough without the additional distractions: their interruptions to ask Zaho a question obviously concerning some attribute of my person, Ilato blowing her nose with her hand and wiping her fingers on her exposed thigh, Helazu casually lifting a wrinkled breast to scratch a conspicuous patch of exzema. Also, my own queries tended to be so obvious, concerned with such everyday things as the names for various plants or garden implements, that Zaho appeared to lose interest, and, indeed, I too found the conversation as strained as a polite exchange of inconsequentials. Any attempt to probe into more important subjects was hindred by Zaho's modest pidjin English and by an irritating obtuseness for which I was partly prepared, remembering the same attitudes in Tofmora, a denial that something existed—a belief, a rule, an interpetation of behavior —that later turned out to be a falsehood. Yet there was no intention to mislead. It was partly that I did not know enough to ask the right questions and partly that every way of life contains a host of unstated terms, attitudes, and ideas so intrinsic to a particular view of the world

that they do not have to be, sometimes cannot be put into words. I had
to remind myself all over again that my work required almost limitless
patience, a meticulous concern for detail, and the abilities of a detective.

If I often forgot to use these qualities the need for them was never
lost, but later on I was not quite so strained or uncomfortable with the
people whom I met in the gardens. Definite progress was shown when
they no longer stopped their work when I appeared, permitting me
to move about as I pleased, to talk to the women wielding their digging
sticks along the newly cultivated furrows, and to observe the men con-
structing the cane fences, sometimes also lending a hand myself, such
uninstructed efforts meeting with good-natured laughter that was loud-
est when I inadvertently chose a task performed by women. My activities were not merely social. I walked through the countryside to learn
and to observe. On the whole the unstructured interviews were more
profitable and better suited to my temperament than formal questions
put to an informant in the privacy of my house. Nonetheless it was
work, requiring a degree of both patience and concentration that became exhausting after several hours. It was then that I felt the benefits
of my surroundings. I simply allowed my objectives to slide from my
mind, no longer bothering to remember or record the details of activity.
At once I became aware of another dimension of experience. The figures
and the landscape assumed a new relationship, a change like the sudden alteration in light when a cloud passes from the face of the sun.
The rows of vines curving across a hillside distilled a tangible warmth,
a visible vibration rising from the topmost leaves that spread protecting
shadows over the roots and ground. A breeze pushed at the cane fences
but found no way to enter; inside their rectangles the air was completely still. People moved at their tasks with a slow, suspended quality,
one action leading to another without a noticeable break. Their voices
came to me from far away, each echoing endlessly in a separate chamber—not dying, simply passing below the level of perception. I lost all
feeling of myself, and when I closed my eyes I seemed to be floating
on the valley, held at each point, lifting with the movement of a sea.

At these detached moments Gahuku life appeared to flow smoothly
through the gardens, one day, one month following another with barely
perceptible changes. There were no obvious signs of the turbulence concealed beneath the uneventful surface. Men carried their bows and the
beautiful, intricately carved arrows to work, but the days had gone
when they might be called upon to use them to repel a surprise attack.

Now they strung the arrows only if a pig broke through a fence or to hunt rats in the long grass on the uncultivated slopes. They had become so limited in use, where man himself had been the principal animal to hunt, that travelers were often seen unarmed on the tracks and government roads. To many who had grown up in other times this radical innovation signified the whole course of events since the arrival of the whites. They described to me how people had walked then, lifting their heads alertly and snapping their fingers, making a sound like that of a suddenly released string. It had been easy to recognize a man, they said, a statement in which I read not only regret for the lost opportunity to display a manly pride but also a recognition, incapable of more precise expression, that independence had gone with it; power had been taken from their hands. Now and then, however, the even flow of events was interrupted by isolated acts of violence. When they occurred, news spread quickly through the gardens and along the ridge until the air seemed charged with its repercussions.

At other times garden work itself assumed a tone that was like an echo, or perhaps a premonition of rhythms obscured by utilitarian routines. It was in the midday sun when I stood at Gesekunimo's stile watching him perform a magic rite to protect his crops from unauthorized intruders. It was in the movement of the russet tassels of the kunai where the Nagamidzuha had erected an ozaha neta many years before, a site long since abandoned, without a trace of its former significance, but still charged with such supernatural power that the prudent avoided approaching it. It swelled to open dominance when Makis distributed the first crop of sweet potatoes from the garden jointly cultivated by two of his wives, Gotome and Guma'e. Perhaps the light and the situation helped to build the atmosphere at this event, for the site lay on an open hillside, visible for more than half a mile, which faced the morning sun. Everything below the garden lay in the shadow of another spur farther to the east, the darkness extending from the base of the hill to the rectangular fence enclosing the action like the proscenium of a stage. Inside the illuminated area women sat in the furrows, their lower legs hidden among the damp vines. The men were higher up the slope, a group of twelve walking with Makis from row to row, stopping every few yards to discuss some aspect of the distribution, now and then retracing their steps to change a decision by altering the position of sticks set up to mark the rows into sections. It was a rather ordinary ceremony, but as I stood to one side I was struck by the intensity of the men. They moved abruptly, speaking quickly in a manner matching their look of puzzled incomprehension when they turned to face a woman who had called to them from the bottom of the garden. Their air of urgency was unmistakable as they readied the scene to their satisfaction, only then falling back and giving over to the chief actor Makis, who performed the part with his accustomed flair, walking slowly and deliberately along the rows, halting to indicate each section with a sweeping gesture and to call the name of the person to whom he wished to give it. It might have been no more than a simple recital of his kinsmen, but his voice filled each name with the resonance of a grand occasion, its tones echoing all those times when he thumped out his pride in the manner that had earned him his orator's reputation. Behind him the hillside seemed crowded with events: slow processions of initiates returning to a village after their long seclusion, waiting throngs leaping to greet them with a tumult of praise, flutes shrilling in the night as the great festivals approached, the voices of people singing in the house of a bride's father on the morning of a wedding, challenges hurled between opposing factions at a gathering of clans, the iridescent orchestration of a hundred plumes tossing an accompaniment to deep-throated shouts of welcome, the high-pitched squeal of pigs slaughtered in the reeking dust of crowded streets. All of Gahuku life was concentrated in the garden at that moment; its discords and divisions and the overstated violence woven into a single pattern with the slow progression of the uneventful days.

My days on the ridge ended as they had begun, in a silence as wide and deep as the night sky over the valley. Darkness came quickly after the sun had set, and by the time my meal was on the table the tilley lamp had been lit. Almost at once the villagers began to arrive, entering through the open door even before I had finished eating. Sometimes there were as many as twenty at a time sitting on the floor, men and boys for the most part and a few of the married women— the wives of Makis, Namuri, and Bihore, who came occasionally but stayed for only a short while. In due course probably the entire male population of Susuroka, Gohajaka, and Ekuhakuka had watched me eat and had examined my few possessions, as well as others from places as far away as Heuve (a good half day's walk to the western side of the Asaro River) who were visiting relatives in the settlement or passing through on business at the government station. When such strangers appeared a stereotyped routine followed. They entered hesitantly and self-consciously, bending down to rub their hands along the shoulders or the thighs of people they knew in the crowd. My own villagers, who had a proprietary attitude toward me, delighted in the puzzled curiosity of these strangers: waiting expectantly for their indrawn hiss of astonished admiration when they noticed the lamp; following their eyes as they took in my bed, the tin boxes containing my stores and clothing, the mosquito net, and the portable typewriter on the folding table. To please them I went along with the game. I took off my shoes and socks when I was asked and joined in the laughter when a newcomer touched my bare foot and drew back his hand in shocked amazement, shaking his fingers as though he had put them to a hot stove. I even became accustomed to undressing in public. It was often the only way to dismiss my visitors, who stayed as long as the lamp burned.

Though Makis cautioned me against it, I liked to keep the door open at night. If there was a moon a narrow stretch of street was visible through the opening, silvered with the incredibly bright radiance that filled the whole valley like a lake. Concealed by the curve of the ground the houses were again fastened and still. Now and then I heard the sound of a plank sliding into place across an entrance, a pig grunting as it settled down for the night, a man's voice talking to a child who had awakened and begun to cry. Long moments passed. Suddenly bare feet went running by the house, and boys' voices called urgently to one another. Then there was silence once again, a quietness so deep that underneath it I could feel the stars vibrate. The mists began to collect in the mountains and the ridge of Susuroka slept.

CHAPTER TWO

▲▲▲

MAKIS

He was known to me as Makis, but I often thought that his battle name, Urugusie, the one by which his enemies knew him, the name chanted as a rallying call by his own people, fitted him more appropriately, its ring a better match for his personal flourish. Even at our first meeting I detected this quality in him; as I descended from the jeep in his village on the day following my arrival in the valley, my feet touched the ground with the curious sensation that it moved beneath me, that the whole landscape swung around my head, and, as it steadied, I found myself clutched to his naked chest, his long hair and his shell earrings brushing my cheek as he embraced me. I was embarrassed by his greeting and overcautious in my response, for he seemed to take so much for granted, and I did not know whether I wanted to live in his settlement. Yet even then his enthusiasm carried me along. His face and figure possessed a quality of ancient beauty—of something perceived in relics from the civilizations of man's beginning —an age-old pride, the mark of grandeur and authority. All his movements as he listened to Young-Whitforde or inscribed the dust with the blueprint for my house seemed to demand attention, displayed, even then, the flair, the swagger that characterized his more ceremonial performances. They were the hallmark of an art that he, like all the orators, had learned, but they fitted him more naturally than others, and even in repose his body conveyed this peculiar grace. Perhaps I was subverted by it at our first meeting, for when I left his village I knew I would look no further for a place to live.

From then onward I saw Makis almost every day. I did not move to his village immediately. The house I occupied eventually took several weeks to build; indeed, its construction taught me my first lesson in patience, which I needed frequently therafter, for the villagers worked at it only intermittently and seemed unable to appreciate my sense of haste, answering my questions with the bland assurance that it would be finished soon.

For a while it was my practice to walk to the village every day to watch the work, hoping also to begin acquaintances that might be useful to me later. It was not a successful enterprise; unless work was actually progressing on my house the village was likely to be empty when I arrived, and there was little opportunity for any systematic work. Rather than spend my time at Humeleveka with nothing to do, I welcomed Young-Whitforde's suggestion that I join him on a patrol journeying beyond the southern ranges among peoples who had not been contacted by the government. He expected to be away for at least three weeks, by which time my house should have been ready for occupancy, and in the interim there would be a valuable chance to see the country. For professional reasons, I could hardly reject his invitation; few of my colleagues have had this particular experience. But when he told me he was asking Makis to join us, I knew I could not refuse. There seemed no better opportunity to get to know him, to form the kind of relationship that would aid me when I went to live at Susuroka.

Makis was a *luluai*, the government-sponsored spokesman of Nagamidzuha, an office that carried little more authority than he possessed already but one that occupied a fair amount of his time, for he had to represent his people in everything touching the white administration. The invitation—rather, the order—to join Young-Whitforde had a dual purpose: first, to indicate esteem for Makis; and second, to use him indirectly as part of the process of extending government law, his presence demonstrating to the new people a facet of their future under white control.

The three weeks we were on patrol were the most arduous I have ever spent. After we left the valley we were never again in really open country. Every day tested me to the very limit of endurance as we circled through the folded ranges, struggling across the interminable ridges on narrow tracks often only a few degrees from perpendicular. I was so concerned with driving my body that much of the country through which we passed is only a vague memory, an undifferentiated background separating our departure and arrival at the sites where we camped each day. From the beginning, Makis seemed to regard me as his special charge. He was always near me to offer a steadying hand as I inched across a slippery log, to show me where to place my feet as we slid down a mountain on the roots of trees, to help me at the last part of an ascent when the few remaining yards seemed more than I could manage. We did not talk a great deal, but the three weeks we spent together became a unique bond, something I shared with none of the other villagers; and when we returned to Humeleveka he had given me the name of Goroha Gipo and called me his "younger brother."

Toward the end of the second week of the patrol, we camped at a village whose people had never seen white men before. The day had been one of continual alarms as we approached, of armed men silhouetted on the ridges in front of us and falling back as our progress brought us closer to their home. The native police who were with us expected an attack. We had come from the territory of traditional enemies of the people who watched us, and we had passed through several burned and abandoned settlements, signs that the two groups were in a state of active hostility. We halted at four in the afternoon at the bottom of the ridge where the village huddled under its grove, waiting there until the men found courage to approach us and we could show them that we meant no harm. After half an hour's debate and a demonstration of the efficiency of the steel knives and axes we had brought as gifts, they escorted us nervously to the crest of the ridge, watching every movement as we pitched our tents outside the protection of the wooden palisade surrounding their homes. We had seen no women or children; all of them had been sent into hiding at the first word of our approach, but at night after we had gone to bed, a remarkable thing happened. At least I remember it more vividly than anything else that occurred during the entire patrol.

As I lay on my camp stretcher listening to the movements of the guard outside the tent, through the open canvas flaps I could see a triangle of silver light, for the moon was full; the mists that shrouded these mountain ridges had not descended yet. Except for myself and the police boy standing watch, the whole camp seemed to be asleep, and I felt the gentle tug of smallness, the intimation of mortality projected on an inner vision of the turning and evolving universe. At this precise moment voices rose in song—a sweet sound, matching my mood of quiet suspension, which took its measure from the stillness of the night rather than trespassing against it. I was so moved that I left my bed and went outside the tent. Several paces distant, the tall palisade was dark against the sky. Its one entrance had been closed, and I made no move to enter it but stood watching the pale glow rising above it, the intermittent showers of sparks tossed by some invisible fire that burned and died with the lift and fall of the voices. Men and women were there, singing together, as I heard them later in Susuroka on many moonlit nights. The words had no meaning for me, but they rang then —and ring for me yet—with peculiar poignancy, the voice of people standing at the threshhold of the future, perhaps beguiled by it already, intuitively drawn to each other and pausing for reassurance as they prepare to step across.

When we broke camp next day, a young boy from the village came with us. He was thirteen or so, certainly not yet initiated, for he wore his hair in braids as the uninitiated Gahuku boys did. No one in our party spoke his language, but this did not seem to worry him. We gathered that he wanted to return with us to Humeleveka, a journey immeasurably greater than the distance involved, virtually a transition from one world to another, a leap through time that took a measure of courage and a degree of foresight almost impossible to comprehend. He attached himself to Makis, who adopted him eventually and named him Susuro, a diminutive form of Susuroka where he lived for the next two years and still remained at my own departure from the valley.

Because of his relationship to Makis and the circumstances under which the three of us had met, he was virtually a member of my household, and I felt a special concern for him. He was an alien like me, though not as much a stranger to everything around him, for his eyes were conditioned already to a similar if not precisely the same way of life. The villagers took joking note of the fact that we were both outsiders, even suggesting a competition to see which one of us learned their language first, a test in which he soon outstripped me. But apart from myself, possibly only Makis could picture him in his village where his future had been decided, and he may have remembered a similar meeting with whites, provoking the same decision in his own past.

Makis had been one of the first among his people to cast his lot with the white man, moved perhaps by the same intuition, the sudden vision that had persuaded Susuro to leave his village with a party of complete strangers. He was certainly older than the boy when the first white explorers came to the valley, probably a young man several years beyond his initiation, betrothed but not yet living with his wife. He had participated in raids and already had earned a considerable reputation, which was possibly noticed by the early government officer who singled him out for special favor in hopes of gaining a recruit for the immediate aims of the administration. Makis also accompanied this man on patrols, experiencing at first hand the power the whites possessed and forming some notion of their ends and of the future they sought to impose on the valley. He chose to embrace what they seemed to offer, following up his initial advantage by identifying with the officials who succeeded his original mentor. His name and influence began to spread beyond his own tribe until his advice and assistance were sought by strangers who had business to transact at Humeleveka, and in time the government, recognizing his reputation, created him luluai of Nagamidzuha, bestowing on him the badge of this office, a small brass replica of the Australian coat of arms, which he wore on official occasions centered among the feathers of his headdress.

Though his career might seem to suggest it, he did not set out to ingratiate himself with my own people. He was not a "grease man," not a flatterer or a sycophant. He always maintained his natural dignity, his pride, the air of grandeur that testified to unquestioned accomplishments in a way of life still sufficiently near in time to merit the approval of the majority of his fellows. He was undoubtedly ambitious, and his nature had spurred him to compete for prestige and a following long before the white man had arrived. Though he cast his lot with the new overlords, he was not a *nouveau arrivé*. On the contrary, this action reflected traits of personality typical of established leaders who under traditional conditions needed both intuition and initiative—the ability to gauge and to foresee where a course of action led, to guide others in the direction they wanted to go, and to know it before they knew it themselves.

Perhaps it was this same incipient talent, this drive, that had led the boy Susuro to leave his home so suddenly. Undoubtedly, he also shared with Makis another tendency, one that was widely distributed and reflected a world view characteristic of an entire culture area. Gahuku are materialists, concerned to the point of exhaustion with the acquisition of wealth and its distribution in a never-ending series of competitive exchanges. They lose interest quickly in ideas and measure the good life in terms of worldly success, bestowing prestige on those who have acquitted themselves conspicuously in the pursuit of its riches. Wealth signifies both power and strength, testifies to the achievements of individuals, of the clan, and of the tribe; reputations are placed on the ballot of public opinion each time the great festivals are held, when the slaughtered pigs, the array of plumes, the necklaces of shell and the breastplates of mother-of-pearl hopefully win both envy and respect.

Both Makis and Susuro had been subverted by the material aspects of my own culture whose first representatives had provided them with a glimpse of wealth and power beyond their comprehension, breaching forever the boundaries of traditional expectations. But the vision impelling them to leave the past was clouded also by a mode of thought that I sensed at my first meeting with Makis.

In Gahuku belief, strength and power, every human achievement testified to the operation of supernatural forces. Men were not thereby the passive recipients of supernatural benefits. Time and effort, the application of human skill and knowledge were necessary to every enterprise, but alone they did not guarantee success. For the universe was informed by a force that was greater than man, by a power transcending any of his natural gifts. It was neither named nor personified and could not be summarized in any single phrase; rather, it was known and revealed through its several manifestations, through everything that signified the good life. It could be perceived in the fertility of men, of animals, and crops; in the wealth of individuals, of clans, and tribes; in victory over enemies; in personal achievement; in the envy and respect of others. Power was *there,* an invisible reservoir waiting to be tapped by means of ritual, but since its benefits were distributed unequally it was clear that the means of obtaining them could differ in their efficacy. The whites, who had so much more of the things power bestowed, must also be more familiar with the manner of its operation, must have a better knowledge of the ways of obtaining access to it, ways that presumably others could learn and might expect to be taught. For power operated in a moral universe, not for the exclusive benefit or aggrandizement of individuals but for the welfare of the larger social whole to which they belonged.

I am sure it was this realm of unspoken assumption that qualified my relationship with Makis. Searching for his motives in asking Young-Whitforde for a white man, I concluded that he expected to obtain from me the kinds of benefits that were provided by European planters in the area, and if these were what he wanted he must have been disappointed when he found that my work and my needs were entirely different. I went farther than necessity dictated in trying to meet such expectations but eventually realized that something more important was involved, that because of it I had to fail him.

I am convinced that his request was essentially an attempt to forge a moral link between the two cultures. I do not mean that he was emancipated from the tendency to see the achievements and the position of the whites in terms of traditional Gahuku notions of supernatural power or that this had not moved him to cast his lot with them so shortly after their arrival. But the initiative he had shown then reflected qualities of personality that were often obscured by the formal requirements of his public role, which masked an insight, a sensitivity that I discovered only after long acquaintance with him. He would not recognize his motives as I set them down now, and it does not matter that they involved a misunderstanding or, rather, a partial understanding of the basis of white affluence. This was to be expected; for no Gahuku could comprehend, had ever seen the complex processes behind the end products of white wealth. Indeed, the artificiality of a colonial society dependent for everything on a distant metropolitan country tended to reinforce or, at the least, to lend support to bizarre notions of the source of its authority and possessions. Yet if these were elements in his decision, I believe he was moved also by his perception and experience of the relationships between the whites and his own people.

The white government at that time was essentially authoritarian and paternalistic. Its representatives were distant figures of respect whose demands, though well-meaning, were often both puzzling and arbitrary. A distance just as great, if not greater, separated the local populations from the whites who were not officials of the administration. Most of these depended heavily on unskilled native labor. The modest wages they offered were the natives' principal means of obtaining the cheap goods displayed in the trade stores, and there were many villages who were willing, even anxious, to provide these whites with a base in return for such dubious benefits. But their interest in the natives was solely practical. They demanded respect because of their color, and for the most part they had no sympathy for the broader aims of government, which they had to see as a future threat to their present position of privilege. In all the relationships between white and black, whether official or nonofficial, the element most conspicuously lacking was moral concern. By this, I do not mean that the government was insensitive to notions of justice and guardianship or that the private segment of the white population was purely exploitive, but there were no personal ties that crossed the barriers of caste, no shared institutions, virtually nothing to indicate the recognition of mutual obligations and of common interests transcending for the natives a strictly limited, practical dependence.

As I came to know him better, I believed that Makis hoped to fill this moral vacuum, that basically this was the motive lying behind the request that had brought me to his village. Essentially, he hoped to establish a climate in which the things he wanted, which my own people possessed, would be given freely, their gift the natural expression of a common bond. It did not matter that in his own view, derived from his tradition, the gift was power or, rather, access to power; what was important was that he saw the necessity for a new relationship between the two cultures, that he was looking for a new door to the future, the one he had tried, which Susuro too had seen, having failed to open for him.

Because his request had to be explained in this manner, I could not escape its implications. Makis wanted more from me than the modest material benefits I was able to provide. In effect, he expected me to introduce a new order, and it was quite beyond all possibility that I could meet his expectations. When I left, the door he had hoped to open would remain as tightly closed, the future he wanted would be no nearer than the day I arrived in his village. It was small comfort that no one else could have done any better, could not perhaps have done as much to show him that personal relationships could transcend the two dissimilar traditions. There were times when I could not avoid his eyes, the expectant look that seemed to be waiting for more than I could give, the quiet glance that seemed to imply an understanding that could not exist. Knowing he asked for the impossible, I had to turn away from him, the pain of my knowledge complicating a relationship that had been difficult from the start.

When my house was ready and I went to live in his village permanently, I attempted to use the three weeks we had spent together on patrol, accepting the view, which he was willing to foster, that the experiences we had shared constituted a special bond between us. I was grateful, too, for the alacrity with which he assigned me an honorary position in his family, for my Gahuku name, which I preferred to the pidjin English "masta," and for the kinship status of younger brother. It was with Makis that I discovered the ridge; the settlement of Gohajaka, shrouded by its trees; Ekuhakuka, open to air and sky, the place where Gapiriha lived; the empty grasslands to the west, the no man's land between Nagamidzuha and Uheto. It was his voice that led me through the alien syllables of their names, his arm that sketched the unmarked boundaries between the different groups. Through him my eyes began to see the broader patterning of life within the valley. He was my introduction to the gardens, to the world one entered by the stiles constructed at the corners of the cane fences, to rows of vines trembling under their burden of dew, to the silence and the sun that suspended thought and time, beguiling every sense with the prospect of a limitless present. In his company I found the shadowed banks of streams, water that was a dark glass mirroring the shapes of unfamiliar leaves, bamboos thrown like a lacquered screen against an ochre cliff. At his hearth I first tasted food from the earth ovens and tried to read on the faces of his family thoughts and sentiments hidden from me by the barrier of language. His house was the first dwelling which I entered, sitting uncertainly on a log while his pigs snored against the wall behind me. And almost every night, he arrived to share my room. Often, his voice was the last sound I heard at night, the signal releasing the vast stillness of the valley.

This is part of what I remember now, but I also see him standing in the village street, limbs dark against the open sky between the houses, his arms gesturing in counterpoint to the controlled measure of his words, the flow of speech, its figures, the references to shared events drawing appreciative murmurs from the people seated on the ground around him. I am beside him as he leads a procession of his kinsmen into another village, feeling the sweep of hair and crimson cloak, the proud lift of his head, the sense of self-awareness as his bare feet tread the dusty ground; and I wait for him to speak for us, wanting the strangers to recognize our greatness. I watch him as he stands among the carcasses of pigs, his hands hefting a club in readiness for the next victim, his feathered headdress shaking its colors at the noon light, a silent echo of violence, of the smell of blood and death around him. He is before me with a long cane in his hands, raising it to whip the naked backs of women who have dared to speak out at a public gathering, but the next instant he is nursing Lusi, the daughter whom I named for him, or laughing in his house with Guma'e, her mother. In all things he seems to carry himself with self-assurance, knowing he has arrived, that his talents and his person are worthy of respect, that he is a man in a culture where maleness represents the highest values.

In the beginning, seeing only the qualities typifying the man of "strength," I developed a distinct distaste for him. I was fascinated by the natural theatricality of his movements, by the manner in which he presented himself to others, but the personality suggested by his characteristic mode of behavior was one I disliked, and I was easily discomforted in his presence, particularly when we were alone in my house, where I either had to talk to him or to ignore him. The latter course, which would have been preferable, seemed injudicious just then, for I needed to know the things he could tell me, and, besides, I did not want to offend him. I continued to seek him out, troubled by the knowledge that I was using him for my own ends and perhaps conveying the impression of a friendship I did not then feel. But in the end, I was glad that I set aside such scruples, for otherwise I would never have discovered the other facets of his nature, would never have lived with the interior echo of his name.

Makis had three wives, Gotome, Mohorasaro, and Guma'e, in that order of seniority. I never spoke more than a few words to Mohorasaro, who lived with their daughter Alima in the first house as one entered the village. Both mother and daughter were rather indeterminate figures, quiet and undemonstrative, never conspicuous, scrupulous in their attention to the work women were expected to perform. Even Alima, who was only seven, had less time for games than other children of the same age. Makis' relationship with his other wives was difficult and passionate, but Mohorasaro never felt the force of his hand or heard him speak to her in anger. Both her cowives and her husband seemed to be indifferent to her.

When I sat with him outside the house of Guma'e, hearing him laugh with her and watching the quality of his attentions, it was impossible to ignore Gotome, several doors farther down the street, who was unable to accommodate gracefully to her rival, but Mohorasaro, cooking for her daughter, seemed content to be alone, and it was easy to forget he was her husband. She was dark, with a wide mouth and high cheek bones that made her eyes appear to be too small, as though they were closed perpetually in a partial squint. Her figure was thin and her ringlets listless and untidy. Even if her cowives did not appeal to me physically, I could see that they might have charms for Makis, but Mohorasaro was no beauty by Gahuku standards, and comparing her with the other women, one saw why her husband preferred their company to hers.

I was puzzled by the fact that the other villagers also seemed to ignore her relationship to Makis, as though they followed the cue provided by his own indifference. In the evenings when people sat outside their houses while their food cooked, there was movement and visiting all along the street, but Mohorasaro and Alima seldom appeared at

the houses where most of the crowd gathered. When Makis went to sit
with them no one else joined him at their fire. Meeting them there, I
often felt that I had crossed an invisible boundary, that the house behind me and its inhabitants were not included in the settlement. Months
elapsed before I discovered there was a factual basis for this feeling.

The relationship between Makis and Mohorasaro was scandalous.
She was a Nagamidzuha woman, a member of his own clan, a "sister,"
someone whom, ideally, he should not have married. That he had done
so was a flagrant breach of customary morality, excusable only because
of his reputation and the dangers to which men of his station were
exposed. For males sexual promiscuity was always hazardous, since one
could not be sure that a sorcerer had not persuaded the woman to
obtain semen from an intended victim. Those who ran the greatest
risks were men of eminence and accomplishment, who were the principal target of their clan's enemies. Because he fitted this bill of particulars, Makis could point out that since she was his own clanswoman
Mohorasaro had fully developed loyalties to him. She was identified
with his interests, his welfare, in a manner quite different from the
wives of other men, who were strangers in their husbands' group, possibly amenable in the first years of marriage to suggestions from those
who wished them harm. If prudence had not been his principal motive
in marrying her, it provided a rationale that others could accept in his
case, though perhaps not in the case of lesser men. But the situation
remained difficult, an affront to normal expectations made tolerable only
by virtually ignoring it.

Gotome and Guma'e, it is impossible to speak of one without thinking of the other rival for Makis' affections. Gotome was the eldest wife,
the mother of his favorite daughter Toho, whom he treated more like
a boy than a girl. She had a rather matronly figure, dark brown skin,
and a round face with an attractive, open smile. Even when burdened,
passing my house on her way home from the gardens, she carried herself with assurance under the bending loads of sweet potatoes and firewood, returning casual greetings with the air of quiet but confident
authority to which she had been accustomed until her husband brought
his third wife to live in the settlement. Gotome must have felt secure
in his affections, not through his regard for her alone, but also through
his deep affection for their daughter, whom he indulged outrageously.

Toho was the complete antithesis of Alima; she could not be ignored.
About thirteen, slim, with undeveloped breasts, she was easily mistaken

for a boy, wearing her hair cropped short and dressing in boys' clothing—a cotton lap-lap wrapped around her waist—instead of the customary fringed apron. Her behavior also suited her dress. She was quite at home in my kitchen, joining the youths who congregated at my fire, never content merely to listen but entering the conversations and expressing her own opinions in a manner that no male tolerated from other members of her sex. She seemed to do only what she chose, and these were not the chores that occupied so much of the time of other girls her age. Though occasionally I saw her carrying a load of garden produce, neither of her parents required her to help them. When I came upon her outside the village, she was usually in the company of a band of boys, and, like them, she spent most of her days in unsupervised games along the ridge.

The freedom Toho enjoyed also contained an element of sadness. With his first two wives, Gotome and Mohorasaro, Makis had but two children, both of them girls. He, like other men, looked with envy on Bihore, whose one wife had produced four sons. Children in general were desired, but sons particularly, for ultimately it was males who assured the continuity of the patrilineal group, upon whom its strength depended, who were essential for the good life. Without a son, Makis apparently turned to Toho as a surrogate, encouraging the independence, even the mode of dress that made her life so different from that of the other village girls. He spoke to her as other men spoke to their sons, and though he plied her with gifts, seldom returning from Humeleveka without some article of adornment, I never saw her dressed like her sisters on ceremonial occasions. Rather, she appeared in plumes and shells, emulating male attire, an indulgence granted only infrequently to certain women in recognition of their services and contributions to the ends toward which men had bent their efforts.

I was fond of Toho, seeing her father in her, perhaps as he saw himself, her eyes alert and direct when she stood in front of me rather than fluttering in shy and giggling embarrassment like so many of her age mates, her gestures almost imperious, informed by the assertive self-awareness of the orators. Yet for all the affection that was lavished on her, the privileges she enjoyed, Toho was a girl, and wanting a son, Makis had taken a third wife, Gama'e, to the great resentment of Gotome.

Guma'e lived in a house directly opposite my own. Though she was clearly a mature woman, she must have been several years younger

than Gotome. She had also been married before, a fact that explained
the circumstances under which she lived with Makis. She came from
the Notohana tribe, where she had been living in her brothers' village
after leaving her most recent husband, the last of three men from whom
she had been divorced. According to Makis, she had noticed him at a
festival, had been impressed by him, and had come to him of her own
accord, eventually persuading him to bring her to Susuroka. Because
of her age and previous marriages he had given no bride wealth for
her yet, delaying until she had borne him a child, an arrangement that
was customary for unions of this kind. When I arrived in Susuroka,
she was pregnant with Lusi.

Guma'e was taller than Gotome and lighter in color, a physical trait
many Gahuku admired. She was no cleaner than the other women, and
her wide, flat nose, pierced for decorations, her high cheek bones, and
her oval chin often reminded me of a conventionalized mask. She tended
to be forward and demanding in her attitude toward me, perhaps
trading on my special relationship with her husband, as in later months
her brothers attempted to do, but it could have been her normal manner
of behavior, exemplifying the barely contained assertiveness possessed
by many of the women, which was rudely checked by men in public
as a threat to their interests. There was no possible doubt that Makis
favored her most among his wives. He seldom went to the houses of
Gotome and Mohorasaro, a neglect that did not seem to perturb the
latter, since she was probably accustomed to it, but a slight that Gotome
was not prepared to suffer without complaint. Day after day she sat
at her fire several houses down the street preparing food that Makis
never ate, fully aware of the domestic felicity displayed at the hearth
of Guma'e, privy to every action and to almost everything they said.
She usually ignored them, preserving the appearance of disinterest cowives were expected to feel and to show through companionship and
mutual assistance. The ideal seldom worked, and Gotome's jealous outbursts were clothed in the justification that, on his part, Makis should
have shared his time and favors with her equally. Not only did he disregard this duty, but he added to her injuries by taking away the
trinkets he had kept in a box in her house. They were not her property, and theoretically he had the right to dispose of them as he pleased;
but removing them from her custody constituted an additional act of
discrimination.

The tempestuous relationhips of this trio were a classical example of the hazards of polygyny, the reason often cited by other men for not contracting plural marriages, though they admitted that the institution possessed attraction for them. Gotome and Guma'e occasionally worked together as they were expected to do, but their mutual hostility was seldom contained for long, flaring into outbursts of anger for which Gotome usually earned a beating from her husband. The domestic tangle was exhibited with full publicity in the street outside my house, the shouts and imprecations of its progress often drawing me to the door to find Gotome sprawled in the dust with the imprint of her husband's foot on her stomach, the other villagers watching the quarrel in silence, perhaps prepared to interfere if matters became too violent, but recognizing the right of husbands to beat their wives. Guma'e did not escape her husband's wrath entirely, though for the most part she occasioned his anger for unseemly independence rather than because of the incessant quarrels with Gotome. Mohorasaro kept aloof from it all and reaped her benefits when Makis was at loggerheads with the other women; then unless he carried his blankets to my house, there was nowhere else for him to go.

The wives often came to me with their troubles, seeking my sympathy and support in a way I found touching but to which I felt I could not respond, at least to the extent of interfering in a situation everyone else appeared to regard as normal. I was particularly sympathetic to Gotome, whose plight seemed the more tragic. After at least twelve years of marriage she had been reduced to watching a rival supplant her with someone of whom she appeared to be genuinely fond. More than once she came to my house when I was alone at night, something that no other woman was forward enough to do, her courage steeled in part by the fact that her husband called me "younger brother" but mostly by her own need. I did not know how to comfort her. Sitting beside me on the floor, her face turned toward me in the light of my lamp, she poured out her sense of injury through tears that washed clean channels through the soot and dust on her cheeks. The welts of his anger on her breasts and legs told me more than I gathered from her choking words. Since she spoke no pidjin English and my Gahuku was insufficient for emotion-laden situations, I called to one of my servants, Hunehune or Hutorno, for assistance. They interpreted my questions dourly, their expression not devoid of sympathy, but constrained, it seemed, by the ethos of their sex, ill at ease because my demands asked them to step outside the customary boundaries of superiority. Other than allowing her the relief of talking, there was little I could do. Even my words, reflecting different conventions, sounded flat and strange on the tongues of my interpreters; they had no more effect than a puzzled, slightly hopeful interruption in the recitation of her injuries.

These domestic wranglings seemed to confirm the impression I had formed of Makis from watching him perform in his official role. In his treatment of his wives I saw a simple extension of the arrogance with which he conducted himself on public occasions. Yet even in the earlier months of our acquaintance, there were glimpses of very different qualities that seemed to suggest that my one-dimensional assessment of him falsified the truth. Little by little, the additional pieces began to fall into place. The dark figure declaiming grandiosely in the village street was not the person I followed through the grasses at the emerald end of day, watching him draw his bow and wait with his arm extended, releasing the arrow like a sigh. And coming back with him to the village, listening to his halting explanation of why he had left the noisy company at his fire to be alone in the questioning air of evening, I became aware of the complexity I had missed.

Much of Gahuku behavior was directed to achieving two ideals that were basically antithetical—"strength" on the one hand, and "equivalence" on the other. Strength did not refer to physical qualities only, for its larger meaning signified a constellation of traits and skills characterizing the ideal man, qualities and aptitudes that the society sought to encourage and instill in all its boys. The "strong" were the precise antithesis of the "weak," who were unassertive and amenable, gentler in disposition, eschewing force and everyday swagger. It was said that the weak, quite undistinguished in warfare, preferred to remain with the women rather than sallying out to best their enemies.

For groups such as the clan, strength was measured in wealth and numbers, mainly numbers of men. It stood revealed at the great festivals, in careening dance and gaudy decoration, in the vast slaughter of pigs and the shouts of pride and accomplishment that prefaced their presentation to the guests. Not so long ago it had been seen in the burned settlements and empty lands of enemies, and though this had gone now without a great deal of regret, important victories and past feats of arms were cited to remind an audience of how high a group's reputation had stood.

With strength a cardinal value, both groups and individuals were

encouraged to engage in a virtually endless rivalry, urged to demonstrations of superiority and dominance. Yet the rules required them also
to recognize the value of "equivalence," to respect and grant equality
to others. In Gahuku thought this was the indispensible basis of stable
and amicable relationships. It meant that one should not attempt to
score at the expense of others or, at least, that what one did should
not place others at a permanent disadvantage such that they could not
show, in future action, that they were able to meet the challenge. This
was the ideal governing the relationships of age mates, the end toward
which young men worked in repaying the debts that had been ac-
cumulated for them at their initiation and marriage. It was one of the
reasons for remembering every gift, the compelling motive in an interminable attempt to break even. It was so important that the rules of
the great festivals, those grandest exhibitions of pride, were designed
to permit the ultimate parity of guests and hosts.

The two ideals were almost incapable of reconciliation, their antithesis creating a tension that set the dominant tone for major areas of
life. Given the ideal of strength, almost any group or individual action
could be suspect, open to the interpretation that it concealed an attempt
to dominate or constituted a covert challenge that had to be met for
the sake of one's own self-image and public reputation. It is possible
that only the "weak men" or the very "strong" were immune to the
effects of the inherent opposition; perhaps men who rose to leadership
experienced it most keenly.

The Gahuku had no hereditary offices. Some authority was associated with certain kinship statuses, fathers having the right to command their children, the senior males of lineage and subclan expecting
respect from their descendants. But general influence was achieved. It
was the culmination of a career in which the ambitious man set out to
gather followers, binding them to him personally through the force of
his personality, his accomplishments, and his contributions to their
needs. Established leaders were "strong," their reputations secure in the
most admired pursuits. They were distinguished warriors and orators,
and also men of wealth. Their mode of presenting themselves was
arrogant, lacking in modesty, characterized by convictions of superiority.
They seemed to be principally concerned with self-aggrandizement. Yet
they trod a bridge so delicate that its passage could not be managed by
either the "weak" or the very "strong."

No established leader commanded any specific instruments of power enabling him to enforce decisions. He could not require, but only persuade and encourage. His position depended ultimately on the willingness of followers to follow, which in turn depended on his recognition that he could not dictate but only guide and encourage consensus. Ideally, all group decisions expressed a group agreement arrived at through interminable hours of debate in which every adult man was entitled to give his opinion. Leaders needed both patience and sensitivity, patience to wait until the many sides of an issue had been ventilated, the sensitivity to gauge when consensus was near, to assess the appropriate time to draw debate to a close by announcing a decision that expressed the conscience of a gathering.

This kind of management was outside the competence of the very "strong," the precipitate individuals who rode roughshod over the opinions and the rights of others concerned principally for themselves and their image of superiority. These were the would-be authoritarians, committed to their own point of view, demanding rather than persuading. By contrast, the leader who had arrived was a more calculating person, not pejoratively speaking, but in the sense that he possessed the talent to manipulate the ideals of strength and equivalence, conforming to one while respecting the other. This required both insight and feeling for the manner in which the system operated. It demanded a considerable degree of self-control, the recognition of limits. But more importantly it asked for someone with foresight and intuition, a man who gave voice to what his fellows felt, who stood for them collectively as the monitor of their aspirations.

In the end, I found all these qualities in Makis. When I watched him address a gathering, the florid gestures of his arms, the stylish modulations of his voice were transformed by my appreciation of the delicacy of his role. His flair, his personal flourish evoked a new admiration as I compared him with men who were "hard." The swagger was real, the flamboyance not feigned, for he was vitally aware of himself and expressed his awareness in the mode his culture admired. But it was not the whole man and knowing there was more, I felt more keenly for his present position.

Makis had reached his place of eminence by the traditional road. He had perceived intuitively where the future lay and had joined himself to my own people. This was his only innovation. The foresight helped him in his rise, and it might have sustained him if time had stopped at that point, arrested where new needs and opportunities kept pace with one another. But having gained an entrance, the force of history crumbled the fortifications of the past, and the future that showed through the breach could not be had by simple accommodations. The roads toward it were untried, the progress down them increasingly rapid, a passage in which the directions of a lifetime were poor guides, where those who had led must learn new signs or give their place to others.

There was nothing new in competition for influence, but in the past there had also been a broad, unchanging base of common experience on which a man could stand to meet a rival. Now it was becoming increasingly difficult for men like Makis to speak for those who had been growing up in the years since the whites had come to the valley. Age excluded them from many of the newer forms of experience. They found it more difficult to learn. They were like men who have been winning in a game but who realize suddenly that the rules were changing, and feeling the play moving away from them, they sought to regain it by the kind of intuitive stroke that had taken Makis to Young-Whitforde's office. It was clear to me that in the future he would begin to lose ground to others; indeed, there were already men in other tribes whose names were becoming better known, rivals on a wider stage whom Makis attempted to disparage.

Yet it was not my apprehension of his ultimate defeat that reconciled me completely to him. The moment of empathy was prompted by events in his domestic life.

Early in our acquaintance Makis told me of his hope that the child Guma'e was carrying would be a son. I had been out on the ridge for most of the morning; I was coming back at noon, anxious to reach the shade of my house when he saw me as I passed a garden where he was working. Recognizing his voice when he called my name, I climbed the stile and joined him in the furrows. I was glad to see him, and I welcomed the thought of a brief rest while we smoked a cigarette. Cupping my hands as I offered him a match, I could feel the moist heat of the earth through the fabric of my trousers. The vines that brushed against my bare arms were hot and dry, the leaves of corn and sugar cane, still in sunlight, bowed under the intangible weight of the storm waiting in the swollen clouds riding the peaks of the mountains. The heaviness of the hour inhibited any desire to talk. In the white light beyond the slat of shadow my hat threw across my eyes, Guma'e was resting on her heels, her arms hanging listlessly between her legs. Susuro sat near her in the vines, facing us but looking past my shoulder to the corner of the fence where I had entered. None of us moved.

Concerned with the details of my own morning, which I needed to record when I reached my house, I had almost forgotten the others when Guma'e spoke a few short words to Susuro. His eyes turned to her briefly before he lowered his head in embarrassment, his lips barely moving as he muttered a reply. Guma'e laughed, extended her arm between her knees, and pushed at his bare shoulder, adding to his confusion as her touch threw him off balance. Makis, who had understood their exchange, chuckled appreciatively. Expressing the affection I had noticed when I observed them together at her fire, he remarked that this woman was not like others, she was not afraid of bearing children. She was strong, the kind of woman who carried only boys. And growing more confiding, he told me he had sought Bihore's help to ensure that her present child would be a son. Bihore, as I could see from his own children, had magic that was particularly effective for this purpose.

Quite apart from my professional interest in the situation, I was drawn into the events of Guma'e's pregnancy and marriage by the honorary place Makis had provided for me among his relatives. This became apparent when two of her brothers visited the village after I had been in residence a month or so. I was working in the house one afternoon when Makis appeared to request some rice and canned meat, explaining that his brothers-in-law had come to see him. Since he generally asked less than people who had fewer claims on me, I gave him what he wanted and also accepted his invitation to join them later, fully intending to do so when I had finished my work. But Guma'e's brothers evidently decided not to wait for me, for after a short interval they came through my door, introduced themselves by calling me "nuguro," the term of address for brothers-in-law, and settled down beside me on the floor.

Even at this first meeting their behavior seemed to have implications that I could not meet; my suspicions were aroused by the fact that they had used the kinship term in greeting me. Though Makis called me "younger brother," and nuguro was therefore the appropriate form to use with his wife's brothers, the social tie between brothers-in-law was a special one, concealing a good deal of ambivalence under the cloak of formal respect and friendship. One could not use personal names in referring to or addressing these relatives, only the term by which they had introduced themselves to me. Brothers-in-law were also

privileged visitors, expecting deference when they came to see their
sisters, as Makis had shown by providing them with the luxuries of rice
and meat. They were the principal channels for exchanging wealth
during the great festivals, and in addition they received a major share
of the bride wealth obtained for a sister at her marriage.

I cannot be certain how much of this knowledge crossed my mind
at this first meeting, but I was wary. I was not very impressed by them,
particularly the elder of the two, who seemed to be bent upon ingratiating himself with me, making sounds and gestures of appreciation
as he studied the contents of my room. They knew no pidjin English,
so our conversation was limited, but I gained a distinct impression that
they had not come principally to talk but to make some other kind of
assessment. The elder of the two, possibly several years the senior of
Makis, had the mobile and expressive face I had come to associate with
men whose characters were "strong." It was he who did most of the looking and talking, the younger being more uncertain and, I thought, the
more likeable. My tin trunks in particular seemed to take the elder
brother's fancy; his eyes returned to them again and again as though
he guessed that this was where I kept the few articles, mainly axes
and knives, that had been bought to use as gifts for special occasions.

While the men were with me, several women came to the door with
vegetables to sell. Since anything seemed preferable to the strained
encounter with Guma'e's kinsmen, I called to Hunehune to take care
of the transactions, almost immediately regretting it as the sight of the
salt, beads, and cash used for payment stimulated the elder brother to
further demonstrations of appreciation in which he rubbed his hands
along my legs. I was always tolerant of the tendency to expect that I
would take anything offered to me, paying more than some article
would bring if it had been carried to Humeleveka, for it was not possible
to explain satisfactorily that my resources had to be budgeted carefully,
that, in fact, I was by no means affluent. But as Hunehune paid for
the goods I was uncomfortably aware of an avariciousness in my self-
styled brother-in-law's interest. After the departure of the women, this
feeling was confirmed when he addressed me at considerable length,
and Hunehune, interpreting for me, told me that the brothers expected
me to make a contribution to the bride wealth of Makis' wife. Even then
it was clear that my share should be generous since there were numerous
references to axes and knives, the most expensive articles available in
the white trade stores.

My uncertainty produced a noncommittal answer. The presumption was annoying, but at the same time I was willing to do something for Makis, prepared to accept, as far as it was possible, the obligations that had been thrust on me. Yet I also knew intuitively that the nominal relationship held possibilities of exploitation simply because I stood outside the system in which I had been granted limited, purely honorary membership. It occurred to me that if I had wanted to do so I could not have made reciprocal demands.

The visit of the two Notohana men stimulated me to make further inquiries about the marriage, in the course of which I learned the circumstances surrounding Makis' acquisition of Guma'e as his third wife and the custom under which he would pay for her when she had borne him a child. Her kinsmen had received wealth for her at each of her previous marriages, but since she was childless some of this had been returned when her husbands had divorced her, for the wealth given for a woman not only established a man's rights to her sexual and economic services but also his rights and the claims of his group to her progeny. The citizenship of her offspring in the patrilineal clan of their father was confirmed by this transaction, though the "gift" of them by their mother's patrilineal kinsmen, their abiding interest in the children's welfare, had to be recognized by further payments at such life crises as their initiation, marriage, and death. Customarily, however, only a token bride wealth was required for a woman of Guma'e's age and experience.

Makis knew that his brothers-in-law were anticipating my contribution, yet he never suggested that I owed him such assistance. I mentioned the matter to him when the brothers left, telling him I would provide some rice and meat for his guests when the event took place and also promising to add an axe to the payment he would have to make. He gave me the impression that whatever I decided to do was my own affair, an attitude others might have adopted more frequently rather than making quite unreasonable demands.

The territory of the Notohana, Guma'e's tribe, was a good two hours' walk from Susuroka, a distance quite sufficient to ensure that there was little contact from month to month between the two groups. Traditionally, Notohana was also allied to Uheto, Nagamidzuha's enemy, a fact that occasioned considerable suspicion. Makis professed not to care about Guma'e's origin, failing to recognize that there was any inconsistency between this lack of concern and the excuses that were made on his behalf for marrying Mohorasaro. It is true that I never heard him attempt to justify this breach of a basic rule. Yet I know he was not emancipated from the generally held belief that women were the principal agents of sorcerers, and watching him with Guma'e, I could only conclude that her personal attractions had entirely subverted him.

In the early months of my visit I saw them more frequently than any other married couple, trading on my relationship with Makis to join them at their hearth in the late afternoons when I wanted a break from the stuffy interior of my house. Very little of what they said to each other was understandable to me. Guma'e never engaged in the obvious demonstrations of affection that were Izazu's custom when she and Namuri were in my house. She and Makis adhered to the conventions of behavior between members of opposite sexes in the public street, but even without the disgruntled presence of Gotome to assist me I could see in their glances and in their tone of voice that they enjoyed each other's company. Watching them and recognizing these familiar attitudes, I felt less strange, lightened by the hope that the whole tradition of their lives would yield eventually to understanding.

As Guma'e's pregnancy advanced the visits of her brothers became more frequent. On the second occasion, Makis and his wife were away from the village. While word of their visitors' arrival was sent to them, the men came to my house, entering in a peremptory manner that irritated me immediately. I sat defensively behind my table while they smoked my cigarettes and studied my room, remembering me now and then with a conventional phrase and gesture of appreciation. The elder of the two had features similar to many Gahuku—the helmet of hair, the band of green beetles above his brows, the filed teeth distilling an air of mercurial pride. But I also felt confronted once more by a personal rapaciousness that repelled me. It occurred to me that I had begun to see with the eyes of the villagers, transferring to him the suspicions that I knew were generated by the very name Notohana, watching him warily—the outsider, the potential enemy. Again he did not disarm me when he called me "nuguro." On the contrary, his insistent use of the kinship term made me withdraw a little further behind my guard.

After several uncomfortable minutes, long enough to finish the cigarette I had given him, the elder brother called to Hutorno, whose face seemed more morose than usual as he interpreted for me, apparently ill at ease in the presence of this man who was an affinal relative of

Makis. His words undoubtedly lost a good deal of their subtlety in translation to pidjin English, a language that does not lend itself to the finer shades of politeness, and in Hutorno's mouth, spoken with a diffidence that seemed to dissociate him from their meaning, they sounded crude, unnecessarily demanding. I gathered that my "brother-in-law" expected me to contribute three axes and four steel knives to the bride wealth of Guma'e. Looking at Hutorno for guidance, I felt I detected a look that cautioned me against agreement. The quantity of goods demanded was not beyond my ability to provide, though in excess, I was sure, of what might be expected from the villagers, and for the first time I saw that my relationship might prove to be a disadvantage to Makis, that others might attribute to it more than either of us intended.

Through Hutorno I rejected the suggestion Guma'e's brother had made, promising, however, to provide one axe for his sister's bride price. Even then he was not satisfied, though Hutorno seemed to approve my statement.

Later that evening when we were alone together, I told Makis what had happened. He listened carefully, his lips etching a look of scornful disparagement that was very different from the polite accommodation of his manner when his brothers-in-law were present. He dismissed the whole episode with an expressive shrug, reminding me that Guma'e's bride wealth, considering her age and past experience, was not a matter for protracted bargaining.

The subsequent visits of the Notohana men convinced me that this was not quite true. What they asked may have been normal, but I felt there were other elements in the present situation that Makis recognized but did not want to admit. The brothers' visits had only one objective, to arrive at acceptable terms for their sister. The subtleties of the bargaining escaped me except where they touched me directly, and here the niceties may have been waived because of language difficulties, the brothers stating their demands with a directness they probably avoided in dealing with the villagers. At least the elder of the two had no compunction about stating the amount my contribution was to be, inflating it far beyond the modest commitment I had made. Although I was handicapped by my uncertainty, the attitude of the villagers hardened my resistance. It was quite apparent that they found the behavior of the Notohana men displeasing. They treated them politely enough, but occasionally their formal manner scarcely concealed the resentment I detected in their voices when the visitors had left. Lis-

tening to them then, I felt a growing suspicion that the Notohana were
trying to take advantage of them, and though they never spoke to
me about it, I also had an intuition that it involved me in a way I
did not properly understand.

Months went by, and becoming more familiar with the villagers, I
began to see less of Makis, finding others who seemed more congenial.
Except when his wife's brothers came to the village, his affairs seemed
no closer to me than those of the others whom I had begun to know
more intimately. Because of this, two days passed before I noticed the
absence of Guma'e, and even then my attention had to be drawn to it.

I was out on the ridge, accompanied by the boy named Asemo,
when I heard the call passed toward us from the direction of Susuroka.
Stopping as Asemo turned to listen, I realized the message had some
reference to us when he shouted a reply. When I asked what it was,
he told me only that Makis wanted me in the village though I tried
to make him ask for further information. Each time he called the reply
came back that Makis waited for me. I gave up the work I had in
mind and returned by way of Gohajaka.

It was relatively early when I arrived, and except for Makis, sitting
outside my house, the street was empty. As I remember it now he did
not seem to be particularly perturbed, though as soon as he began to
speak I realized he must have been worried, otherwise he would not
have made a suggestion that was entirely contrary to custom. Guma'e
was in labor, and he wanted me to see her. Since men were never
present at childbirth, I knew that something must be wrong, and I
asked him when her labor had begun. He replied vaguely that her
pains had started two days before.

I am quite unschooled in most medical matters and in none more
so than the present situation. Yet two days seemed an inordinate
length of time for delivery, and I felt that something ought to be done
though I knew there was little I was competent to do myself.

Following Makis, I was so concerned about the situation that I
hardly noticed where he led me. We took the path to the river, skirted
a garden belonging to Gotome, and turned aside under the trees clothing the lower terraces. Our feet made no sound on the narrow track,
which was flanked by stands of marbled crotons whose leaves stroked
my legs with moisture. Makis seemed to increase his pace, his dark
figure almost slipping out of sight in the shadows, the urgency of his
movements increasing my feeling of uncertain anticipation. The ridge

was out of sight above us, a dazzling thought behind the dappled green light in which we walked, a world so removed from the stillness near me that I wondered if it would be there when I returned to the boundary of the trees.

Makis had not said a word to me since we had left the village. I considered asking him if others would approve of what he was doing but put the question aside, too concerned with my own role to query his right to flout convention.

After half an hour we reached the edge of the stream. I was several paces behind him when he pushed his way through the trees and stood aside to make room for me. It was a place I had not seen before, a small bay undercutting miniature cliffs hung with ferns and creepers, a place of deep shadow and dark green water set against the main body of the stream coursing over its stony bed in a flurry of white light, its sound hushed by the intervening branches that almost touched its surface. Makis squatted on his heels, indicating we had reached our destination.

At the foot of the bank a natural causeway of stones led out toward the main stream, ending at a large rock that rose several feet above the water, its smooth surface partly in the shadow of the trees and partly in the sunlight flashing beyond their curtain of leaves. Momentarily, I wondered why we had come there, for I could not immediately discern the figures on the rock—three women whom I recognized as Izazu, Guma'e, and the wife of Bihore. Guma'e was seated lower than the others, leaning forward on her swollen belly, her legs extended, the water dividing around her feet. She had removed the bilum women usually draped around their heads and, unconfined, her hair fell forward, hiding most of her face. Her two companions squatted beside her, bathing her shoulders and back with water squeezed from cloths they dipped in the stream.

The sound of the stream, so much louder where they sat, probably prevented them from hearing our approach, for they gave no sign that they knew we were there, and I felt uncomfortable watching them. Minutes passed. I wanted Makis to speak, to reveal our presence, wondering what he expected me to do. He gave me no clue to his intentions, squatting impassively on the bank, seemingly unconcerned, a man looking down from his superior station at something that mattered only to women. Yet I felt this was unfair to him, that he would not have called me and brought me there unless he had been troubled.

He broke his silence at last, calling across the water to the women. Guma'e did not move, but the others stopped their ministrations, turning toward us with a startled look that changed to embarrassed confusion as soon as they saw me on the bank. Izazu answered for them all and drew a further query from Makis, commencing an exchange that lasted several minutes. At the end of it he rose and gestured for me to follow him down the bank.

The rock was hardly large enough to hold us all, yet Izazu and Bihore's wife insisted on greeting me properly, reaching around Guma'e to rub my legs in a manner that hardly helped me to maintain my footing. It was immediately apparent that, prompted by Makis, they expected me to take charge, inching away to let me sit near the patient. Makis was below me, gazing up in a manner that meant I had to make a decision. I was completely at a loss. Guma'e turned her head briefly to look at me and to speak my name, the tone of her voice echoing the dull appearance of her eyes and the lines of exhaustion or pain running from her nose to the corners of her mouth. Her hair and body were wet with sweat and water.

The rock seemed a most unlikely place to give birth, and when I asked why they had brought her there, I learned that she had gone to the garden house of Izazu when her pains had started two days before. When nothing had happened the midwives had brought her to the stream to cool her, their notions of the therapeutic value of water linked, as I knew, to conceptions of magic. Heat carried the power of spells, and anyone entering a dangerous situation, including illness, sought the protection of the opposite condition—coldness, which had the character of a nonconductor, erecting a "field" to resist inimical forces.

Trying to be helpful, I put my hand to her stomach, wanting to gain time as much as anything else. Makis and the two midwives watched me with a quite misplaced confidence, for I did not even know the first rudimentary questions to ask. Guma'e was completely passive under my hand, which I held on her for about ten minutes, until reassured that there were no contractions. It was possible that they had misinformed me on the time when her labor had commenced; yet she was so close to exhaustion that there seemed to be only one thing to do. Turning to Makis, I suggested that if she could walk we should take her back to the village, where a litter could be made to carry her to the station hospital.

When I recalled my decision, I remembered that Makis accepted it immediately, and I felt myself move closer to him because he had shown me this confidence. It added another ingredient to the quality of our friendship.

After ascertaining that Guma'e could walk, we left the river and set off through the trees, Makis leading, followed by the three women, I in the rear. I was anxious to reach the ridge as quickly as possible, but our progress was slowed by Guma'e who needed to rest after every hundred yards. While we waited for her in the green light, Makis called for the help we would require when we arrived. Answering cries came back as the message was received and passed ahead, the disembodied voices unrolling like a line guiding us out to the world above.

Reaching the crest of the ridge, I was surprised by the number of people in the street, but I paid them little attention, attributing their presence to curiosity aroused by the messages Makis had sent ahead. Guma'e collapsed on the ground outside her house, where several other women immediately joined the two midwives, their bare, solicitous backs hiding her from sight. Most of the men watched silently from the opposite side of the street, only a few of the younger ones, including two of my own boys, responding to the directives of Makis, who had brought an axe and a worn blanket from the house he shared with Guma'e. Watching them move reluctantly to his commands, I became aware of something that in retrospect I believe I might have expected.

Listening to Makis, I detected a quality in his voice that I could not place immediately. His tone was urgent, perhaps a little exasperated with the men helping him to make the litter, but searching for something else that had disturbed me, I realized that his words sounded unnaturally loud against the hard silence of the crowded street. Momentarily, my mind swung from the activity around him to the dark, watching figures lining the fence outside my own house, puzzled by their detachment from the plight of Guma'e. It was not the first time that I experienced a rising impatience with their fairly prevalent tendency to stand aside from crises in which they were not personally involved, but though my first reaction was to try to shake them out of their indifference, my defenses also gathered to combat their hostility. At the time it was no more than an intuitive reaction to the quality of their watchfulness, a brief stab of apprehension that was forgotten quickly, though later the same night I recalled the scene vividly—the bright light that seemed to shrink the row of thatched houses and the figures bending over Guma'e, their curiously diminished size intensifying the feeling that they moved in the presence of some invisible threat.

It took no more than half an hour to make a serviceable litter from the blanket and some bamboo poles. When Guma'e had been placed on it, four of the younger men raised it to their shoulders and carried her down the street. Makis turned to me briefly, his movements momentarily arrested, as though there was something he wished to say. His eyes seemed to reflect such a troubled need to speak to me that my feeling of apprehension returned. But while I hesitated uncertainly, wondering if I should go to him, he turned abruptly and followed the litter down the street. I watched him until he was out of sight; then, vaguely disturbed, I went to my own house, the silent men standing aside to let me pass through the fence.

I remained in the house the rest of the afternoon and evening, writing down the day's events. While I placed them on paper I was aware that the crowd in the street had not dispersed. I could not see very far through the door, which was opposite my table, but could hear the low-keyed voices of the men when I lifted my head to stare at the bright rectangle of light that changed from white to burnished gold as the hours passed. There was no alteration in the subdued quality of the exchange outside, even during the evening meal when, as a rule, the street filled with relaxed laughter and the shouts of children. On this night the village seemed to be going to bed with something new on its mind, and the feeling grew that whatever it was, I was centrally concerned in it. No one came through my door, an omission remarkable in itself, and even Hunehune, when he lit my lamp and brought my meal, appeared unusually subdued, as though he was privy to something that touched me closely and felt embarrassed because of it.

After I had eaten I attempted to return to my work without much success. I felt more alone than at any time since my arrival in the village, and trying to locate the reason, I decided it was not simply because there were no visitors to receive. At other times I would have welcomed some respite from their attentions, and it was not their absence but rather the reason for it that disturbed me. In writing down the day's events I had been reminded of the current of opposition that met me on reaching the ridge with Guma'e. The more I thought of it, the more important it became. The silent immobility of the men

did not seem to indicate indifference, but linked to the concern Makis
had shown before he turned away from me, remembered in conjunction with the quality of the conversation in the street throughout the
afternoon, it increasingly came to stand for some threat I did not completely grasp.

Putting my work aside, I tried to read, but the hiss of my lamp
against the darkness of the night interposed a barrier between my
mind and the words on the page in front of me, and after several
hours I decided to go to bed.

I had closed my book and had started to move from the table when
my head was brought abruptly round toward the door by the sudden
appearance of Makis. Startled by his unannounced entrance, I recovered with a flood of relief as soon as I recognized him, my manner,
the tone in which I formed his name, showing my undisguised pleasure
as he sat beside me. My mind was crowded with questions, but many
of them were too personal to ask. Reticence prevented me from seeking his confirmation or denial of the matter most important to me: the
suspicion, now virtually a conviction, that I had provoked the anger of
the villagers.

His voice was matter-of-fact as he told me what had happened since
he left the village. They had seen the white medical assistant, who
had examined Guma'e and had sent her to one of the hospital wards
—a long, thatched shed dimly lit by kerosene lamps, where the unwashed patients lay on pallets spread on hardwood stands. He had
left his wife there, attended by the two women from the village.

While I listened to him, his unemotional recital lessened my concern, but at the same time I found myself reacting with disapproval to
the flat tone of his voice, to the bald description of events in which I
read a total lack of personal involvement. I looked toward him, suddenly sure that the difference in our attitudes could not be bridged.
His face was in profile, turned toward the door, his features hidden by
the sweep of plaited hair that caught the light in a net of bright,
metallic points. His shoulders, the curve of his back, even the arms
resting on his thighs seemed to be relaxed, confirming my impression
that Guma'e's condition did not move him. I told myself there was no
reason why I should expect more positive concern from him; yet even
allowing for differences in convention, I seemed to find an absence of
essential sympathy that alienated me. Then the ambiguities of my own
situation returned to trouble me, raising doubts as to whether I should
have interfered.

In the silence following his account I felt myself drifting farther away from the whole pattern of life his attitude represented, from its indifference to suffering and mortality, to the concern I was accustomed to expect in interpersonal relationships. Therefore, when he turned to me suddenly I was unprepared for what I saw in his face and heard in his words.

It was the first time he had looked at me directly since he had appeared out of the darkness, and I immediately noticed the intensity of his eyes, the emotion that also showed on the chiseled planes of his face and in the lines at the corners of his mouth, which seemed to be deeper than I remembered them. I intuitively wanted to help him, responding to the appeal his expression conveyed and also to my own need for reassurance, his patent distress breaching the isolation that had been encroaching on me. I waited for him to tell me what he wanted to say, aware that he could not find the words he needed. His inarticulate struggle seemed harder in contrast to his customary eloquence, and when he managed to speak his halting voice moved me more deeply than the virtuosity of any of his public speeches, for the unstudied phrases ignored the conventions of superiority and overrode the formal division between men and women. He told me simply that Guma'e must not die, phrasing his words imperatively, "This woman cannot die," as though the form of command might help to prevent its happening. He added in his next breath that he did not want to lose her, that his feeling for her, touching his hand to his stomach, killed him inside. Remembering the manner in which he had summoned me that morning, our journey to the stream, and our subsequent return, I realized that his affection for her was deeper than it appeared to be from any of his outward expressions. I had never seen him like this before; nor had I heard a comparable confession from any other Gahuku. The conventionalized expression of sorrow was familiar to me. The ritual keening, the cries that ran along my spine like fingers were surely informed with genuine emotion. Yet the medium of its expression separated me from the mourners, and I had to be a witness not a participant in grief. I felt a difference now. Makis would not have spoken so directly to the villagers, and for once I was grateful for my position, moved that it enabled him to meet me at the level of his personal need, searching for words to contain his apprehension of loss. I wanted to respond in a way that he could understand, but I was also drained by helplessness, unable to find the phrases of comfort and reassurance.

We sat in silence, the room crowded with thoughts neither of us could express. He had turned away from me again after his brief declaration, but now his shell earrings jangled against his other ornaments as his head lifted toward me, and he set aside his own worries to tell me something I had to know. His marvelous eyes were bright points of concern in the shadows of his brows; his lips moved carefully as he tried to make me understand, preparing me for the import of the words I could not believe.

"If this woman dies, you cannot stay with us." For a moment I looked at him without speaking, not even sure that I had heard him correctly. Then he hurried on, answering the question I had not asked. "If she dies, they will say it was your fault. You saw their faces when we brought her back from the river. They were talking, saying she should not go to Humeleveka. They said she should stay here, among us, at Susuroka. Now they will say you sent her away, and if she dies no one will talk to you. Listen to me, friend, your work is finished. Leave us—go away. Brother, you cannot stay here any longer."

I knew that what he said was true, that it was this I had suspected hours ago. It was the reason I had waited for him to come to me, in the afternoon and evening, unable to work, growing increasingly alone as the sky darkened and silence descended on the valley. Now that he had confirmed what I had known, I was relieved, strangely lightened, and closer to him than at any other time in our acquaintance. I did not blame the villagers or question their right to their opinions. I knew their strong aversion for the native hospital, for the wards crowded with strangers, many of whom belonged to enemy groups, and earlier in the day, examining Guma'e on the rock where we had found her, I had been aware that my suggestion would not win me any popularity, though it was the only thing to do. I also realized now that I had not expected Makis to agree so readily to what I said. On past occasions he had expressed approval when I questioned this obvious reluctance to take advantage of white medicine, but he had never managed to convince me that his words reflected his convictions, that his modernism was real, an article of faith rather than mere lip service to the views I held.

It was this, more than anything else, that made me feel so near to him: he had asked me for help and he had also overcome his scruples, had put aside his own misgivings to act promptly on the only advice I was able to give. I was not particularly concerned by my own situation as he had just described it to me. All that mattered to me was that I was linked to him in a way not possible previously. Moments before I had been trying to reach him through the troubled air of the room, wanting to give him more than merely intellectual support; now I did not have to try. The untoward conjunction of our lives had created a climate, a common apprehension of change, in which we were temporarily extensions of each other.

After his brief outburst he did not speak again, and there was nothing I wanted to say, could say, so we sat for a while listening to the night outside my house. Half an hour passed and then he left me briefly, rising with a gesture of his hand that told me to remain and returning after several minutes with his threadbare blanket, which he spread on the floor near my trunks. I waited until he had settled down, then I went to my own bed, taking the lamp and placing it beside me on the crate that served as a table. I reached out from my sleeping bag and turned the valve that cut the light. The incandescent mantle pulsed for a moment. The plaited walls wavered, gradually dissolved, disappeared in the darkness that filled the whole valley.

When I woke next morning, he had already left for Humeleveka. I did not go out that day but tried to work at home. The village emptied early and all my boys left to wash my clothes in the stream below the ridge, with the exception of Hunehune who remained on call in the kitchen. The sunlit street seemed even more silent than the previous night when the fastened houses had been filled with sleeping animals and people, and now that Makis had gone I became more concerned about my own predicament. I could not quite accept the finality of the statement Makis had made, but the possibilities it raised killed my ability to concentrate. I did not form any definite plans to meet the eventuality he spoke of, but the prospect of such a radical change became increasingly unsettling as the hours passed, magnifying the problems it would bring. Even if I had to leave Susuroka, it would not necessarily mean the end of my work, but I did not relish the thought of having to start again in another village, compelled once more to surmount the difficulties of establishing a personal relationship with its people. Indeed, I was uncertain whether I could bring myself to make the effort and foresaw the likelihood that I would leave, preferring to face the necessity of explaining why I had abandoned my study rather than subjecting myself to the strain of a new start in a new place.

After lunch the heat pressed against the thatched roof like a heavy, invisible body, its weight increasing as the afternoon wore on. I went once to the door and stepped outside into a blinding light. The whole sky was covered with opaque clouds becalmed above the valley, motionless, their stillness echoing the monumental silence of the row of houses and the listless heads of grass. Suddenly unable to face the empty street, even to walk across it to the weak shade of the bamboo where I often sat, I went inside the room again, relieved as the familiar safety of its walls closed around me.

I lay down on my bed and closed my eyes, feeling the heat, the stillness seep toward me through the thatch. Eventually, I must have dozed, for I sat up at the sound of my name and found Hunehune standing near the table. He was diffident, uncertain whether he ought to wake me, but his information that Makis was calling to me brought me to my feet at once. I followed him outside to the corner of the fence that faced toward Asarodzuha. Even as we arrived, I heard the voice coming from the settlement on the far side of Galamuka. Hunehune answered with the long "oooh" of recognition, and after a moment's pause the voice replied, sounding a little closer, as though its owner was moving rapidly toward us. The conventional form for passing messages, the extended, lengthened sounds, distorted the words, and I could barely recognize my own name, Goroha Gipo, among them. I waited for Hunehune to translate for me, disappointed when he remarked perfunctorily that Makis was on his way and wanted me to wait for him. Unable to check my impatience, I told him to ask the question uppermost in my mind. When he turned to me again his face told me everything I had to know. The relief in his eyes released my burden of uncertainty, and his words simply confirmed what I knew already, that Guma'e had been delivered of a child at Humeleveka.

It was only after returning to the house that I remembered there was much more I needed to know: whether she and the child were well and whether she had borne a boy or girl. The answers to both questions came as soon as Makis arrived, entering with the familiar, self-assured gait, the jingle of shell, the toss of hair, and clasping me to him in a way that assured me all was well. The child, he said, was a girl, and momentarily my relief was overlaid by disappointment for him, knowing how much he had wanted a son. But neither then nor at any other time did I hear him voice regret, and my opinion of him rose because, as far as I could tell, his disappointment had no effect upon his feelings for his wife or daughter.

Later that evening, the villagers came to my house as usual, but their attitude was distinctly different, informed by a new familiarity, a new ease and acceptance. A short time before they had been ready to blame me if Guma'e had died, now they credited me with her successful delivery, and the episode earned me such a reputation that in the following months I was called from my bed at night to examine several other women in labor. Makis himself attributed everything to me and asked me to name the child in recognition of the part I had played.

When Guma'e returned to the village with the baby, preparations for paying her bride price began almost immediately. Her two brothers were early visitors, reviving my distaste and my uneasiness with their ingratiating attitude, wide smiles, and fulsome exclamations of appreciation, while their words skirted obliquely around the reason for their visit. I was sufficiently worried by their behavior to seek reassurance indirectly from Makis. Although he was again his customary self, he also felt the change recent events had effected in our friendship. The night we had shared the possibility of Guma'e's death had altered my perception of him completely. The overstated qualities of his personality did not bother me any longer. I had found the individual beneath his public façade, and when he was with me now we seemed to meet at the level we had found intuitively in the moment of recent need. But if he shared my suspicions of the Notohana men, he professed to be unconcerned, remarking that the matter of the bride price was not really important, that it was something he could handle easily.

I was not convinced that I was wrong. Even though he turned my tentative questions aside, I still felt that the Notohana men were trying to use my presence as an opporunity to inflate their demands, sure that Makis and the other villagers could count on my help to meet them. I was not especially concerned about my own contribution; rather, I saw the villagers, particularly Makis, being manoeuvered into a position where, in order to maintain face, they would have to give more than custom normally required, more than they could afford. None of them indicated directly that they were aware of this, but I felt they knew it and also included it in their calculations as they readied their separate contributions to the bride price.

A month passed, and the day arrived to formalize the marriage of Makis and Guma'e. In the morning Makis killed two pigs that had been in the care of Mohorasaro. He had intended to take one from

each of his senior wives, but Gotome had refused to accept his decision. Her attitude had occasioned a heated altercation the previous
evening, the sounds of the quarrel bringing me out of my house to
find her in tears at her fireplace, the bilum on her head askew from the
blow she had just received from Makis who stood above her, his face
distorted with anger as he lashed at her with obscene imprecations.
Later, Gotome, completely discredited, took a bundle of belongings and
went to her kinsmen at Gehamo, avoiding any part in the celebration
of her rival's marriage.

Beginning on this angry note, the day continued with the squeal
of the pigs as they were bludgeoned to death in the dusty street. Makis,
Namuri, and Bihore split the warm bodies open, spilling blood and
entrails on the ground, the steaming smell attracting other animals who
snorted distrustfully near the scene of carnage, ready to retreat from
the blows that were aimed at their probing snouts. I did not remain
long at the preparations for the feast. The total absence of shade was
more than I could bear; so I returned to the house where, from my
knowledge of many previous occasions, I could use the sounds of the
street to inform me of the progress of events. Though my head was
bent above my notebooks, I could see the pyres of firewood laid across
the mouths of the earth ovens, their flames flickering like a mirage
against the white glare. In the babel of voices, the cries of reprimand
and expostulation, the laughter, the demanding wails of children, I
recalled a dozen other times when I had sat among the crowd while
the piles of refuse grew, spreading around us like a stain that ate at
the dust, and the air became heavy, nauseous, with the odors of raw
flesh and singed bristle, the sweet smell of corn husks and crushed
greens. Now, as then, torpor settled on the village in the early afternoon when the ovens had been sealed with cones of earth and people
retired to the walls of the houses, huddling in the bar of shade beneath the eaves. Even the pigs abandoned the street, and while the
light hummed against the walls my head nodded over my work.

It was four o'clock when I decided to join the gathering, prompted
by sounds that told me that the feast was ready. The air had cooled
with the approach of evening, whose shadows had begun to stain the
western mountains. I breathed it gratefully, crossing the street to the
house of Guma'e, self-consciously prepared to accept the welcoming
faces that lifted at my approach. I recognized her brothers and met
them in the manner of greeting expected of me. Glad to have this over

I went to Makis, accepting the seat he made for me on a log near his door. Once settled among the villagers of Susuroka a feeling of anonymity returned to me as, rendered almost invisible by their concern with their own affairs, I was able to study them from a clinical distance.

I gave my immediate attention to the guests from Notohana who numbered about twenty. Though some of them mingled with the Susuroka people, the majority sat apart, behind the piles of sugar cane and tobacco leaf that had been presented to them on arrival. Searching their faces, I saw nothing to confirm my suspicions. They were quite relaxed as they watched the opening of the ovens, a little restrained perhaps, conventionally polite, but no more wary than people ought to be in the company of strangers, their watchfulness no different from the care I had noticed, and also felt, when I had sat with my own villagers at Gama or a dozen other settlements belonging to different tribes.

My study was interrupted as the food was brought from the ovens and my own portion was handed to me, the presentation accompanied by the usual gestures of appreciation, the smiles, the words that encouraged me to eat, the expectant pause as I broke the food and tasted it, as though they did not quite believe that I would eat, perhaps anticipating rejection and always pleased when it did not come, finding in the simple act of eating an acceptance of their way of life that was rare in their experience with others of my kind. I had learned that no one ate to completion at these formal gatherings, so I availed myself of the custom and placed most of my food aside; Bihore solicitiously wrapped it in leaves and called to Hunehune to take it to my house when I was ready to depart.

Possibly an hour passed while the whole company concentrated on the feast, men rising now and then to accept their joints of pork as their names were called by Makis and Namuri, who squatted over the meat debating each cut with the elders, apportioning it with the care necessary to ensure that everyone received his proper share, the precise portion to which he was entitled by his status and his relationship to Makis. My attention wandered, passing above the heads of the crowd to watch the light as it began to liquify along the staves projecting from the thatched roofs of the houses, returning again, however, as soon as I sensed by a subtle variation, a drop in the level of chatter, that the moment had arrived to hand the bride price to the Notohana.

Makis had brought a wooden box from his house and had placed it in the center of the crowd between the villagers of Susuroka and his Notohana kinsmen, who had drawn to one side during the feast and now sat together in a double row, attentive and expressionless. I understood very little of his speech, gathering its temper from the sound of his voice, from the confident flow of words and the pride of his stance, the imperious gestures of his hands, the lift of his head and the firm self-assurance in the hard lines of his legs. When he had finished he turned dramatically toward the house where Namuri presently appeared, leading two pigs, which had been tethered to a post throughout the afternoon. Taking the halters, Makis held them out toward his wife's brothers. The ensuing pause held me completely still, my mind tight with the premonition of disaster as I felt the same gathered alertness in the people near me. I relaxed as the eldest Notohana brother cleared his throat and, rising, accepted the pigs with a few brief words, ending with a polite but hardly enthusiastic shout of appreciation that was echoed with greater feeling, I thought, by some of the older men in the visitors' party.

Makis turned to the box between the two groups, and while he spoke again I realized that this was the part of the ceremony for which the Notohana had been waiting. Though I am sure they had not moved, they seemed to have drawn closer to the box, almost bending over it, so intent that I doubt if they heard or understood much more than I of the speech of presentation. When the lid was thrown back I jumped involuntarily, my movement similar to the sudden, unrestrained eagerness that brought the Notohana forward while Namuri and several other men moved quickly to the side of Makis.

The seeds of disorder seemed to be there from the start. There was no pretence at politeness now as the box was virtually hidden in the throng of bending bodies and Makis, answering the eagerness of his wife's kinsmen, revealed its contents in rapid succession: four axes, including the one I had given him, bush knives, strings of beads, lengths of red cloth, and an assortment of traditional valuables—plumes of the bird of paradise, ropes of small cowries, and a necklace of white shells. I was astonished by the amount, remembering his assertion that his marriage to Guma'e called for only a modest outlay of wealth, and I knew at once that my previous suspicions had been right, that he and his kinsmen had been drawn into a struggle for prestige, forced to accept the inflated demands of the Notohana or to admit that this image of their wealth, their strength was wrong. The array of objects disgorged by the box was a counterchallenge, a display having its own aggressive implications, clearly intended to silence the Notohana, to overwhelm them, to force them to admit the superiority of Makis and his followers. But nothing was certain in these competitive situations, and the Notohana held the better hand, since it was not their reputation that was being judged.

Makis stood back from the empty box, tense, his chest fluttering with excitement as he waited for the Notohana to react, possibly expecting to hear the conventional shouts of accliam. They were huddled over the articles of the bride price, debating its merits, and several minutes passed before they moved aside, giving room to the eldest of Guma'e's brothers who spoke from where he sat, his face and eyes hard with rejection and vindictiveness. The Susuroka reaction came at once, a stunned silence broken by an angry outburst from Namuri, whose words tightened the expressions of the Notohana. Makis was still, caught on the edge of uncertainty while Namuri replied again to the Notohana. His immense figure strained with outraged hostility, and running to his house he returned at once with a knife and a length of cloth, throwing the articles on the pile in front of the Notohana.

The visitors' eyes calculated this addition to their wealth and rose again as adamantly as before. Namuri seemed ready to explode. He pushed his way through the crowd and stood near his house, his hand clutching the thatch while his words flew over the heads of the villagers to strike at the impassive Notohana. Galvanized, reacting to the challenge to their reputation, others followed his example, throwing additional contributions on the pile. The Notohana were unmoved. Completely out of patience, Namuri swung away from the crowd, his words and gestures, tossed across his shoulder, clearly intended to end the whole transaction. But I never learned what might have happened at that point. Makis, who had been standing aside, inactive while Namuri had taken charge, suddenly thrust himself through the throng, almost running to the door of Gotome's house. His hair swung free of his shoulders as he bent to pull aside the rough planks, the motion of his arms matching his spate of words. Disappearing inside, he returned almost immediately, rose to his full height as he passed the threshold of the door, and stood for a moment in commanding silence, his arms folded around a heap of colored cloth, an axe, and several strings of beads. He gave no heed to Namuri's quick expostulation, ignored the cries of restraint that lifted his other kinsmen to their feet. Walking carefully, his shoulders taut with pride and contempt, he passed through the villagers and faced the seated Notohana. His chin was raised. His eyes were perfectly steady in the shadow of his brows. Even the feathered halo in his hair seemed to respond to the will that sat so firmly on his lips, the airy plumes, held in quivering suspension, extensions of the self that he presented to his wife's kinsmen as he opened his arms, adding their contents to the goods as though he dared the visitors to raise another question.

The rest was anticlimax. One of the Notohana, an old man sitting to the rear, rose unsteadily to shout acclaim, forcing the others, even the brothers of Guma'e, to follow his example. In his triumph Makis was magnanimous, relaxed, laughing, trading jokes with the visitors, submitting royally to their hands as they took their leave, his own arms passing lightly down their shoulders, barely caressing, politeness satisfied but also leaving little room to doubt that he had vindicated his position.

Later, in my house, Namuri and Hunehune were still enraged by the avariciousness of the Notohana, telling me, for the first time, that what I had suspected had been true. Guma'e's brothers had hoped to capitalize on my presence in the village, certain that the people of Susuroka must have put me to the same use, hopeful, too, that Makis would take advantage of our personal relationship. I could not express my gratitude. Aware of the Notohana design, all of them had rejected it at a cost they had only partially anticipated. But my mind moved particularly to Makis. Of them all, he had been in the best position to use me; yet he had hazarded his reputation without requesting the help he must have known I would give. I felt the warmth of an acceptance that I had hoped for but often never thought to find. When I watched him on later occasions, I often saw him as he had appeared that afternoon, ignoring the attempts to restrain him, walking from his house in all his pride of person to empty his wealth at the feet of the Notohana, his reckless act another link in the chain that binds me to him.'

CHAPTER THREE

▲▲

ASEMO

Asemo was fourteen or fifteen, a little younger than the age of initiation for most Gahuku boys. He was slight and serious, never playing the buffoon like Piripiri, his age mate, who stirred up gales of laughter in the street by hopping around with his head between his knees, flapping his elbows and crowing like a cock. Though Asemo joined in the laughter and shook his head with pleasure, he was a more dignified and thoughtful boy. I seldom encountered him among the groups of his peers whom I met on my walks along the ridge, and he seemed to avoid their rough-and-tumble games. He lived at Susuroka, where I noticed him first among the older people who met almost every night in my house.

These gatherings began soon after my evening meal and sometimes even earlier, for when I was still a novelty to the villagers even my food and the manner in which it was served were worthy of close attention. The first callers came shortly after Hunehune brought the tilley lamp and placed it on my folding table. As they entered from the darkness of the street, crouching to pass through the low doorway, they greeted me by calling my name, Goroha Gipo, and settled down on the complaining bamboo floor to watch me from the shadows. I returned their greeting, offered them cigarettes, and tried to ignore their chatter while continuing my record of the day's events. But I could not isolate myself from the sound of their voices, from a scuffle taking place below the level of the table, or from the low laughter that followed some remark I had missed; so I closed my books with the justification that observing my visitors was better employment.

The hours when they were with me paid me well in new information. With its light and its larger size, my room had some obvious advantages compared with the crowded, smoke-filled darkness of the village houses. These qualities, quite as much as my own peculiarities, which became blunted by familiarity, drew people to the room in times

95

of crisis, and listening to the give and take of their discussions I discovered nuances of thought and feeling that might have been missed
in more formally structured situations. My position did not allow me
the freedom of their houses, and in the public street where I saw them
most often, accepted limits of expression drew a screen around many
intimacies; but in my room, responding to the strange surroundings,
they sometimes lowered the guard of convention and let me see into
the private lives that lay beneath the formal patterns of relationships.

For more than a year, until Makis built the clubhouse, my room
served as a partial substitute for that traditional men's gathering place.
These buildings were still a conspicuous feature of many of the older
settlements. Oval rather than round, and two to three times as large
as the ordinary dwellings, their thatched roofs rose to a series of peaks,
each of which supported a wooden pole surmounted by a clump of
orchids. Open to women only on rare occasions, they symbolized the
basic division of Gahuku society, in which the men were the continuing
core of every village. Men monopolized the religious symbols and the
esoteric rituals associated with them, controlled subsistence activities,
settled disputes, and decided the appropriate time to hold the great
festivals. Women were only second-class citizens whose rights in the
community were conferred by marriage rather than birth and were
dependent to a large extent on their bearing sons who would carry on
the corporate interests of the men. The facts were a little different,
as Hunehune and his friends knew, but the subtle departures from the
official version had to be viewed against the uncompromising rigidity
of formal distinctions.

Traditionally, the clubhouse had been the focus of male dominance,
the inviolate center that every boy entered after he had passed through
the painful rites of initiation. But there had been many changes by the
time I arrived in the valley. Lutheran missionaries had been working
in the area for at least twelve years. They had not gathered many
converts nor effected any fundamental changes in religious thought, but
they had introduced ideas that were influential because of their association with the dominant white minority, and they had denigrated
the more conspicuous and accessible forms of pagan belief and practice. In some communities nearer to the center of their activities, the
sacred flutes had been burned in public, the ritual associated with them
had been abandoned, and with it had also gone the principal supernatural justification for the men's organization. In other villages less

influenced by their teaching, the younger men were leaving in increasing numbers, free to travel under the peace established by the white man as they had never been before and lured away, at a time when they would have been serving their apprenticeship in the clubhouse, by the opportunity of earning money in underpaid and unskilled employment by the Europeans.

When Makis founded Susuroka there had seemed to be little purpose in spending time, materials, and effort on a men's house. There were fewer than a handful of boys nearing the age of initiation, and in the changing times it was virtually impossible to maintain the system of control and surveillance that had been a major function of the men's association. But although husbands now slept in the women's houses with their wives and children, they often hankered after the older custom. Makis was the first to see how my room could be turned to their advantage; he came to me with his blanket one night and announced that he intended to sleep on the floor. I did not want to give up almost the last vestige of my privacy, but his imperative manner gave me no alternative. Resenting his demand, I pulled my sleeping bag up to my ears and fought my way to sleep through the added irritation of his snores.

Other men soon followed his initiative, and hardly a week passed without one or more of them arriving with their skimpy bedding and settling down against the wall. It never occurred to them that they might have been imposing on me. In their view of the world, too close and constant an association with the opposite sex, even with one's own wife, could impair a man's vigor or retard his growth during the critical years of adolescence. Youths were cautioned against it and criticized if they were too frequently in female company. Older men who ignored the convention risked premature old age. This belief was still sufficiently powerful, even in these changing times, to overcome any diffidence the men may have felt when it first occurred to them that my room could provide a handy substitute for the protection of the clubhouse.

Little by little it became for some of them even more than a place to sleep occasionally. After Makis again showed the way, they began to use my tin trunks as safe deposits for their personal belongings, replacing my own dwindling supplies with small amounts of cash, shell ornaments and feathers, lengths of cotton cloth, sticks of trade tobacco, and articles of more indeterminate use—a magpie assortment of possessions, stained and smelling of smoke and dust, to which I kept the keys. Sometimes it appeared that I had less right than they to the house, although I had paid them for everything but the land on which it stood. They never asserted it in so many words, but as the months passed and they grew more accustomed to me, their proprietary attitude increased until it seemed perfectly natural when the sacred flutes were kept in my rafters throughout the great festival.

In spite of any of the professional advantages of this close association, its total effect over the years probably contributed to my eventual illness. I could not relax completely with the villagers. There were too many differences to promote complete ease, too many uncertainties to lower every guard. Even toward the end each day was like a meeting with strangers, seldom entirely free of the disconcerting strain of seeking for a familiar value in their attitudes or trying to recognize the hidden implications of their words. They reached their own judgment of me quite early, and possibly their task was much easier. The whole manner of my life with them set me apart from other whites whom they knew, and if they never understood my purpose they accepted me for what I seemed to be. The readiness of their acceptance surprised me, frequently moved me deeply and increased my feeling of indebtedness, but the strain remained, and their invasion of my house prolonged my exposure to it.

Occasionally, as I sat at the table trying to follow the conversation of the men who crowded the floor, one or more of the village girls poked their heads through the door, entering uncertainly with a quick retort for the younger men who tried to embarrass them, but ready to escape from the teasing cuffs as they tried to find a place to sit. While there they sucked in their breath and shook their fingers in astonished admiration of everything they saw, watching me all the while with a white-eyed combination of fear and coyness that appeared more feigned than real. The wives of some of my closer men friends were more frequent visitors, particularly Izazu, the wife of Namuri. She usually arrived later than her husband, invariably taking a place beside him and often bringing their son Giza with her. Watching the three of them in the lamp-lit circle I was virtually unaware of the other figures who merged into the shadowed background, fully occupied by the discovery of a dimension to their personal relationships that was normally obscured by the formal prescriptions of intersex behavior.

Namuri was about thirty-five years old, a large man whose chest and thighs expressed the Gahuku ideal of male strength. In him, however, this physical vigor was not accompanied by any complementary flamboyance or aggressiveness. He possessed the self-awareness that was such a noticeable characteristic of Gahuku male behavior, showing a conscious pride when he stood for his photograph, yellow flowers tucked into his long hair, his legs assertively apart, and his fingers curled tightly around his bow. But he was not ambitious nor eager to lead, content rather with the generalized respect due to an older man who had proved himself in the valued male pursuits. Namuri moved with a sureness and a certainty that seemed to indicate an unquestioning acceptance of the privileges accorded men of his kind, and I also felt that he was very much aware of his physical attractiveness. His wife had similar qualities. She was near his age, taller than most of the women and still firm breasted. Her skin was rather light in color, pale café au lait as the lamplight fell on the flesh of her inner thighs, shading to a darker, satiny hue beneath her arms and in the hollows of her neck where her hair cast a triangle of shadows. Her features were not particularly attractive, but she had a lively and possessive eye, a manner of tilting her head back with a jingle of shell ornaments and a commanding toss of her plaited hair that showed that she was used to attention and ready to exercise the more subtle forms of authority her sex possesses.

She was obviously enamored of Namuri. As they sat side by side on the floor she linked her arms around one of his legs and leaned against him. His shoulder filled the hollow above her breast, and when she turned to him, moving with an impulsive need for closer contact, their hair met, and her teeth were white against the darkness of his neck.

He sat unmoved through her displays of affection, maintaining the aloofness appropriate to his sex, but when their son was with them their joint interest in the boy seemed to breach the need to observe the formal limits of social distance. Giza was undeniably spoiled. As he stood between his father's knees he turned and twisted with the petulance of children who know how to take advantage of love, reaching toward his mother's breast only to reject it when she cupped it in her hands, turning instead to bury his face in Namuri's shoulder. While he was there, husband and wife seemed to be oblivious of everything around them, caught in the uncompromising light of my lamp in a manner entirely different from the appearance they presented in the street, forming so close and intimate a circle that sometimes I felt impelled to look away from them.

This embarrassment was due not only to their uninhibited displays of affection, but also to the knowledge, which I shared with the villagers, that Giza was not their own child. Izazu and Namuri had had no children. Giza was the son of Bihore, Namuri's younger brother, whose prolific wife was the envy of men who were always ready to suspect that women did not want to bear them children. This charge was one of the most frequent and conventional expressions of sex antagonism and one of the most common causes for divorce. Childlessness was never attributed to male inadequacy but always to female perversity, to their fear of pain and possible death, which caused them to resort to their carefully guarded knowledge of contraceptives, withholding from men the natural right of fatherhood. Whatever the reasons, the incidence of barrenness was sufficiently high to confirm the standard male view of essentially opposed interests. It placed the childless woman in a particularly vulnerable position, provided a ready excuse for polygyny, and underscored the prevalence of adoption.

No one spoke openly of the true parentage of children like Giza. Since they received as much attention as any other child, the conspiracy of silence seemed to reflect the anomalous position of the foster parents, perhaps particularly the touchiness of husbands, but also I thought, watching Izazu, the basic insecurity of women. Everyone knew that Namuri was thinking of taking a second wife. The woman, who had been aroused by his dancing at a festival, had sent word that she wanted him to bring her to Susuroka. His increasing overnight absences left little room to doubt his intentions, and they provoked a characteristic protest from Izazu who sat sullenly in the street while he was away, refusing to work and muttering that she would kill her rival if he brought her back with him. Sometimes it seemed that he delayed only from genuine affection for his wife, encouraged to a move that no man would question but held back by the intangible tie his language could not express, caught, it seemed, by the dependence to which his sex ideally was immune. Perhaps Izazu, circling his thigh with her arms, could keep him for herself, but if he chose to send her away no one sitting on my floor would speak seriously in her defense.

Like Namuri and Makis, the men who came to me most constantly were relatively young, all of them probably under forty. They had a more lively personal interest in the world I represented than the older villagers, to whom it would always remain a puzzling and possibly unwelcome intrusion. Maniha, the elder brother of Makis, was one of those who came seldom, spoke little while he was there, and stayed for only a short while, sometimes only long enough to accept a cigarette when I handed them round the circle. He must have been close to fifty, already a little stooped but quite vigorous and quick in his movements. There was little physical or temperamental resemblance between the two brothers who had been born to different mothers. Maniha was smaller in build than Makis but still wiry and capable of working day after day in his gardens. He was not assertive and never given to levity. Even when he was young he had probably not possessed either the talent or the ambition to be an orator. Yet he had a lively mind and was capable of exercising more subtle kinds of influence. No one questioned his right to be called a man of strength. In his youth he had been known for his skill in fighting, although his reputation did not equal that of his father nor even of Makis, who had had less time to earn a name. None of his exploits were given the heroic embellishments that elevated the deeds of some men to the status of legends, to be recounted whenever there was need to reaffirm the glories of a past no longer possible, but he had been a reliable if unspectacular warrior, showing in this, as in everything else he did, a firm commitment to the basic values of the life to which he had been reared.

He was one of the village conservatives, valuing tradition and still wearing at his waist the vomiting canes whose use I learned later, implements that had symbolized the world of men and the shared interests for which they stood together. The canes were seldom used now and never worn by the younger generation. Age had added to the respect in which he was held, and when I knew him he was one of the Nagamidzuha elders—the select body of men, past their prime but versed in customary lore and procedure, whose advice did more perhaps to form opinion than the ranting oratory of clan spokesmen or the hotheaded wrangling of those who were still chasing their ambitions. Like others who had achieved a similar position, Maniha used his influence unobtrusively, seldom rising to state his views openly at any gathering but moving quietly around the perimeter of debate to find the ear of one man and then another, gradually encouraging the semblance of consensus with which all group discussions were supposed to end. He was never a leader in any matter touching the new ways that were altering every life so rapidly, having little time for either the new proscriptions of the white man or the broader range of experience that beckoned so enticingly to others, but he was always present, always alert and ready with advice whenever the things he knew, and seemed to love, were under discussion.

Maniha had three children, a married daughter and two sons, the elder of whom, Bin, had joined the native police, a body officered by whites, and had been away from Susuroka for three years. Asemo was his younger son. I had liked him as soon as I noticed him in my house, watching him sit quietly in the second row of men partly outside the circle of light, his chin raised, and his eyes occasionally catching and reflecting a small bright spark as he studied everything I did. There was a difference between him and the other youths who were noisily bumping shoulders with one another or trying to best a neighbor in some other permitted form of aggression. Asemo was not disdainful of their rowdiness. Now and then his eyes left me to catch some particular action in the scuffle, drawn to it by a rapid interchange of words that parted his lips in an appreciative grin. But he always returned to his quiet study of me, and he remained long after his age-mates had left for less confined surroundings. He had a quality of contained but relaxed participation—his hands held loosely in his lap, shoulders slightly to the fore, his back a supple curve from the base of his neck to the crossed legs that carried the weight of his body. Asemo's head and eyes showed that he was taking stock of everything around him, yet he also seemed to be aloof, watching from some inner vantage point where his mind made its own judgments and decisions. My affection for him built gradually in subsequent months, developing to the point where he was one of the few Gahuku with whom I was ever entirely at ease.

By the end of a day spent mostly in working at my table, the air inside my house became unpleasantly stale. A musty smell rose from the ground under the bamboo floor increasing my vague discomfort, which came from a combination of sudden, irritable distaste for the sagging camp stretcher and the jumble of boxes and stores, and the strain of working too long in poor light. I often sought relief for my eyes and mind by leaving my compound in the late evening when the sun had dropped behind the western mountains but the whole valley still glowed with a golden light.

When I crossed the street, it required a conscious effort to reply civilly to the unwelcome, imperative interest my presence always provoked. My dissatisfaction with myself was transferred to the people who sat idly beside the ovens, to the scavenging pigs snorting distrustfully as I approached, and to the piles of garbage, which seemed to spark a sudden realization of the alien quality of everything around me, confronting me with the difference between my present circumstances and the things to which I was accustomed and sought in my other existence.

I sat down at the edge of the path that ran down the hillside to the garden areas, choosing a place where a dense clump of bamboo many years old provided the only permanent shade in the settlement. From here I obtained one of the most encompassing and dramatic views the ridge afforded. At my back the houses soaked the light so thirstily that their walls seemed wet with a liquid brilliance. Overhead, the bamboo leaves hung a dark frieze of spears across the sky, moving only slightly in air that was still warm but that carried a hint of the chill rising up to meet the night from the lower terraces. At the bottom of the hill a thin blue veil had descended over the deserted gardens, softening the edges of the stalks of corn and the neat rows of vines. More than a mile away, beyond the trees at Gohajaka where the quilted pattern of the gardens ended and the grass began, a small arc of water held the sky in an embrace, its emerald surface slipping around the base of a shadowed cliff where a track mounted to the nearest villages of the Uheto. On the higher ground groves of casuarinas were flushed with the memory of the sun, pinpoints of light still flickering intermittently in the darkening distance, going out one by one in the hanging valleys where night had already claimed a score of other settlements.

Asemo was frequently one of the crowd of children who joined me under the clump of bamboo. Unlike the others he hardly seemed to intrude, even when he stayed on when the rest had returned to the village. Only a few feet would separate us as he squatted beside me on his haunches, looking across the valley in the direction of my own eyes and keeping so silent that I often forgot he was with me until some slight movement of his bare feet as he altered his balance recalled me to the present.

At times like this I became most clearly aware of the areas of Gahuku life into which I would never be able to enter. In a crowd, or even with two or three people, it was much easier to believe that I could recognize their thoughts, their motives, and emotions, penetrating to the deeper layers of their lives through doors that were opened by the tone of a voice, the expression on a face, and the graphic movements that lent additional point to their words. With only one of them I had none of these clues to his thoughts, particularly when we had exhausted our range of talk. The silences had been more frequent and more distressing during the early months of my visit, and as they grew and lengthened I had manoeuvered desperately to put an end to them, searching for a question to help me across the widening gap. This self-consciousness passed as I became more familiar with the people. Eventually I no longer felt compelled to talk or, failing to discover an appropriate word, to escape from the situation with the excuse that something else required my attention. When the silences fell I used them as a welcome respite in which to draw into myself and rest, allowing my mind to move in an orbit unrelated to any of my immediate ends but coming back at last to the point of departure.

As the circle closed, bringing the present back with renewed intensity, I was sharply aware of the different paths my companion and I must have traveled in the intervening minutes. At least from our outward appearance Asemo and I could have been engrossed by an identical purpose, but he could not be expected to bring a similar perspective to bear on the visible features of the valley any more than I could share, except vicariously, his range of experience. It was not that I was unable to relate what I saw to the pattern of life in which I was partially involved. Out of the events I had seen and the past that had been recalled for me, everything became informed by a distinctive quality, so that the high ground beyond the river was not simply an expanse of grass barred by the contrasting alternations of sun and shadow but also a no man's land separating traditional enemies. Each point of reference carried a specific implication, was colored by knowledge that was certainly shared by Asemo or any other man who sat beside me; yet there was no way of telling if there was any common ground in our perception of the same object. Occasionally I had an intimation of meeting them at a level that transcended any visual conventions, as on one early morning at the summit of the ranges to the far northwest, while we were returning home after an absence of three weeks, Makis had caught up with me a moment after my first view of the valley, lying perhaps a thousand feet below us, and grasping my arm had directed me to look into the distance, over the foam of clouds and the columns of smoke melting into the irridescent light of day, toward the ridge where Susuroka still lay a good day's walk ahead of us. The pressure of his fingers seemed to convey the essence of what we mean by home, its hundred meanings and associations, but even as I felt a quickening response I knew that our basic connotations of the word had to be different, that I could never say precisely what he saw, and that lacking the necessary schooling in introspection he could never explain it.

I was continually at odds with this basic difficulty. Even as I think I know what Asemo wanted it is possible that this is attributing too much to him, enveloping him with an aura of tragedy visible only from my own perspective.

Sometimes, leaving the house in the early morning, I saw him among the crowd of younger people who had invaded my kitchen. Apart from my staff, there were usually a few others who were about his own age. Lithe but still immature they sat on the ground beside the open fire where my meals were cooked, their long headdresses fanning across the dust. The moment I appeared my name was spoken with the sharp intonation of a warning and several heads swung round to face me, eyes white and muscles gathering for quick flight. The difference between Asemo and his age mates was very noticeable in this mercurial company. Though he had not been initiated, he wore his hair short, without the distinctive artificial plaits, and always wrapped himself in a lap-lap. This was the new mode of dress, replacing the traditional vees, and was now mandatory in every white household. It was therefore worn by every man who was oriented toward the world the whites represented. A lap-lap was not necessarily more sanitary, though perhaps it was more modest than the older style. Soap was difficult to obtain in the village, and when a dirty undershirt completed the outfit the total effect was often extremely disagreeable. Somehow, Asemo managed to keep his clothes clean, but though he was personally attractive, well formed, with a bright, engaging smile, his figure lacked the picturesque bravura of his age mates whose long hair, responding to every movement, accentuated their restless fluctuations of interest. Compared to them he seemed more stolid. Yet he was far from dull, and perhaps his quietness and apparent reserve simply reflected a more precise appreciation of the future and what he wanted from it. At least this is what I began to suspect on the rather rare opportunities I had to observe him. It was confirmed when he entered my household and I saw him every day.

After the marriage of Hutorno, who was supposed to help prepare my meals but who was never in the house when he was needed, I had an adequate excuse to discharge him from the household staff, the explanation being that his involvement with his new obligations prevented him from giving sufficient attention to my needs. I had no real intention of filling the vacancy his departure left but should have known that once a position had been established it was almost impossible to explain why it was no longer necessary. A day or so later, Hunehune said that he had found someone to take Hutorno's place. For a moment I felt like replying that I did not intend to engage a new boy, but when he added that it was Asemo, I gave in once more to the fairly common tendency to tell me what was best for my own interests.

In the following months there was absolutely no reason to complain about Asemo. He was even more attentive than Hunehune who, being older, was able to pass on to him many duties that were properly his own, in this way finding more time to attend to his other interests. Asemo always asked my permission before absenting himself for more than a hour or so at a time, and when I was away from the house he chose usually to accompany me rather than remaining in the empty village where, had he been like Hunehune, he would have spent the hours stretched out on the kitchen floor singing himself to sleep.

At first we had little to say to each other, not much more than had passed between us on the afternoons when we had shared the shade of the clump of bamboo. I wanted to know him better and kept reminding myself that I should make the effort, but other matters always seemed to be more pressing. Finally he assumed the initiative and placed our relationship upon an entirely new footing.

I had been working in the house and had begun to feel an urge to seek the open air when Asemo appeared across the table from me holding a grimy schoolboy's notebook. He hesitated to show it to me, self-consciousness competing with pride as I took it from him. A dozen of the stained pages were covered with penciled words, a childish script whose uncertain form showed the concentration and effort of putting it down. Obviously it was schoolwork of a kind, simple sentences of Gahuku expressed for the most part in phonetic symbols. Like all children's writing it was peculiarly affecting, evoking an innocence that calls us back from the distance of maturity into a forgotten past crying for protection, but finding it in the present circumstances added something entirely different to the act of sudden recognition. It spoke not only of the inevitable changes lying within the individual life but also of the forces and events shaping the larger world through which one has to find a way, always with knowledge that is incomplete. Almost as sharply as though it was pictured there, the page in front of me forced a realization of the basic posture of the people with whom I lived, suspended precariously between a past where changes are infrequent, unrecorded landmarks in the slow progress of time and a future less than a generation old that was hurrying them into history. No one in the village was exempt from the implications of Asemo's writing, but it was his age group, not the old or the very young nor even the youths in their twenties, who would taste the real bitterness. In the succession of generations it was these adolescents who would have to discover the difficult balance between reality and hope.

Looking up from the book to Asemo, I felt the unaccustomed burden of seeing farther ahead than his own eyes could penetrate and of being unable to tell him what I saw, a heaviness that from then onward qualified my perception of everything he did. The book contained his own work, the result of over a year's intermittent attendance at what was called generously a mission school in the Gehamo village below the ridge. The instruction was given by a native evangelist representing the Lutheran church whose local headquarters, staffed by a white American and his wife, were eight miles distant on the opposite side of the Asaro River. The man was not a Gahuku. He came from the coast, which no one in Susuroka had seen, where he had attended a Lutheran training center, had been baptized, and had been taught to read and write after a fashion in a vernacular called Kate, one of two languages out of the total of several hundred spoken in New Guinea that the mission used to spread its message. Like other lay evangelists he was attached to an outstation on the completion of his training. There he picked up a local language and eventually became the spearhead of mission activity in an assigned area, living in a particular village where he was supported by the local people but also traveling through a much larger parish whose boundaries barely kept a pace or two behind the government's continual effort to extend the limits of its own control.

In a country where people had lived out their whole lives within an area of a few square miles, an evangelist was almost as much a stranger as myself. He had no established niche in a village unless he married a local woman, and he depended ultimately on charity, though it was phrased as support for the services he rendered. These were supplying the natives with the enlightenment of the scriptures and the salvation of baptism, but possibly of more immediate importance to the group that gave him land and built his house, he was also expected to teach the children to read and write. For many of the older generation lit-

eracy had an almost mystic, perhaps a magic virtue. They had not yet
grasped the social and economic implications of color, but they were
increasingly aware of the barriers of caste, and literacy seemed like
the miraculous bridge that would lead them to the wealth, the privilege,
and the power concentrated in the Europeans. Left to the mission and
its lay evangelists, the bridge would prove to be a chimera, for they
offered only the bare rudiments of learning, sufficient to string some
semiliterate sentences together and to read, with difficulty, a few
sacred texts transcribed into a tongue no white man would bother to
try to comprehend.

Asemo had arrived at his own negative opinion of the mission
school. He was clearly pleased by the interest I showed in his work, but
when I looked up from the final page he took the book from me and
closed it in a gesture of dissatisfaction. Looking into my eyes, the tone
of his voice an odd but affecting contrast to the uncertain stance of
his figure, he commanded me to teach him English. At least his words
were phrased as a demand, a convention to which I had become accustomed gradually but that struck me now with an entirely new feeling
of misgiving. There were insuperable difficulties to granting his request. Even if I had been able to take the time from my other work I
was not equipped with the necessary technical skills to guarantee success. But this could not be explained to his satisfaction; it would not
occur to him to doubt my ability to give him what he wanted.

Once again the uncomfortable feeling came that wherever I went I
was the focus of unvoiced expectations. The evidence was slight and
inconclusive, often no more than a watchful flicker in the brown eyes
that studied everything I did, or perhaps a subtle inflection to a question and the even less tangible sensation that some deeper level of
meaning was given to my answer. At times the unreality affected me so
strongly that I seemed to be walking precariously on a tightrope of
unstated assumptions, as if I were somehow acquiescing in the view
that I knew more than my plain statements conveyed. Criticism was not
involved; rather, we were all members of a silent conspiracy whose
terms were understood but never stated; and we all knew the reason
why my answers were never complete.

I was most conscious of uneasiness with Makis, but I also felt the
current of its implications disturbing the air of the room as I tried to
persuade Asemo of the impossibility of his request. Even as he assented
that I was too busy to take on an additional task, the look in his eyes

seemed to withhold any substance from my explanation. The futility
of combating the mirage of the villagers' assumptions won him an
agreement. I told him I would help him in my spare time.

At best our lessons were irregular. In agreeing to help him I had
had some hope that his interest would fade quickly, absolving me
from any need to carry out the bargain, but this never happened. He
appeared in my room with almost ritual precision toward the middle of
the afternoon carrying the book and pencil I had given him and he
settled himself on the floor to wait until I was ready. His characteristic
attitude seemed to imply a willingness to sit there indefinitely. He sat
cross-legged, resting his forearms on his knees, his steady eyes leaving
me only when someone passed along the street beyond the open door.
Now and then the sound of a distant voice thinned by the heat outside
the house lifted his head alertly, and his face was crossed by an expression that seemed like an invitation to share what he had heard. I
worked without interruption through his silence and his steady scrutiny.
Occasionally the brief flashes of recognition passing between us seemed
to express a mutual understanding and a bond of companionship rare
in my relations, and on impulse I would put my work aside so that
we could start our lesson.

We never accomplished very much. While he took my chair I sat
on an upturned crate beside him holding his hand to help him to form
the letters of the alphabet, sounding each vowel and consonant as we
made it. We progressed from there to the words for simple objects in
the room, but verbs seemed to be beyond my reach, and by the time
our lessons ended Asemo could manage to speak only a few broken
sentences of English.

I never doubted his ability to learn from proper instruction, but I
was impressed most by his ambition for knowledge itself. Almost everyone in the village had acquired a need for something out of the white
man's world, but Asemo wanted more than a steel knife or axe, tobacco,
or trade-store cloth and beads. It was not that he was any less ma-
terialistic than other Gahuku. If he had phrased his wants they would
have included everything that the whites possessed in such abundance,
but he was seeking for something for which money and goods were
only a material expression or symbol. It was the intangible something
lying beyond them, that which made them possible, that he hoped to
gain. Colored by the culture in which he had been reared, his name
for it may have been power, specifically the vague but overarching

supernatural power that governed all success. But shorn of the overtones of magic, it was knowledge that he sought.

He was committed to the world of Humeleveka where the ugly
European houses tried to emulate suburbia and where, before long, a
curfew would exclude people of his color from the streets when night
fell. He was not aware, I am sure, that the rich hues of his skin would
be held against him. He had not yet felt the indignity of being a black
man in his own country, and he had the simple belief that those who
possessed what he wanted would be willing to share it with him.

I had begun our lessons without enthusiasm, but as the weeks
passed it became increasingly difficult to evade the implications of
their quality. Sitting alone in the cluttered, shadowed house and watching Asemo's awkward efforts with his pencil, I could feel the sun burning along the ridge outside, bending the tassels of the grass and drawing
off the frail color of the casuarinas, and Asemo's head, bending over
the book, seemed suddenly threatened and defenseless.

At such times the pattern of life to which he had been reared, the
traditional interests of boys of his age, and the future for which they
had been prepared were like a physical presence in the house, a background that seemed to impose itself on my words even while I was
speaking to him, compelling me to acknowledge the contrast between
his studious concentration and the groups of long-haired youths whom
I met on my walks along the ridge.

The small world of these boys standing at the threshhold of manhood already prefigured the uncompromising divisions of adult life.
Although they had not been admitted to the status of men, they were
clearly members of the Gahuku elect, still somewhat constrained and
uncertain in the company of their elders, but among themselves, in
their free and largely irresponsible life on the ridge, they showed
they were aware of their worth and of the privileges waiting for them
just below the horizon. In their relations with each other maleness,
even more than kinship or age, was the ultimate principle of association,
the common factor that held them together. Arrogance and aggressiveness, tempered by immaturity, were the qualities that earned respect,
and the movement of their naked limbs, the thrust of a hip bearing the
body's weight as they rested with crossed legs, was like an echo of the
assertiveness of orators.

Two formal situations impressed me as particularly telling expressions of the anticipated shape of a boy's life—one celebrating a woman's

first pregnancy and the other taking place when a group of youths, age mates who had passed together through initiation, received the official approval of their elders to have intercourse with the girls to whom they had been betrothed. I watched the first rite one afternoon at Gohajaka, when Goraso's pregnancy was about six months advanced. Earlier in the day her own and her husband's close kinsmen had hunted for bush rats in the grasses of the ridge and had cooked and feasted on their catch. As evening approached, Goraso, wearing a wide pregnancy belt, sat on the ground in front of them, making her lap a perch for a small boy who carried a child's bow and arrows. While they remained in this position first her husband's kinsmen and then her own relatives wound the woman and boy in lengths of bark cloth, forming a cocoon that covered them completely. Then the men reversed the procedure, stripping the wrappings from them one by one. As the last piece of cloth was removed the boy leaped from between her legs and scattered the adults with his arrows.

The second rite established individual households for a group of age mates. The young men, in their early twenties, had been betrothed several years before at the time of their initiation. During the intervening period they had been required to avoid their future wives, waiting until their elders considered they were physically mature and ready for cohabitation. At the final marriage ceremony the girls formed a line in the village street, each exposing a bare thigh in the direction of her husband. The men approached in an armed procession, each taking a position in front of his wife. The bows in their hands were strung with an arrow called "anger," a three-pronged weapon used for hunting birds and smaller game but not considered lethal for any fair-sized animal. The arrows struck the bare thighs from a distance of a few paces, not penetrating deeply enough to maim, but often printing the flesh with a lifetime reminder of formal submission.

Between these two rituals the ideal shape of a man's life was rounded out by the innumerable details of a boy's observation. From his earliest years the club house stood for his future. Everything concerning the collective life of the village centered upon this place where his father slept, and even while very young he must have begun to appreciate the extent of the formal division that separated the adult members of his family.

The traditional male view of Gahuku life, seen from the perspective of the mens' house, was what a boy was encouraged to see and to perpetuate in his own attitudes and behavior. As he grew up, if he learned his lessons, he believed in the superiority of the interests that united his sex and strove to exhibit the qualities that would earn him a reputation for strength. It was an exaggerated view, distorted by the effort to keep the contrasting patterns of male and female apart, for the overbearing character of men masked an uncertainty that often seemed as deeply seated as their expressed convictions of superiority. Male ends, male security, were opposed by the views men held of female sexuality. The perpetuation of the group was threatened by a woman's mercurial attachments leading to broken betrothals and frequent divorce and by an unwillingness to bear children. Legend held that the most sacred and most secret symbols had been discovered by women and thereafter taken away and appropriated for male use only, to be viewed by the women on pain of death.

It was this life, presented in such sharp contrasts, containing few halftones, that seemed to force itself into my room through the dazzling interstices of the bamboo walls as Asemo bent over his book. Our lessons often continued until the afternoon was almost over and the street outside was filled with the voices of people returning from the ridge. His complete absorption seemed to challenge the pattern of existence whose sounds ran up and down the street. It affected me the more deeply, summoning a stronger impulse to protect him, because I had no illusions concerning my ability to instruct him. But something else was even more difficult to explain to him; the future he hoped to gain with my help was quite beyond the reach of anyone his age. In any plans to help to secure it for his tribe, Asemo was expendable, already too old to warrant the investment of the years of formal schooling necessary to realize even his most modest hopes. The tension between the future he sought and the past he was trying to leave behind gradually dominated our lessons on those quiet afternoons. Asemo had not felt it yet, perhaps would not feel it for many years, but events in which he was soon involved underscored in a highly dramatic way his basic predicament.

They began six months or so after he had joined my household. It was the dry season of the year, a period of heightened social activity when most festivals were held. There was a special quality to these days, a buoyancy; I woke with every sense alert. The mornings often broke without the usual low ceiling of clouds and the mists that muffled

the village in opalescent cotton, clear nights giving place to equally
clear days in a quiet transition.

I awakened one morning with the feeling that something new had
been added to a familiar situation. The village was completely silent,
yet the air seemed to vibrate uneasily against my ear, prompting me to
recall the unidentified sound that had broken into my sleep. For a
while I lay still and listened intently for anything that would give it a
recognizable shape, but there was nothing to which I could fasten an
explanation. The day had barely begun. It was far too early for any
movement in the houses, and the sound that had left its track on my
mind must have come from outside the settlement. I started to dismiss
it as imagined when suddenly it came again, lifting me up to my elbows
with a sense of shock.

In later months the same notes came at many times of day, but they
always carried the quality of this first encounter—the predawn air chilling my arms and shoulders, the glimmer of light in the empty street,
and the whole valley lying exposed and unsuspecting as it slept. Their
sound eludes description. It had too many different elements and contradictions, and the music was based on an entirely alien scale. The
clear air offered it no resistance, and the notes, coming from a distance,
seemed to wind at will through an echoing void, tracing such a ca-
pricious path that their origin was successfully concealed. They struck
with a hollow, pulsing beat in the bass register, a continuous explosion
of notes like a cry of hunger torn from a distended, disembodied throat.
More shrill calls played in and out of this rhythmic background in repe-
titive patterns that after a while could be identified as tunes. Both
elements were deliberately joined, contrasting and complementing, designed to produce a unified effect. The shrill notes fluttered avidly
around the deeper cries, possessed of the same need and urging the
stronger on to fulfill it like vultures wheeling in a cloudless sky, dependent on their predatory fellows.

Even as the first calls troubled the morning air people began to stir.
Currents of speculation ran through the village, subsiding gradually into
a listening silence. Outside my room the predawn light grew slowly
more intense; then the strange cries ceased as abruptly as they had
begun, leaving only a momentary echo on the threshhold of day.

In the street later, I found that the sounds were the principal topic
of conversation. There was no doubt what they were or where they

came from. They were the sacred flutes of Gama, and at this time of year their appearance could mean only one thing, that the Gama had decided to hold the greatest of Gahuku festivals, the *idza nama.*

These festivals were a complex of activities; their principal components were male initiation and the ceremonial exchange of enormous quantities of pigs, the principal measure of traditional wealth. They occurred infrequently, at intervals of five to seven years, timed to coincide with the maturation of each succeeding group of adolescent boys, but also dependent upon the state of the group's resources, for they were competitive displays of strength, a celebration and affirmation of the values that gave life its characteristic shape and tone. No other activity took so long to arrange, engaged such a large number of people at one time, or involved so much visiting. Secondary ceremonies signified the completion of various stages in the preparations and pointed to the climactic events with which they closed. Each one of them provided an opportunity for self-display, a chance to stress the dominance of men and the bonds uniting their sex, to assert the wealth of tribe and clan, and to obtain prestige and influence. All the richness of their lives found expression in this context, played out in the flashing, gaudy colors of paint and feathers and towering decorations that added several feet to the normal height of a man. And when the festival was over and people returned to their routine tasks, a whole pattern of existence had been displayed.

Adding to the extraordinary character of the events, indeed, sanctifying and setting them apart, the sacred flutes invested them with the mysterious power of the supernatural. From the moment that their first dawn cries served notice of the group's decision their calls marked the beginning of every day, beat against the tight, dry air of noon, and wound a magic thread through the silver silence of the nights. Gahuku are not philosophers or theologians. They had no priesthood devoted to the interpretation of doctrine, the preservation of dogma, or the management of ritual. Their religious beliefs are not formulated precisely, not stated in a more or less coherent system that is available for objective examination and discussion. No other side of their life proved so difficult to penetrate, was so elusive, less amenable to definite statements yet also so pervasive, so intrinsically a part of the world as it is seen through their eyes and minds. Inference was almost the only key to entering this realm of thought.

In Gahuku religion there are no gods to whom men are responsible and few demons, apart from some bogeymen—horribly deformed simulacra of human beings who are encountered sometimes by solitary individuals. Yet the world and everything within it depend on supernatural force, an impersonal power operating as the force of life, having no name nor any specific location, vaguely ancestral in character, and ultimately the source of all success, indispensable for everything men hope to achieve. The religious quest is essentially a search for this power, an effort to tap it and control it, to discover its source, and to enlist its aid in securing a bountiful life, It is a search beset by fundamental uncertainties; for the nature of the power sought is not known completely, and it is possible that there are alternative ways of obtaining access to it, some giving a more certain control and bringing more abundant rewards than others. Individuals, even whole groups of people, may differ in the efficacy of the methods they employ, in their knowledge of the source of power, and their control over its operation, but everyone has need of it. This force is not malevolent; it neither punishes nor condemns. There are, however, potentially harmful spirits who entice women away from the paths and gardens, seduce them, and after intercourse reveal their true identity by spitting in the women's faces. Death results from these encounters, and sometimes illness is caused by the ghosts of the recently dead who feel neglected or displeased by behavior that failed to show them proper respect.

Ritual is the means men use to tap the fountainhead of power and to divert it to man's ends. In periodic cycles spanning the better part of a generation the villagers renew their whole lives in it, building the ozaha neta whose meaning had been so difficult for me to ascertain. The unspectacular object fashioned from stakes and roughly hewn timber is like a flume thrust into an invisible stream, drawing it off and channeling it down to men, establishing a supernatural reservoir whose mystical influence sustains them through the following years. This rite is the supreme act of faith and aspiration, the dual impulse of fallible human nature lying at the heart of all religion. But the crude table and the bleached bones almost concealed by sprouting leaves speak less clearly of the continuing concern with power than the pulsing cries of the flutes echoing along the paths of morning.

These sounds are explained to women as the calls of mythical, carnivorous birds, *nama,* which abide periodically in the men's house and carry off the adolescent boys during the crisis of initiation. It is a graphic and pertinent description of the effect produced by the bamboo instruments, and sitting behind the closed doors of the houses, whenever the flutes are played in the open street, the air seems to be roiled by the beating of invisible wings. Yet the nama are more than a symbol of male dominance, a picturesque way of telling women their proper place, and the simple deception, which possibly fools only children, is one of their less important features.

On a characteristic occasion, I was with a procession of twenty villagers returning along the ridge to Susuroka from the floor of the valley below Ekuhakuka, where the morning and early part of the afternoon had been spent feasting at a secluded garden dwelling. While the men gossiped or slept in the shade, the nama rested in pairs inside the house on a bed of colored leaves and flowers. They were unremarkable instruments, hollow sections of bamboo closed at one end, about two feet six inches long and six inches in diameter, with a small round hole that a player held to his mouth. There was no external decoration and they had so little material value that they were broken and burned at the end of the festival. In spite of their ceremonial bed and their food, salt and cooked pork placed in each mouthpiece, it was difficult to associate them with the extraordinarily moving cries that began and closed each day at the height of the festival season. But it was the tunes that carried their wealth of symbolic implication.

It was nearing midafternoon when we returned from the floor of the valley to the ridge. The climb to Ekuhakuka was short but steep, and I was out of breath when we reached the crest, thankful for the brief pause as the men formed a single file just beyond the dilapidated, empty settlement. For a mile or so, from here to the outskirts of Gohajaka, the ridge was narrow, falling away abruptly on either side of the path. The grass was stunted in many places and the slopes were gashed with the red and chocolate scars of recent slides that had carried away the covering of crotolaria, leaving the track completely exposed, almost miraculously suspended in light and air, so open that anyone moving along it was plainly visible from the gardens below, their figures silhouetted on the breathless arch of sky. As we reached these barren heights the men nearest the flute players extended branches of leaves to hide them from sight, though even this attempt at concealment must have seemed a trivial subterfuge to any curious eyes directed upward from the gardens by the sound of the music. The men were absorbed by the performance, speaking only when the flutes were passed to a new group of players. It was impossible for me to tell what they felt, though the startling brightness was a perfect match for their rapt expressions. I was struck by the thought that they may have wanted to be seen, that they were aware of the effect they made, that each step filled them with a mounting pride and drew them closer together in the bonds of a common emotion.

A short distance from the entrance to Gohajaka, Gapiriha, holding a formidable length of cane, pushed his way to the front of the procession, going ahead in order to clear the street for our progress through the village. He was running past the houses as we entered the street, beating against the barred doors, scattering the terrified chickens perched on the thatched roofs and the ubiquitous pigs scavenging near the fires. The music of the flutes rose to a new pitch of intensity as the players seemed to double their effort, inspired by the submissive, unseen audience behind the walls, the throaty shouts of the other men who had followed the example of their herald, and the answering welcome of old Alum whose age allowed her the privilege of staying outside her house, where she leaned against her staff and faced the nama, her eyes closed fast and her thin, bent body shaking with shrill cries.

Later, back in my house with the flutes laid carefully on the floor, the men were like contestants in a game that had tested their strength and concentration to the limits of their endurance. They were almost drunk with excitement, balanced on the edge of exhaustion, their nervous energy so recently strung to its highest pitch seeking to return to its normal level through incessant talking. Hunehune's eyes were bright with feeling. His voice trembled perceptibly, like his hand, which rested lightly on a pair of flutes, while he tried to make me understand and share the wonder of the sound we had heard. The aesthetic thrill he hoped to explain was closely linked to the fact that each tune required two flutes, bass and treble, point and counterpoint, melody and rhythm, joined as parts within a whole. One without the other carried no emotional charge whatever, but played together, complementing yet intertwined, the effect was magical, a mystery for which he had no adequate words. Gesturing helplessly with his hands, Hunehune turned to Bihore and remarked that his playing had so deranged him that if he had been a woman he would have had to come to Bihore's house. There was no mistaking the implication of his words, the attribution of sexual qualities to the nama. Male sexuality was a manifestation of power, the very force of life, the basis of existence; the flutes not only symbolized power in its most inclusive sense but also linked it to the structure of relationships that bound each man to his fellows.

Each tune was the common property of a different subclan, that group of men who were descended through males from a common ancestor. Passed down, according to tradition, from the most remote ancestral times, they stood for the continuity of this group and the inviolate character of its bonds and associated attitudes, internal harmony, mutual support, and solidarity before the world at large. In the tunes of the nama each subclan expressed and experienced its common purpose and identity, celebrated the goals it sought, and the invisible medium of power in which it was steeped.

In the following weeks the sounds of the nama were threaded through the background of every day. The Gama flutes could be heard quite clearly from Susuroka, but as the season progressed other tribes and villages signified their intention to hold the festival, and on any morning the calls seemed to speak to each other from a dozen different places, harshly insistent from the grasslands to the south, thin and troubled like the last notes of an echo, from the hanging valleys in the western mountains. Though they became a customary part of experience, I was never able to sleep through their cries, always waking as their notes beat at the threshhold of dawn and carrying the memory of them in my mind as I waited for them to return in the blue and golden air of evening. Their inaudible vibration hung upon the intervening hours, pulsing in the sunlight and the purple underside of clouds, following a breeze along the leaves of the cane fences, filling the whole landscape with the quickening tempo of life.

The speculation the Gama flutes had started continued unabated in Susuroka, veiled, however, by an attitude of formal disinterest. The villagers shrugged aside my questions when I asked if the Gama intended to hold an initiation as well as the ceremonial exchange of pigs. Perhaps they did not know the answer, but there was also a carefully studied attempt to underplay the significance of the events taking place so close to them. It was clear that among their other functions, the idza nama touched the most sensitive areas of pride and reputation; they stimulated an urge to meet their challenge, to establish the equality demanded in Gahuku society. Morning and evening the flutes seemed to question this equality, taunting other villages to show their strength or, failing, to admit at least a temporary inferiority, and inevitably they started a round of discussions concerned with the ability to reply.

Such discussions were taking place in Susuroka. They were completely informal, a careful testing of opinion led by men who resented the delicate position of the village, which was compelled to watch passively while the Gama asserted their strength. It was essential to act with the greatest circumspection, avoiding anything that might carry an insulting reference to the events on their borders. Makis was my chief informant, and apparently there was only a remote possibility that our own flutes would speak for Nagamidzuha. So much hinged on the festivals that it was necessary to secure the agreement and participation of every segment within a tribe, and, in turn, this depended upon a precise assessment of individual resources and committed contributions. The majority opinion doubted that the tribe could marshal sufficient wealth this year. Nagamidzuha would have to wait for some future occasion, even though this decision was opposed by some of the villagers.

Susuroka was in the same position one month later when the past reached out to assert its claim on Asemo. I was alone in the house, working, quite late at night. No one had come to bother me in the earlier part of the evening and the circle of my lamp light was a solitary clearing in a pressing forest of darkness. A movement in the doorway lifted my head abruptly, my mind a split second or so behind my eyes in recognizing the two figures as they entered; it was Makis and his half-brother Maniha, their dark bodies parting the yellow glare as, crouching slightly, they sat on the floor beside my chair. Even at rest it was impossible to disassociate Makis from the splendid public figure who declaimed with such flourish at clan gatherings. His fingernails were quite as long, if not as carefully tended as a woman's; they drew my eyes to the hand that held his cigarette, the wrist lightly flexed, poised for one of the studied, sweeping gestures that punctuated the flow of his speeches. In profile against the light, his back was an alert, assertive curve, tensed for sudden movement like the muscled thighs of his crossed legs. His chin was raised to look at me through the marbled wisps of blue smoke, the extended line of his throat merging into the portion of his chest visible below his naked shoulder. Farther to the rear, Maniha faced me, obviously older, his skin beginning to wrinkle where the cushioned muscles shrank closer to his frame, its color fading under a slightly chalky bloom. Maintaining his usual taciturnity, he allowed Makis to do the talking, interjecting a brief phrase only when he needed reassurance that I understood.

I was not very attentive, wanting to get back to the work they had interrupted. The unfinished sentence in my typewriter nagged at my mind, and when their talk lapsed into a familiar pause it was almost impossible to hide my impatience. I looked at my watch, then remembered that the signal of dismissal was quite meaningless. Short of my ignoring them or going to bed, nothing would move them until they were ready to leave. Makis began to speak again.

His words had almost slipped past me before the meaning came, that the Gama had decided to initiate a group of boys. Forgetting everything else, I began to ply him with questions, eager for all his information on a still unseen ritual, so engrossed in drawing him out that his increasing hesitation was scarcely noticeable. His replies grew more oblique the harder he was pressed for details. Realizing slowly that the purpose of their visit was connected with the Gama festival, I waited for them to show their hand. The night pressed closer to the lamp's circle of light. The moment for confidence was passing, and I wondered what could be done to retrieve it, but Makis caught it a second before I was about to speak, asking what white men thought of these customs.

I replied carefully, trying to make it clear that my own attitude had nothing to do with the position taken by missionaries or government officials. Makis listened attentively, turning now and then to answer Maniha, who evidently had more difficulty with my inadequate Gahuku. At the end both of them seemed satisfied, though I was never sure that my explanation of these distinctions in the power structure was successful. It was not simply a matter of language; rather, the difficulty stemmed from their own inability to distinguish among the various categories of whites whom they knew and their tendency to impute to all of them a common purpose, mutually supporting one another in anything that touched the local population. After a moment's consideration Makis changed his position on the floor, lifted his eyes to look at me directly, and asked if I objected to Asemo taking part in the initiation.

I was taken completely by surprise, quite unable to grasp the implication of his question. Seeing my hesitation, both of them began to speak, their explanations coming so quickly that I couldn't keep pace with them. Maniha wanted to initiate his son. He had opposed the villagers' decision not to hold their own festival, pointing out that there were several boys who should be initiated and also offering to provide four large pigs for the occasion, a gesture of munificence with which he had hoped to swing the balance of opinion in his favor. One of the most conservative men in Susuroka, he did not approve of the shape life was taking under the influence of Humeleveka. He probably suspected, with good reason, that the men's organization was losing ground to the new opportunities opening to boys of Asemo's age. The work his son did for me indicated the direction of these interests and ambitions, and Maniha knew that if I left Asemo would find employment with some other white. Even now, he felt it necessary to sound my opinion before arranging his son's initiation. I was the boy's mentor in the life he had chosen, possibly closer to him in some respects than his father, who wanted to know if it was possible to reconcile the disparate values for which we stood.

Having no simple answer to his question, I looked away from him. Maniha had never been one of those who irritated me with their continual attentions and innocent attacks on my privacy. I had not spoken more than about a dozen words to him; certainly he had never addressed me directly; yet I always knew when he arrived and left and had often felt compelled to look at him, catching his eyes briefly in the moment before they turned away. His reserve had seemed to come from indifference, but now it had other implications, an undercurrent that had been responsible for the sudden pricking of discomfort when I found him watching me so closely. Strangely, I did not feel that he disliked me or opposed my relationship with Asemo, though he almost certainly regarded me as an adversary. It was not my person but the life I represented that provoked his wary interest. He looked at me as though he was measuring his enemy, trying to assess the terms demanded by the future.

Similar situations had occurred previously. Toward the end of an interview an informant occasionally interrupted me with the identical question Makis had asked when he was pressed for the details of initiation. Each time it happened, it was as if our discussion had tripped a shutter in his mind, that suddenly, through the unaccustomed task of description, he had found himself standing aside and observing his customs objectively. The eyes watching me were always slightly puzzled by this experience, the voice defensive, its guard lifted against the doubts crowding to the edge of recognition. To explain to Maniha that my attitude had nothing to do with that of the missionaries and the government seemed entirely inadequate for the present circumstances. His question was prompted by something more than a momentary shift in the ground of certainty; it asked for more than reassurance as the opening shutter revealed the unexpected possibility of alternative standards of judgment. As he leaned toward me in the harsh light, silent, waiting for a reply, I felt he was asking me to foretell the future. He could see the direction in which it was moving, and like a man who senses his ultimate defeat he threw Asemo's initiation at the challenging shape ahead, hoping to find a place for his tradition in this altered world.

My honest answer should have been that it was already too late for the kind of accommodation he wanted. The qualities that had made his reputation, the traditional knowledge for which he was respected, and the goals he had been taught to seek could not survive unaltered the changes my own people had set in motion. For men of his kind, unable or unwilling to shift direction, the future offered only an increasing isolation and the bitter experience of watching leadership pass to other hands. But I could not accept the responsibility of confirming his suspicions and did not want to accept the role he had assigned to me or to join the conflict for Asemo. Withdrawing to neutral ground, I disclaimed any right to an opinion.

I did not think of Asemo until the following morning, when the cries of the flutes woke me once again. The shadowed silence in the room and the contrasting bar of light through the open doorway had become a familiar background to the music, but while I listened to the sleeping village, the open notes seemed nearer than before, their urgency suddenly reminding me of the final minutes of my interview with Makis and Maniha when I had asked if Nagamidzuha commonly sent their boys to Gama for initiation. Makis replied that he could not recall another occasion when this had happened. Suddenly uncertain, he consulted with Maniha who answered my question, explaining that Asemo's mother's brother, a Gama man, would act as the boy's sponsor. The arrangement was unusual and it confirmed my interpretation of Maniha's motives. The cries of the flutes became the voice of Asemo's basic predicament, and of all those caught between the past and an uncertain future.

An hour or so later I found that Asemo had left the village on the previous afternoon, going to the house of an elder "sister" at Meniharove. His abrupt departure might have been a protest against his father's plans or simply a means of avoiding embarrassment, the "shame" the younger people felt at public exposure. In the kitchen, the boys casually accepted the second explanation for his absence. I also learned that I was the only person in the village who had not been aware of Maniha's plans for several days.

People crowded the street that morning, long past the hour when they had usually left for the gardens. They had an air of restrained excitement, as though the previous night's decision had lifted their spirits in anticipation of a treat they had not expected to share. No one mentioned Asemo. I was left alone to wonder what he was feeling at Meniharove.

Two weeks passed before I saw him again. I felt his absence more than I could have anticipated. The time we had spent in the afternoons had proved to be a welcome change in my routine, a break that I missed now when I returned to the empty house. Coming home, the path along the ridge seemed to be interminable. Even behind dark glasses my eyes ached from the glare, and the weight of the grass made breathing difficult. My legs were impelled forward only by the thought of the waiting house and the relief when its shadows closed around me. But I was also most vulnerable to loneliness and doubt when I was tired. My work seemed to be proceeding too slowly; knowing the villagers seemed no closer than on the day of my arrival. But this anxiety only served to conceal a more fundamental personal question: whether I was doing what I wanted to do with my life. These misgivings were brought about by my lack of interest in many of the formal aspects of professional scholarship and, at still a deeper level, an increasing sense of isolation that made me question my ability to touch others, and to be touched by them, in the way I needed.

These moods of depression had not occurred since my lessons with Asemo began. At first reluctant, even resentful of his presumption when I found him waiting on my return to the house, I slipped gradually into acquiescence and discovered surprisingly that tiredness drained away easily as I sat beside him. Our conversation was limited to the essentials of instruction, and while he worked we were often completely silent, he absorbed in the task set before him, myself detached, listening to the street sounds as though they were faint, vaguely remembered echoes from another existence. His quiet figure provided me with a refuge from my work and also from the doubts that crowded my mind when I looked beyond my present situation to the life I had to resume on leaving the valley. His need and his trusting diligence suspended my own difficulties, and in the process generated a reciprocal dependence.

After his sudden departure I looked for him wherever I went. Coming unexpectedly upon a group of boys, or seeing their slight figures approaching me along a path, I searched for his familiar features. On one occasion, returning from Meniharove with Makis without any certain recollection of the purpose of our visit, I was aware that my trip had been made only in the hope of finding Asemo, and the entire time had been spent watching for him while the men conducted their business. He did not appear, and unnecessary reticence prevented me from asking after him. His absence may have had no connection with us, but it could have been deliberate avoidance, his own reluctant choice, expressing his intuition that momentarily at least the world I represented and which he hoped to enter had yielded him to a past fighting tenaciously for self-preservation.

This feeling overshadowed every subsequent detail of Asemo's initiation. I followed the preparations from a distance, questioning my house boys. The frank accounts of their terror when they had stood in his place joined me more closely in sympathy to Asemo and added to my burden of doubt and responsibility. It was not enough consolation to know that the dangers he faced were exaggerated by the boys: initiates seldom died from the rites. I could not help wondering whether or not he knew that his father had asked me to make the decision, and, knowing it, what he thought of my response, how he fitted it into his prospect of the future.

Days passed, and except for my continuing concern there was an atmosphere of anticlimax in the village. Maniha was seldom at home now, apparently spending most of his time at Gama, where life had taken on a pace that was quite different from the normal routines still occupying the villagers of Susuroka. Following them about, I felt completely isolated from them, unreasonably expecting them to share my undivided interest in the events drawing so close to us. Our relationships were often colored by mutual impatience, on their part of justifiable irritation prompted by my continual demands to know the precise day on which Asemo would enter the men's organization, and on my part increasing dissatisfaction with their noncommital answers. In the long run I could have saved myself a good deal of unnecessary bother, for I was not informed until the night before the ceremonies took place at Gama.

For the first time in many weeks the flutes were silent that morning. The day broke in fountains of light, and clouds piled high above the mountains, leaving the whole valley open to the sky, a vast green arena waiting for the events that had been so long in the making. As I dressed, the village filled with the sounds of preparation, and Hunehune, bringing me my breakfast, had exchanged his cotton lap-lap for a bright new male skirt in the Bena-Bena fashion, a style from the east that some Gahuku chose to wear at important ceremonies. In the street later the men put on their finest decorations, standing patiently while boys dressed their long hair or, like Makis, studying the effect of every precisely placed feather in a trade-store mirror propped between his knees. The sun flashed on mother-of-pearl that had been smeared lightly with crimson oil. Feathers fluttered on every head, shaking their colors— bright yellows and reds, peacock hues of blue and green—over skin shining like dark glass under a new application of grease. Familiar features were entirely transformed by paint or barely recognizable behind bone ornaments inserted through pierced septums. Coronets of emerald scarabs and bands of white shells circled every brow, barbaric contrasts to deep-set eyes flashing with anticipation in their wells of shadow.

Entering the street, I was hailed from a dozen different directions with an uninhibited effusiveness that urged me to share the excitement. I took a seat near Makis, moved by my reception and trying to express, by my closeness, the gratitude that always rose to my throat when I encountered this ready acceptance. Over the heads of the men, southeast of the ridge of Asarodzuha, the green trough of the valley had begun to shimmer in the morning sun, reality already succumbing to the illusions of heat. A dozen Gama settlements were identifiable by their groves of casuarinas, each standing below a column of pale blue smoke. The silence in the landscape, compared with the noisy preparations close at hand, pricked my skin with anticipation. The things I wanted to see were happening there, hidden from my eyes by distance. My mind bent toward Asemo on the morning of his manhood, wishing him more than he could possibly achieve.

The men dallied so long over their dressing that we were late in setting out for Gama, forced to maintain a pace that taxed every muscle in my body as I tried to keep up with them. In front of me, Makis had looped his long ceremonial bilum, which he wore like a cloak, across his right arm, holding it high, like a woman protecting her skirts from the wet grasses of the trail.

Almost an hour passed before we reached the outskirts of the nearest Gama settlement, entering it near a new clubhouse that had been built to receive the initiates. I had expected a noisy welcome, but the village was completely silent, a double row of houses flanking a street whose exit was hidden by the twisting contours of the ridge. The men entered it boldly, knowing their destination. Groups of women standing near the houses allayed my anxiety that we might have arrived too late. They noted our presence with a few cursory greetings, not moving from their waiting positions, their eyes returning immediately toward the hidden end of the village. Many of them wore mourning, the mothers of initiates who had smeared their bodies with clay in ritual recognition of their separation from their sons, who were formally crossing over to the male division.

As we advanced, the silence seemed to gather itself into a tight coil. The eyes of the women were dark, sightless sockets in their masks of grey clay, their chalky limbs motionless, skeletal figures arranged in rigid attitudes of listening concentration. An answering response came from the men. Their pace increased to a fast trot, then suddenly, signaled by a shattering explosion of sound, they broke into a headlong run that carried us into the concealed end of the street.

The noise and movement were overwhelming. Behind us, the shrill voices of women rose in keening, ritual, stylized cries informed by genuine emotion that were like a sharp instrument stabbing into the din around me. The ululating notes of male voices locked with thumping shouts, deep drum beats expelled from distended chests counterpointed the crash of bare feet on the ground, and, rising above it all, came the cries of the flutes, which I heard at close quarters for the first time, a sound like great wings beating at the ear drums, throbbing and flapping in the hollow portions of the skull.

For several minutes utter confusion filled the street. Abandoned by the villagers of Susuroka, I tried to draw back from the engulfing sound, to impose some order on the scene in front of me. At least fifty men were in the clearing, decorated in the full panoply of war, chests and faces daubed with paint or pig's grease mixed with charcoal, some armed with shields, others with only their bows and arrows. The dark skin of their bodies was punctuated dramatically by the whiteness of shell, the yellow of the plaited bands that clasped the muscles of their arms and calves. The tossing array of plumes, parrot and bird of paradise, which fluttered like attendants over their heads, was a coruscating, swirling mass of brilliance matching their movements, swooping low as they bent from the waist, flying back again with their lifted heads, circling the space between the rows of houses. Dust rose under the rushing feet, a haze separating lower limbs from glistening torsos, and, as the minutes passed, chest and shoulders from the extended line of a throat, from faces that were almost expressionless in their ecstatic communion with an invisible force.

Asemo and his age mates were somewhere in the middle of the throng, almost certainly blinded by the dust, carried along by the press of stronger bodies, their heads, like mine, spinning with the noise and the shrilling of the flutes. Other youths had told me, laughing, of their panic during these opening minutes of their day-long ordeal, their fear of being trampled and the chilling effect of the flutes, apparently no less moving because they knew of the simple deception practiced on the women. I could only wonder with pain what Asemo felt, reaching out to him across a distance immeasurably greater than our respective years. For suddenly a barrier that had lifted briefly during the past few months had dropped between us, foreclosing any possibility we might have had of meeting each other on the same side.

For the rest of the day I carried this feeling with me, a curiously ambiguous mixture of closeness and detachment from the whole sequence of events that followed the initial eruption of sound in the Gama village. At times of group crisis I felt most alien, the outsider who became virtually invisible. But on other occasions there was a personal identification with the individuals that transcended the boundaries established by our different backgrounds, the very strength of the feelings displayed before me drawing me into the tide of a common emotion. This time it did not happen. Partly, perhaps, the reason lay in the fact that what I saw that day revolted me. At one level I could appreciate the drama of the rites, their arrogant sweep through the valley, their staging, observing them as a splendid spectacle, and beneath the physical acts I could see a more important symbolism, meanings not particular to the Gahuku context alone but drawn from the universal range of human experience. But the violence, the aggressive overstatement also laid me open to a rejection of it not uncommon while I was in the valley and the basis of my frequent need to contrive a screen between myself and this life.

Nothing could have contrasted more sharply with the periods I had spent alone with Asemo; perhaps nothing else could have served so dramatically to promote awareness of our inevitable separation. Indeed, as the events unfolded I felt the separation had been accomplished already, that I had had all that I was entitled to expect from our relationship, forced to stand aside while the stream of his own life carried him away from me.

I was not far behind the men as they burst into the arena of the valley. Released from the confinement of the trees, the flute calls and the shouts leaped toward the sky, spinning across the grasslands to the distant mountains. The forward rush of the men carried them along a path, almost too narrow to contain them, that ran between high fences of pit-pit. Those on the outskirts of the throng were pushed against the fences by the press of bodies in the center, the blows from their legs and shoulders thrashing the leaves of the cane until the entire space above our heads seemed to toss to the music, a frantic dance that followed us through the length of the gardens.

Passing the last patch of cultivated land the men changed direction abruptly, turned from the path and plunged down the side of the ridge. For an astonishing moment I stood at the place where they had disappeared. They were already far ahead of me, careening down the steep slope, legs lifting to the level of their waists to force a passage through the grass that fell behind them in a lengthening wake. The whole hillside seemed to shiver under the momentum of their rush. Bright stands of crotolaria broke under their feet, scattering their yellow flowers on the trampled grass; saplings bent to the ground like ravaged derelicts. As I hesitated at the edge of the path the flute cries and the shouting were answered from other points in the valley, filling the sky with a shrill vibration. In a sudden vision I saw the clans of Gama streaming down the neighboring ridges, turning aside from the well-worn tracks, taking to the slopes and the broken ground in the same symbolic show of strength, surging irresistibly toward their meeting place at the river.

It was more than a mile away, farther by the normal paths that kept to the high ground above me. I was virtually alone, outstripped by the men, following behind them on the sound of the flutes, my feet slipping and sliding along their trail of devastation. The sun was high and hot, draining the landscape of its color, veiling the mountains in a smoky haze that obscured their shape and reduced their shadowed folds to fading bruises. As I stumbled and fell I was not aware of any feeling other than the need to reach the river. The abrasive grass, cutting my hands as I clutched it for support, and the confining wetness of my shirt were almost unnoticed as I listened to the different streams of sound converging in the distance, meeting and leaping towards a turbulent climax, a final drumming of voices, of wheeling and beating cries that tore at the roots of the mind as I reached a knoll above the water.

A scant six feet below me, the river curved around a wide gravel spit. The sun struck its surface from directly overhead, splintering painfully on the shallows, where stones kicked the water into a white flurry, sliding like a mirage across the deeper reaches near the opposite bank. A vast crowd of men, drawn from all the Gama clans, were gathered on the spit. Most of them faced the water where, above their heads, I saw what the initiates in the front ranks had been brought to see, perhaps a score of naked figures, standing or lolling in the shallows, openly displaying their genitals. Even by the normally outspoken standards of the Gahuku this ritual exhibitionism was frankly overstated, a direct and obvious demonstration of the sexual aspects of male strength, the actions of the figures in the water keyed to hooting shouts of admiration and encouragement.

My immediate reaction was neither one of surprise nor shock, having nothing to do the men masturbating in the stream below; rather, it was as though the scene below me was totally unreal, something that might give a puzzled tug to my memory at a later date, like an unplaced name or face that causes a momentary and fruitless search through the past in an effort to locate it. All the brightness of the sky seemed to be concentrated in front of me. Distant landmarks, the mountains, the rolling sweep of grass were blurred and indistinct, the action on the spit detached from any larger context, occurring in some independent world of experience, close to me yet immensely remote.

I am not sure how long I stood on the knoll. When at last I went down to the crowded spit the naked figures had left the river and the flutes were silent momentarily. The heat was intense, rising in almost visible waves from the stones, stabbing back at my eyes from the surface of the water. Though the beach and the bend of the river were completely exposed, plainly visible from the elevated ground behind us, the air was close and stifling, heavy with sweat and grease and the cloying odor of unguents, with the biting smell of the overwrought emotions of the crowd. I remained at the edge of the throng where many of the younger men, not long past their own initiation, were watching their elders prepare for the second act of the ritual. The shouting had ceased, but voices were raised excitedly above their normal pitch, creating a general level of noise in which it was impossible to distinguish the individual commands and instructions of the clan leaders.

Gradually, purpose and direction began to emerge from the apparently disorganized movements of the crowd. Past the ranks in front of me I noticed a movement toward the river, several men stepping out until the water parted around their calves, its dark stains eating into their trailing crimson cloaks. As they turned to face the beach my eyes fell on the youth who stood between them. No older than Asemo, his head reached only to the shoulders of the men who held him firmly by the upper arms, the tightness of their grip forcing his soft flesh into folds between their fingers. Against the violence of their paint, his figure looked slighter than it was, his nakedness touchingly immature. His knees were slightly bent, as though his legs swung helplessly in the currents of the river. When he raised his head, the eyes looking toward the bank were wet with panic.

Suddenly, if only momentarily, the screen that had separated me from the action seemed to part. The noise, the smell of several hundred bodies, the dazzling light swept over me like a rush of stale air from a sealed room. Drawn involuntarily into the crowd, feeling the lick of its tension, I searched for Asemo, filled with a need to be near him, to expiate the betrayal for which I felt unreasonably guilty. Thinking I recognized Makis, I tried to push my way toward him through the crush, but was several yards from my goal when a ringing shout went up from the beach and the cries of the flutes bit into the sky above my head. I was forced back from the water as the crowd around me retreated, clearing a path along the margin of the spit.

Several men had appeared on this narrow stage in front of the initiates. One of them, a man in his early thirties, was Gapiriha of Nagamidzuha. He was above average height, very powerfully built, his skin shining like metal through rivulets of sweat and grease, the musclature revealed as sharply as the detail of an anatomical drawing. There was a striking Mayan cast to his features, the curving nose almost meeting lips that were feminine in their fullness, their sculptured lines partly hidden by the circular bone ornament hanging from his septum. Known as a "hard" man, he was given to sudden outbursts of violence, too forceful and self-assertive to care much for the opinions of others, too impatient of the subtleties of persuasion to attract and hold a following, but nevertheless a man of reputation, direct and aggressive, clearly identified with the more obvious male virtues. His chest shuddered and his eyes were intensely bright, a shine that lacked the slightest flicker of recognition, looking out from some pinnacle of personal experience, some private state of feeling and awareness that distended the veins of his neck in explosive, inarticulate shouts.

I watched him with fascination and disbelief, the combination of recognition and rejection that is sparked by any violent display of emotion. He moved out into the river and faced the crowded bank where the water swirled around his calves. He was holding two cigar-shaped objects fashioned from the razor-sharp leaves of green pit-pit. Flourishing them like a conjurer in a spotlight, raising them above the level of his shoulders, he tilted his head back and thrust the rolls of leaf into his nostrils. My flesh recoiled in shock, nerves contracting as though they were seared by the pain that must have swept through his own body as his fingers sawed at the protruding ends of the wadded leaves, thrusting them rapidly up and down inside his nose. I felt sick with distaste, wanting to turn from the exhibition of self-mutilation that provoked a chorus of approving shouts from the crowd, a sound climaxed by the familiar ululating cry of accomplishment as he withdrew the bloody leaves and lowered his head toward the water. Blood gushed from his nose. His fingers, holding the instruments of purification, dripped it onto the surface of the river, where its cloudy stain divided around his legs. His knees trembled, seemed almost about to buckle under him as he bled, and when he raised his head to stagger out toward the beach his lips, his chin, and his throat ran with bright red.

Even before he reached the gravel spit the crowd's attention had returned to the river, where half-a-dozen men were following his example. As though surfeited by the excess, my initial shock dissipated into a feeling of detached revulsion, not yet connecting the events before me with Asemo. My ears rang with the clamor that rewarded the exhibition in the water. The odor of blood, warm and cloying, added a new ingredient to the acrid smell of the crowd, its presence a sharp reminder of the patterns of thought and the motives lying behind this violent mistreatment of the body. The action taking place in the river was not an isolated or infrequent occurrence, but a standardized performance by which men sought to promote their strength and vigor. For all their protestations of superiority, their perception of women was tinged with an element of envy, and in objective moments they sometimes made unfavorable comparisons between the inevitable processes of maturation in the sex they despised and the less certain, because less obvious, indexes of male development. Women's natural advantages were linked to menstruation, and the proud male sought to engineer the same effect by self-inflicted bleeding, starting at initiation. Once introduced to the practice, men who had the right concern for their health bled their noses regularly, using the wads of leaves to purify their flesh, to rid their bodies of the contaminating influence of women, and to ensure that they faced the dangers of their position in a cleansed condition, ritually protected from the hazards of aggression.

As with every event that occurred that day, notions of physical growth, of ritual pollution, and of social separation of the sexes were blended in this act of characteristic violence, and the assumption of manhood, the formal identification with the masculine side of life was sealed with the shedding of the initiates' own blood. For the crowd-rousing demonstration in the shallows of the river was designed primarily for the edification of the row of youths whose arms were pinioned by older men, a graphic, overacted prologue to their own role in the unfolding drama.

The implications for Asemo were brought home to me suddenly as the last of the blood-stained figures staggered up the gravel beach and the center of attention shifted to the row of waiting boys. My search for him, interrupted by the entrance of Gapiriha, had brought me within several paces of where he stood. Like his age mates, his arms were held by two men, Makis on one side and Bihore on the other, the contrast of their plumes and paint investing his own unadorned nakedness with almost sacrificial innocence. I recalled his elder brothers' descriptions of their feelings at this precise moment, their minds numb with the apprehension of pain, the urge to struggle and escape constrained only by the greater fear of shame. I am sure he did not recognize me. His own eyes saw nothing but the need to marshal the defenses of his body for the imminent act of violation, and he could not have been aware of the manner in which my heart rushed toward him. It was not simply the thought of his suffering that closed off my senses so that momentarily we were alone in the shimmer of light and water, facing each other across a void, the noises and the smells of the crowd nothing more than a remote intrusion beating unsuccessfully at the boundaries of recognition. Everything I had gradually learned of him in the past few months returned to me, rendered more vivid by the weeks of separation, so that I realized suddenly the gap his precipitate departure had left; and the loss stabbed the more sharply because I saw him, now, clearly projected against a screen of impersonal events whose sweep ignored the justifications for his present predicament.

I was probably the last of my kind to witness the action taking place in the river, and generations of Gahuku younger than Asemo would know it only at second hand, as an element from a past that in moments of frustration and disillusionment they might romanticize and regret. But I was seldom successful in maintaining the required clinical distance between myself and the villagers, and at this moment my relationship with Asemo imposed its own particular construction on the scene. He stood for the inarticulate aspirations of a people thrust unwillingly into the uncharted sea of time, and I was struck suddenly by a feeling of poignant futility, a compound of sympathy for those who acted as though the past still showed a viable perspective on the world ahead, and a deeper pain for those whose visions of a possible future blinded them to the externally imposed limits of reality. This was precisely where Asemo stood. The figure of his Gama sponsor concealed him from me as he received the thrust of the purifying leaves, but when the older men moved aside, his violent mission done, the bright blood flowing from Asemo's lowered head was like a hopeless offering for peace between embattled opposites.

My recollection of the day's subsequent events is curiously anticlimactic, though in fact the tension and the violence grew in intensity, building up to the wild, running chase that carried the men back to their settlements. But everything of personal importance had been said to me when Asemo's blood reddened the water, and the things he suffered after this seemed like an unnecessary reiteration, an example of the Gahuku's exhausting tendency to seek excess.

It was past midday when the initiates' first ordeal ended. The light and heat, magnified by the reflecting surfaces of stones and water, had built toward the blinding point. A dozen men moved out into the shallows, their features totally unrecognizable behind the masks of paint crusted with drying blood. The fingers of the man nearest to me worked at releasing the length of cane that circled his waist twice, above the broad, plaited band supporting his vees. Though I had often noticed this item of apparel (it was worn by some men as an everyday part of their attire), I had never ascribed any significance to it and had not thought to ask its purpose. Now I experienced a sudden apprehension as he shaped it into a long, narrow U. Leaning forward from the waist, he placed the rounded section in his mouth, straightened, tilted his head, extending the line of his neck, and fed it into his stomach. My throat contracted and my stomach heaved, compelling me to look away. When I turned to him again most of the cane had disappeared, only two small sections, the open ends of the U, protruding from the corners of his mouth.

I have no idea how long he held this grotesque stance, his straining abdomen and chest racked with involuntary shudders. Already sickened by the display, I stiffened with shock as he raised his hands, grasped the ends of the cane and sawed it rapidly up and down, drawing it almost free of his mouth at the peak of every upward stroke. The fervor of the crowd mounted to a clamorous pitch, breaking in wave upon wave of pulsing cries, the final surge matching my own relief when he dropped the cane, bent from the waist, and vomited into the river.

A new, sour smell threaded through the overheated odors of the beach. The palms of my hands were wet, and my mouth filled with the taste of nausea. I had to force myself to look when the men repeated the performance on the boys, my distaste and the urge to turn away checked by apprehension of their danger. Though it was surely less painful than the first ordeal, there was a serious risk of internal injury if the initiates struggled while they were forced to swallow the canes. Fortunately, or perhaps it had been deliberately planned, they were already too exhausted, too shocked and weak to resist, but I watched anxiously for signs of blood as their sponsors held the boys' heads between their knees. When it was over, I was giddy from the light, the noise, the acid smells, a revulsion so strong that I had to turn my back to the river.

All this time I had not seen Asemo from whom I had been separated in the interval between the two ordeals. The action had moved from the water before he came to view again, standing limply between Bihore and Makis, clearly in need of their supporting hands. Self-consciousness checked my immediate urge to go to him. I did not know what he felt, or what he was expected to feel, any more than it was possible for me to enter into and share the emotions of the older men who had bled and vomited. My sympathy probably was not expected, and I made no move, feeling more alien than ever before.

Though the flutes had ceased their shrilling and the shouts had ended, the crowd milled about the beach, clearly preparing for the final act. Older men strutted importantly near the group of sadly bedraggled boys; the agitated flourish of their red cloaks matched their rapid interchange of words and their brief, intense glances at the heights above

us. For the first time in many hours the world outside the narrow beach
came to mind, and following the direction of their eyes, I turned toward the ridge cresting like a pale green wave against the sky. The
entire landscape seemed completely empty and devoid of life; yet I
felt a faint but unmistakable premonition that this first impression was
erroneous. There was something slightly ominous in the gestures of the
men, signs of a new, untoward excitement that made me search the
grass again. More than a mile away, farther by the paths in everyday
use, the Gama settlement we had left that morning huddled below its
casuarina grove, the trees blurred and bruised by the heat of midafternoon, their spired shapes fading into a virtually colorless sky. The
intervening distance pulsed and trembled, the grasses bowed under
the weight of light. There were no clumps of denser vegetation nor any
shadows to offer places of concealment, and thinking of the journey
home I forgot the reason for my careful scrutiny, anticipating with misgiving the toiling return to the summit of the ridge.

On the beach, the crowd was preparing to leave. Some of the
younger, stronger men had lifted the initiates to their shoulders, support
their dejected, limp condition seemed to need. The remainder of the
company surrounded them shoulder to shoulder, a noisy corps of pro-
tectors who appeared to disregard the voluble, possibly conflicting instructions of the older leaders. No particular person was in control nor
was any single command given, yet the entire body of men moved off
together, jogging up the path they had avoided earlier in the day.

There was little superficial resemblance to the spectacular surge of
the morning's procession. The pace was slower, the flutes silent, out of
sight, and even the voices were stilled. Yet there was no mistaking the
undercurrent of aggressive maleness, the concerted, rhythmic tread of
naked legs, the calculated bravado of tossing plumes, the feeling of alert
anticipation that pricked at the mind like the intermittent, flashing
reflections of light on ornaments of polished shell. I followed close
behind the throng, thankful that they had taken the easier route listening to their laboring breath, the thump of their feet, the jangle and
click of their decorations, the medley of sounds superimposed like an
insistent, premonitory thrill on the silence of the afternoon.

We mounted higher, now out of sight of the river as we reached the
shoulder of the ridge, a point where the path widened considerably
between the walls of grass. The pace increased as the forward movement met the gentler gradient of the land, but the quickening of step

was also prompted by some other expectation that no one had bothered to share with me.

The confrontation came as we rounded a concealed bend in the track. A tempest of shrill cries fell on us like a rain of arrows, and hordes of women suddenly appeared among the grasses. Galvanized, the men broke into a run, lifting their voices in a thumping celebration of strength that rose and fell with their pounding legs. At that precise moment a stone hit my shoulder with a stinging blow. Startled, but trying to maintain my pace, I looked around uncomprehendingly, searching for the source of the attack and finding it the next instant when the man ahead of me, struck on the side of his neck, turned his contorted face to shout abuse at the screaming women.

In the ensuing confusion it was impossible to estimate the number of assailants. Keeping pace with the men, they ran through the grass bordering the track, stumbling and falling as it wound around their legs. The grotesque, clay-streaked figures of an earlier hour capered wildly at the edge of the group, skeletons with wierdly flailing arms and legs, but the brunt of the attack was carried by other women who were armed with a mixed bag of weapons—stones and lethal pieces of wood, an occasional axe, and even a few bows and arrows. There was no mistaking the venom in the assault. Even the men, who had known what to expect, seemed to be taken aback by it, startled by its force and the intuition that it threatened the established limits of expression. It was not the first time this thought had occurred to me. These graphic rituals of opposition spoke of deep-seated divisions in Gahuku life, not only the formal, ceremonial structure of male and female relationships, but also the avowed notions of superiority and a schism that often revealed itself in open antagonism; men held the upper hand, and they used it. Female resentment had few avenues for direct expression, though men suspected there were many indirect ones, and perhaps the superior male was aware of this on occasions when custom allowed the overt demonstration of opposed interests. As an outsider who had seen the high-handed treatment the men meted out, I could understand their concern when they faced these situations, the perceptible rise in tension correcting any tendency to regard them as a ceremonial charade; for they knew that prescribed boundaries were a poor defense against the inflammatory potential of sanctioned retaliation.

The fury of the present assault convinced me that the ritual expression of hostility and separation teetered on the edge of virtual disaster.

The men had bunched together as they ran, so closely packed that they struck each other with their legs and arms. In the center of the throng the initiates, riding the shoulders of their escorts, swayed precariously from side to side, their fingers clutching the feathered hair of the head between their legs. The noise reached out to every corner of the world, the shrill cries and imprecations of the women beating against the stylized male chant that answered them in rising volume, swelling in a concert of defiance. For several minutes the two groups kept apart, an occasional stone or piece of wood hurtling from the sidelines and usually striking home, for it was almost impossible to miss the running target. The outraged shouts of those who were hit spurred the bolder women on to closer combat. Leaving the protection of the grass they darted at the flanks of the men's procession, wielding their weapons with every intent to hurt. Several victims staggered under their blows, lost their footing and their place in the crowd, and separated from their fellows, threatened on every side, took refuge in temporary flight, turning when they had reached a safe distance and hurling back their outrage in abuse. Fresh blood appeared on shoulders and legs. There was a genuine need to fear more serious injury. Neither the axes nor the arrows had been used, as far as I could see, but the pieces of wood were large enough to lay open a skull if they made direct contact, and the initial successes of the women urged them on to more heroic efforts. Undoubtedly the proper, the expected thing for the men to do was to carry on through the assault, ignoring the flying sticks and stones in a telling demonstration of strength, a graphic assertion of male values, but the women's heat had pushed the whole activity beyond the limit where it was possible, or wise, to maintain this composure. Individuals began to turn under the blows, and to follow up their shouted sense of outrage with direct action. The women held only for a moment before they sought the safety of the grass. Scattering in front of their pursuers, they were soon left behind by the main body of the procession, which reached the settlement unmolested, entering the shelter of the trees as the medley of angry cries changed to the keening rise and fall of ritual anguish.

The day ended with the clans departing for their respective villages, taking their own bedraggled and exhausted boys with them. During the night the flutes cried again from every men's house where the groups of initiates had been placed for their long seclusion.

More than six weeks passed before the final act was played in the

Gama village. During this time I thought often of Asemo but did not visit him in the men's house where he remained with his age mates. Instead, I followed his progress through his subsequent trials at second hand, gathering information on this period of tutelage. It would have been a simple matter to see him, even though the villagers of Susuroka, not as directly involved as the Gama, had returned to their own affairs, and I told myself I could not spare the time away from them. The truth is that I suspected seeing him would only add to my distress, sharpening that sense of his personal tragedy that had qualified his initiation. I could not close my mind to the contrast between these recent events and the motives that had led him to seek my help.

Because of this, I not only kept away from him but also had little heart for the final ceremonies in which his manhood was accepted. The pride and the tumult of praise greeting his assumption of his rightful status had overtones of sadness for me unexplainable to anyone present, and this private perception flavored the clamorous events with a peculiar bitterness.

They began before dawn, an hour conducive to moods in which we see farther than we permit ourselves at other times, and the urgent anticipation of the villagers sparked no answering response in me as we set out for Gama. The atmosphere was grey and lost, the mountains hidden by the veil of darkness, the sea of grass a silent, heavy presence bordering the track. Mists were still thick beneath the trees surrounding the Gama clubhouse where most of the men had gathered before we arrived. There was a great deal of activity but little noise, the hushed voices tuned to the hour and the stillness of the thatched house, where the initiates were being readied for their ceremonial return to life. Standing to one side, deserted by Makis who had been with me all the way from Susuroka, I shivered from the chill rising up my body from the soaked fabric of my trousers. The air had begun to stir faintly as it often does in the pause between night and day, a barely perceptible breath that shook cold splashes of water from the trees. Near me, a group of watchers hugged themselves for warmth, standing above a small fire that sputtered and smoked in the dampness.

The light increased, a gentle greying that gradually revealed the refuse of many meals littering the clearing. In the east a narrow thread of gold appeared in the sky above the mountains, counterpart to the first hint of color in the cloaks and feathered decorations of the men. Makis joined me and suggested that I go with him to the village to await the arrival of the initiates, who, garbed in the finery their kinsmen had made in the preceding weeks, were almost ready to leave the clubhouse.

It was only a short walk, but by the time we reached the street the whole world was dressed in the full panoply of dawn. Crowds of women lined one side of the avenue between the thatched houses. Every few paces, down each side of the street, ovens emitted plumes of blue smoke. The smell of aromatic greens, of blood, and of raw meat hung heavily on the air, aftermath of the vast slaughter of pigs that had taken place the previous day and harbinger of the distribution of cooked food that would close the afternoon. While Makis stopped to receive the greetings of several women in the crowd, I found a place behind them where I could look above their heads toward the entrance to the village. Almost at once a signal traveled down the line in front of me. Propped against the eaves of the house at my back, I looked to the end of the street, where the garden fences trembled in the golden light. Above the leaves of the cane, massed feathers shook their colors in the morning air as though the whole landscape had blossomed with strange flowers overnight. Knowing the Gahuku's dramatic flair, I had no doubt that the effect had been intentionally contrived, and my admiration for their showmanship increased as the procession of invisible figures delayed their entrance, winding back and forth along the garden paths while the light grew and the excitement of the women broke in a rising chorus of welcoming calls.

They entered the street when the cries had reached a peak of anticipation; the vanguard of older men trod the ground slowly and firmly, their heads high, their bows strung tight with arrows. Even at a distance I recognized the pride stretching the muscles of their calves and thighs, and I felt an answering lift as their silence erupted in the familiar, shouted celebration of accomplishment heralding the entrance of the boys, now men—changed persons, not recognizable as what they had been before.

Armed warriors walked beside them as they came down the street, stepping slowly like the others, their pace geared to the weight of the enormous headdresses that had been fashioned for them during the night, coil upon coil of bark cloth wound around their hair and projecting from the back of the head in a huge bun that strained the muscles of their necks, the whole surmounted with opossum tails and cassowary feathers. Now the women broke their lines, ran between the escorts seeking sons and brothers, feigning to mistake them in their new guise, keening and crying when they made the right identification. Darting back to the houses, they fetched lumps of fat and bamboo tubes containing pork, rubbed the youths' limbs with grease, and broke the tubes on the ground in front of their moving feet. Clouds of dust rose into the golden light, and long after the sun came up the village rang with the clamor of the welcome.

The remainder of the day was carried by on a vast volume of sound and the rushing of hundreds of feet as parties of visitors arrived to dance in the settlement. Stirring at first, the careening dance, a rush of men in the center of the street, grew stale with repetition, and I waited impatiently for it to end, restrained from leaving only by the thought that I had to record it all for future use. My personal interest had ended during the first set, when the street had been momentarily quiet and the initiates, after their welcome, had gathered for their own performance.

There were a dozen of them standing together in light that still carried the caressing glow of early morning. Bereft of their escort, they seemed uncertain and shy, no older or more experienced than the day they were carried to the river while the flutes ate at the sky above their heads. They moved unsteadily under ungainly decorations, and I failed to see the splendid, stirring change that had been apparent to their elders' eyes. But dignity touched them when they began to dance, a slow measure based on the assertive stepping of the men but held to a restrained, promenading pace by the weight they carried on their heads. For a moment I was one with the crowd of admirers, silent now, and perhaps like myself bending toward the slight figures who symbolized the promise of human life, forcing us, as we watched, to recall the hopes once held for ourselves, our own temerity in stepping out to meet the future. Asemo was in the front rank of the dancers, his legs moving in unison with his age mates, his face, like theirs, expressionless, his eyes fixed on some distant point only he could see.

CHAPTER FOUR

▲▲

THE AGE MATES

There was no way of knowing what Asemo saw that afternoon as he trod the street carefully under the heavy ornaments of manhood, no way of sharing the private vision in the eyes that looked above the painted, feathered throng whose voices were the very sound of time receding. Perhaps he saw no farther than the walls of my own house, hoping for nothing more than the pattern visible in the lives of the older youths who worked for me, but though he stood behind them chronologically the waves of change had also lifted him ahead of them. His future, if he gained it, had to be different from the lives of these others whom I studied daily.

When I set up house in Susuroka my real needs were extremely modest, someone to help prepare my food and to wash my clothes, far below the scale imputed to me by the villagers who measured by what they saw in the European houses at the government station. It had been the same during my first period of fieldwork in New Guinea. Then I had not been sufficiently sure of myself to resist when the unnecessary help was foisted on me. Now the same suggestions were accepted with only minor reservations; my household staff could be a valuable source of information. For the same reason, only people from Susuroka were employed, even though that policy had personal disadvantages. My staff's own affairs, their schemes and the demands of their kinsmen, often seemed more pressing than their household duties; they had a regrettable tendency to be absent when most needed. At one point I had to complain to Makis who told me what I knew already, sensibly suggesting that I hire my assistants from outside the village. It would have been easy to do. Itinerant Chimbu from the densely populated valleys beyond the western mountains often came to Susuroka looking for work. A few were even employed as garden help by Gehamo men, and in a moment of extreme irritation I decided to add one to my payroll as an "outdoor" man to fetch my water from the spring below the ridge and to tend the patch of vegetables behind my house. No one objected to my plan, agreeing that the move was justified by my difficulties. Yet the experiment failed, perhaps was sabotaged deliberately. The "foreigner" was accepted with poor grace, often subjected to ridicule, and seemed to be more lonely than I. At the end of a few weeks, when he was accused of fomenting trouble, I let him go; thereafter, whenever other Chimbu appeared in the village they were quickly chased away.

The number of my paid helpers fluctuated rather sharply. At the peak period there were six, for a few weeks, only one, but for most of the time there was a staff of four: a cook, who had worked briefly in the kitchen of a house at Humeleveka, a boy to clean the house and wash my clothes, one to carry water and firewood, another to tend my garden and the flock of scrawny chickens I managed to acquire. The staff changed fairly frequently; only one remained with me from the beginning to the end of my stay. But of them all, the four who were with me longest, who with the exception of Asemo are the ones I remember best, are Hunehune, Lotuwa, Hasu, and Hutorno. They were all between the ages of seventeen and twenty-one, as different from one another as any four young men chosen randomly from such a group. Hunehune was the only one for whom I developed a close affection; Hutorno I liked least of all, but severally and together they exemplified the problems of their generation, and their presence in my house helped me to appreciate the quality of the tie that formed their principal bond.

The formal patterns of Gahuku life placed considerable emphasis on differences in age, both between generations and chronologically within the same generation. Sons were expected to obey and to respect their fathers and, by extension, all other men of their father's generation in their clan, whom they addressed by the identical kinship term. These older men were the arbiters of conduct, vested with the right to discipline the children, yet very seldom exercising it. The young ran at the edges of adult life receiving little guidance, little formal training until their initiation, when their elders' demands and criticism increased dramatically, beginning a period of subordination that lasted until they had reached their middle thirties. The submission required by the generation above them often rankled, yet it probably occasioned less resentment than the formal dominance of their older brothers, a superiority lasting through adolescence and well into early manhood. In the

▲▲▲

The photographs that follow are of people and places that appear in the pages of the book and of activities related to those described. All of them were taken by the author and are from his collection. The **anthropologist**, Mr. K. J. Pataki, drew the maps.

▼▼▼

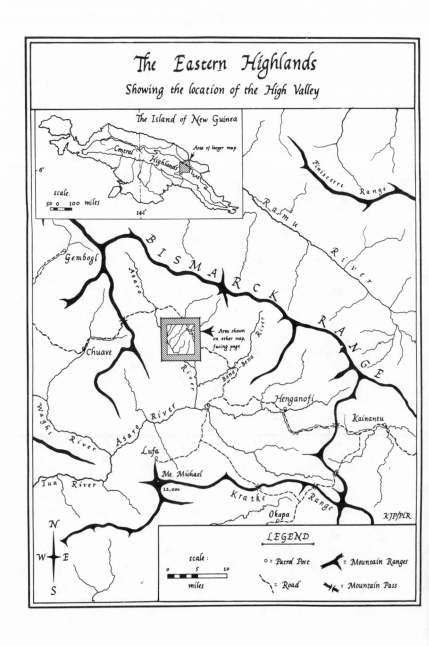

The Eastern Highlands

Showing the location of the High Valley

The Island of New Guinea

Area of larger map

Central Highlands

scale:
50 0 100 miles

BISMARCK RANGE

Finisterre Range

Ramu River

Gembogl

Asaro River

Area shown on other map, facing page

Chuave

Bena-Bena River

Henganofi

Kainantu

Waghi River

Asaro River

Lufa

Mt. Michael
12,000

Tua River

Kratke Range

Okapa

KJP/PLR

N
W E
S

LEGEND

scale:
0   5   10
miles

○ = Patrol Post

⋏ = Mountain Ranges

= Road

⋎⋉ = Mountain Pass

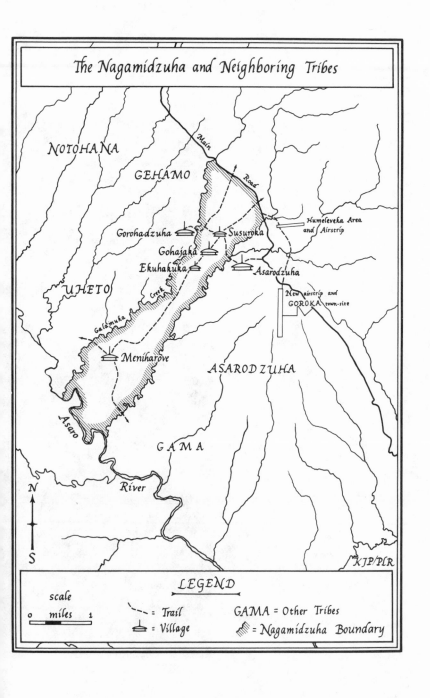

The Nagamidzuha and Neighboring Tribes

NOTOHANA

GEHAMO

Main

Road

Humeleveka Area
and Airstrip

Gorohadzuha   Susuroka

Gohajaka

Ekuhakuka   Asarodzuha

UHETO

New airstrip and
GOROKA town-site

Creek

Galamuka

ASARODZUHA

Meniharove

Asaro

GAMA

River

N

S

KJP/PLR

LEGEND

scale
o   miles   1

---- = Trail   GAMA = Other Tribes
🛖 = Village   🛖 = Nagamidzuha Boundary

*The ridge of Susuroka,
looking south from Gohajaka
toward Ekuhakuka.*

A section of the street of Susuroka. The poles projecting from the roofs of the houses are topped with a clump of orchids. The boy in the foreground is an uninitiated youth.

Women weeding in a garden among sweet potato vines. In the background are a pit-pit hedge and casuarina trees.

Boys playing in a clearing. Their long headdresses indicate that they are uninitiated.

Makis dressed for a festival. He holds a drum in his left hand.
His headdress is made of feathers and shells with alternating
bands of fur and green beetles above his eyebrows.

*Susuro sitting in the
street of Susuroka.*

*The brothers of Guma'e sitting outside Makis' house; the
elder is on the right.*

The villagers of Susuroka assembled for the marriage feast of Guma'e and Makis. They are surrounded by refuse from the ovens.

Men dancing on the final day of Asemo's initiation.

A newly initiated youth walking in the village on the final morning of the ceremonies after his long seclusion in the men's house. His artificial beard signifies his manhood.

Lotuwa dressed in a pullover and a cotton lap-lap.

Sesekume, his son Hasu (left), and two of his grandchildren in the street of Susuroka. The infant is peeling a stick of sugar cane.

Tarova and Gapiriha. Gapiriha is butchering a pig with a bamboo knife.

Gihigute, Tarova's father, preparing food on a banana leaf.

Four of Tarova's age mates setting out for one of the courting parties following her betrothal.

Zaho dressed for a festival.

'Men and women appraising the cooked carcasses of pigs
that are part of a ceremonial exchange of food.

world of uninitiated youths and children, it was the voices and the hands of elder brothers that were raised most frequently against the boys. Ideally, an older youth moved through the status structure always one step ahead of his younger sibling. He was privileged to command; he expected both obedience and respect. Though he also had reciprocal duties, such as helping to provide the bride price for his younger brother, the relationship, seen from the junior partner's point of view, was one of constraint, generating tensions, latent rivalries, and antagonisms that modified the ideal of sibling accord and mutual support. After achieving independence, few men chose to associate daily, intimately, with the elder brothers to whom they had submitted for so long electing rather, to make common cause with an *aharu,* an age mate, one of the group of youths with whom they had been initiated.

The quality of this tie was unique among the bonds linking a man to other members of his clan, for it alone carried no implications of superiority and subordination. Males of roughly the same age, within a chronological range of one to five years, were social equals. They moved through the social structure on the ascribed principle of strict equality. They were initiated as a group and, hopefully, betrothed as a group. They were married together, became fathers at the same time, and if all went well achieved their independence by establishing separate households at the same time. They were friends and confidants, virtually always together, sharing the most important experiences—courting, raiding, and stealing pigs together, roaming the ridge and the garden lands as a group and, as a group, listening with passive resentment to public criticism and to the exhortations of their elders. The pattern of their relationship was set long before initiation, encouraged by adults who found amusement in introducing toddlers to one another as aharu; it was fostered too by the young nursemaids who cared for them after weaning, so that when boys were six or seven its lines were already clear, observable in the heads bending together in the sun, heard in the murmur of children's voices watching the antics of a captive insect, developing and broadening with the increasing scope for adventure as they approached their teens.

By the time each age group faced the ordeal of initiation, its members had incorporated their formal rights as social equals and, on occasion, expressed their resentment dramatically when such rights could not be achieved. After the trial that made them men, while they were secluded in the clubhouse, their fathers and elder kinsmen set out to buy them wives, carrying a token bride price to the settlements of eligible girls. Often unsuccessful, they returned again and again, trying one village and then another while the novices waited in the men's houses, their return to normal life delayed until a girl had been obtained for each of them. At least this was the aim and the novices' due, but sometimes the plans failed, leaving a boy without a bride on the day his novitiate ended. Most of the youths in this position probably accepted it, knowing their elders would return to the quest at a later date, but now and then one of them felt his indignity so keenly that he ran to an enemy group. His suicide, for his action meant death in most cases, protested his kinsmen's failure to provide him with equality.

The age group's jealous concern for its rights extended also to its own members if their behavior flouted conventional expectations. Several years elapsed before the youths were permitted any contact with the "wives" who had been procured for them after their initiation. Each couple was supposed to meet on only the most formal, public occasions when perhaps they might furtively watch each other from their places in the crowd, finding the opportunity to silently arrange an assignation. Such encounters were necessarily secret, concealed from even the other members of the age group, but little harm was done unless the girl became pregnant. Then outraged age mates of her "husband," resenting this breach of formal equality, had been known to kill her, their action reflecting the characteristic male propensity to blame all violations of sexual rules on the forwardness of women.

Times had changed so much when I arrived at Susuroka that neither of these forms of protest was open to the boys who worked for me. In the succession of generations, many elements of their situation were unique; yet the essential quality of their bond remained the same as it had always been, and watching them, following each through his personal crises, I could see their continuity with their elders, with the men who built their houses near each other, who worked their gardens together, and who walked hand in hand along the garden paths, paired like the sacred flutes, the marvelous nama whose extraordinary, complementary cries were designated by the same term, aharu, which signified to everyone his own relationship with his age mates.

Lotuwa was the first of the group to join my household, selected by Makis before my arrival in the village because he had worked in a white house at Humeleveka. I never enquired what his experience had been and did not expect very much from him as we unpacked my belongings, though he took charge of my modest supply of cooking utensils as though he knew what he was doing, arraying them in a manner calculated to impress the crowd that had gathered to watch. He was the youngest son of the luluai of Meniharove, a man of commanding size and presence whom I met much later. The father, Gasieto, visited me now and then, but I knew him only slightly as an older person to whom Makis frequently deferred. His village was larger than any of the Nagamidzuha settlements on the crest of the ridge and also nearer to Gama, where he had many close associations. His reputation had been made long before the arrival of the whites, and he was too old, too firmly committed to the values of the past to bother trying to understand the ways of the alien government. He never learned any pidjin English and seemed to depend on Makis to interpret the demands that reached him from Humeleveka, though in all the traditional areas of life he was probably the younger man's superior and mentor. "Gasieto wants me," was often the explanation for Makis' journeys to Meniharove, when he left his work to respond to the call passed along the ridge from the distant floor of the valley.

I could not see much physical resemblance between Lotuwa and his father, though almost certainly my eye was deceived by their different manner of wearing their hair. Lotuwa, like all his age mates, followed the new preference and wore his hair short, in a modified crew cut that exposed the whole face and neck, a mode so radically transforming that I often failed to recognize a man who had recently cut his hair, compelled to rediscover a face that had been only partly known to me. Lotuwa was handsome; he possessed by the standards of my own culture a physical attractiveness not uncommon in Gahuku men but seldom, if ever, seen in their women. He was my own height, five feet seven, straight, and beautifully proportioned, not overmuscled but possessing a natural grace of body that shamed the physiques of most whites. His skin was brown rather than black, suffused with chestnut lights, his features Latin rather than Negroid—the lips full but not greatly everted, the lids of his dark eyes pulled slightly upward toward his brows, the nose straight and long, not broad or overfleshed.

Yet his good looks were tempered by certain traits of personality for which I did not greatly care. He was circumspect in front of his elders, maintaining the proper attitudes of respect, and he was always polite to me, diligent at his work, and rather quiet. This demeanor contrasted with the personality he presented to his age mates and the younger boys, when his behavior struck me as a brash complement to his slick appearance, to his air of self-importance and a distasteful veneer of sophistication. He fancied himself as a person of some accomplishment in the areas of life that had been opened by the coming of my own people. He handled the modest materials of my kitchen with an air of authority, responding with flourish to the silent observation of the long-haired boys who gathered to watch him, their eyes white with admiration for the mysteries he performed so casually. His attitude toward them was both demanding and condescending. Even his movements when bending over the fire or arranging my food on the plate seemed to be overlaid with a shiny, superficial gloss that was very different from the impression created by his best friend Hunehune.

Hunehune, like each of the other members of my staff, was recommended to me by Lotuwa. They were the same age, twenty-one at most. Hunehune was shorter than Lotuwa and not as dramatically good looking, though he possessed engaging qualities that the other entirely lacked. His face was pleasant and open, his expression usually serious but now and then lightened by a slow smile expressive of his whole personality, the reflection of a genuine vein of humorous self-appraisal that always drew an immediate, accepting response from me. He began as a second-in-command of the house but later replaced Lotuwa, performing his additional duties well enough though he lacked the experienced efficiency of his friend. He had a good deal of spare time, and on days when my work kept me at home, and the two of us were alone in the village, I could hear him singing to himself in the kitchen, his voice gradually faltering, becoming drowsy, trailing off into silence as the weight of the day increased. When he answered my call, the sleep on his face was visible as his eyes attempted to return to me and my needs in a manner that made me forget that my lunch was two hours late. His slowness often tried my patience, but the moment I had decided it was time to speak to him about it, his apologetic, gently humorous face disarmed my anger. It made little difference if he was late, and I even felt grateful for it, lightened by a disregard for the demands of a routine belonging to another world and another life. In time, I knew an affection for him that was almost as deep as anything I felt for Makis or Asemo.

Hasu was the tallest of the boys, about five feet eleven, with a physique that was suited to his height. He was darker than Lotuwa, with a strong but rather somber face expressing a personality not given to levity. He was not morose like Hutorno, but he stood aside from the joshing that frequently filled the kitchen with laughter. In the rougher games in the village street he played with silent intensity, his concern to win echoing the violence that often flashed from his hand as he cuffed a smaller boy who interfered with him. He was the youngest son of Sesekume, an old man nearing the end of his active life, whose patrician face, framed by a short grey beard, spoke of his past accomplishments and his present place of respect as one of the elders of Ozahadzuha. There was a physical likeness to Sesekume in his son, but Hasu also possessed a hardness his father lacked, a will-fulness, a touch of the arrogance that sat on men like Gapiriha. Though the qualities of strength were softened by his youth, their incipient marks were visible. He was often alone and did not take kindly to Lotuwa's orders, resenting his age mate's place of command in the household. Hasu's own interests seemed to be his closest concern, fore-shadowing an adult attitude of scant respect for persuasion. In other times he might have acquired a considerable reputation but surely not a following, for his will was not tempered by the sensitivity of men like Makis.

Hutorno was a younger son of Gihigute of Ozahadzuha. He had his father's rather large mouth, dark coloring, and slim build, but the re-semblance ended there. He was more talkative than Hasu and lacked his incipient arrogance and independence, but had no other redeeming qualities. He was sullenly slow, responding reluctantly to my few de-mands and neglecting his duties to attend to his own affairs outside the village. When he returned from one of his frequent absences, his scowl increased my irritation; but reprimands had no effect and I began to avoid him.

The comradeship of the four boys was thoroughly impressive. The bond of age they shared with each other seemed to transcend the strik-ing differences in their personalities, holding them together in a re-markable manner. It was obvious that their closeness was expected of them. Indeed, it was difficult, at first, to distinguish the subtleties of suspicion and antipathy from the ideal that had been imputed to the relationship, and watching them from day to day I was often sharply envious of their easy accord and its contrast with anything that lay in my own young manhood.

In the beginning I understood very little of their exchanges in the kitchen, but there was no mistaking the tone of their voices, the laugh-

ter, the low murmurs, the sudden ripples of excitement, which drew
an image of companionship as clearly as though I had been able to
follow their words, and in the street in the late afternoon as they ran
with a crowd of younger children, their cries of *pren*, pidjin English
for friend, their search for each other's attention, released in me a
warmth that also seemed to be in the eyes of the adults watching
them near the smoking fires. They were not yet fully franchised men.
In many important respects they were more subservient to their elders
than the younger, uninitiated boys whose days passed largely without
any adult supervision; for if they were privy to the secrets of the clubhouse and privileged to be present when the men gathered to arrive
at group decisions, they were also under closer surveillance, their presence encouraging a constant criticism that their younger brothers
escaped. In the places where the men met to transact their business—
the garden houses, camouflaged by overhanging trees, separated from
the rest of the world by the living fences whose leaves returned the
light like the sandy shallows of a pool—the members of their age group
prepared the stones for the earth ovens, split the firewood, and drew
the water from the streams. They moved through the dappled shadows
with their bamboo burdens on their shoulders, answered directions, and
sat down at a respectful distance while their elders argued a decision,
and later, as the food cooked slowly under the steaming cones of mud,
when the air was breathless, heavy with the weight of afternoon, they
held themselves impassively, faces contained and expressionless while
the older men temporarily released from the matter in hand examined
their conduct and usually found it wanting. Later, they ventilated their
animosity against the younger boys, returning in kind the carping appraisals to which they had recently listened.

In time I discovered more to their relationships than showed in the
public picture of close companionship, rivalries that qualified the
formal character of their bond, preferences that could not be stated
openly but that were revealed to me occasionally in confidence, my
position providing the boys with a license to express verbally what
others probably read in more subtle forms of behavior: in glances they
could interpret from their own experiences, in the intonation of a word,
in a momentary reluctance to share something an age mate had demanded. It became clear that the quality of the relationship between
Hunehune and Lotuwa was different from anything they shared with
Hasu or Hutorno. With them pren carried the connotations of personal

choice and mutual affection subsumed by its cognate form "friendship." Their responses to one another transcended the formal demands of equality, were informed by a lightness and a regard that altered the whole character of an action, so that in them could be seen the proto- type of the older men who sought each other's company in preference to that of closer kinsmen who had controlled them in their youth. Yet even if they reminded me of familiar attitudes, their glances, the hand impulsively searching for a companion's shoulder recalling needs I also knew, their relationship could not be transposed into a precise equiv- alent in my own culture. For this freedom, the accord visible in the heads that touched as they bent above my fire, was possible only be- cause they were age mates. Other ties did not contain the possibility of similar expressions.

Hunehune and Lotuwa probably knew that I preferred them to Hasu and Hutorno, and seeing their own antipathies reflected in my attitude, they were often critical of the other boys. Their confidences, haltingly expressed when we were alone, provided me with informa- tion no amount of formal questioning would have obtained, but want- ing to be fair to their age mates, I was never comfortable through the exchanges, taking my attitude from their own caution, from their white- eyed watchfulness as they listened for the cushioned sound of bare feet on the ground outside the walls.

As I watched the boys from day to day it was difficult to visualize them as they would have been if my own people had not come to the valley. They were at the age when many of their elders had already earned considerable reputations as warriors. Of them all Hasu was the one who would have applied himself best to this most admired form of masculine expression. He had the build of the "strong," the figure to command respect and admiration, and his youthful taciturnity pre- figured the hardness of men like Gapiriha, an arrogance that grew im- patient with the interminable subtleties of debate and the conventions of equality. Lotuwa and Hutorno might have made conventional war- riors, doing the expected and finding satisfaction in the painted violence of their world, but Hunehune was more difficult to place against the background of that life. He was no less fond of self-display than his age mates, no less proud of his appearance dressed for a festival in bark-cloth vees, his head decorated with plume and shell, his skin oiled and his features, hidden under glowing pigments. He danced with the inner concentration of the strongest men, beating his drum and singing with a hoarse ecstasy, shifting his weight deliberately from leg to leg, every movement acknowledging the presence of the crowds whose admiration he hoped to win. He accepted and delighted in the privileges of being male and jealously protected them, yet he was also capable of standing aside and commenting with wry objectivity on the men's pretentions to superiority. His essential gentleness was no mate for ambition, and he was lucky to live at a time when service for Europeans could substitute for the traditional apprenticeship in violence.

None of the boys was old enough to remember very much about the ambushes and battles still so alive to their elders. Except for an occasional spontaneous show of force, the government had imposed an uneasy peace on the valley by the time they were about ten; they had only vague recollections of exile and the stronger taste of fear as they clung, with contorted faces, to the hips of women scurrying to a safe distance. None of them showed any regret that he had been spared the test of war, yet they were not impatient or unresponsive to their elders' unflagging interest in this aspect of the recent past. They listened with intense interest to the recitals of heroic deeds and rose, at the end of a discussion, with their shoulders a little more square, their heads a little higher with pride in the achievements of their group. On these occasions their carriage probably reflected more than a momentary, vicarious identification with the boldly aggressive past, for they, too, had been feted as successful warriors, winning their acclaim on a field where legs and arms were used instead of spears, where the reputation of their group rode with a hard ball of bark cloth as they struggled to place it between the wooden posts of their opponents' goal.

These football "games" were not mere sport but a substitute for feuding, *hina*, the forceful retaliation for injuries that disrupted the relationships of friendly tribes. Feuds were instigated by acts of adultery, by the theft of pigs, or by homicide, and unlike warfare, *rova*, the interminable hostility associated with enemy groups, the fighting ended when the injured party had redressed the wrong. Under the government-imposed peace feuding was proscribed, but groups that had been injured frequently issued a challenge to "futbol," meeting their opponents in a contest that adhered to traditional rules of redress. The game was modeled loosely on rugby, but during the encounter, which occasionally lasted several days, the numbers of the opposing teams fluctuated sharply: at critical moments, as many as thirty men on each

side might face each other. The team representing the offending group
entered the field with a score of one in its favor, standing for the act
that had to be redressed. Its opponents, representing the wronged
group, aimed to even the score—not to win by amassing a greater
number of points but simply to "back" the goals its rivals gained. In
the heat of the encounter careful scoring was almost impossible. The
game invariably degenerated into something closer to hand-to-hand
combat than organized competition, yet eventually the ideal was up-
held. For the contest ended when the elders of both groups, watching
its progress from the sidelines, decided that the scores were even, and,
honor satisfied, the challengers left the field.

It was customary to give the defending team a feast. I went to one
such celebration at Gehamo, advised beforehand that the feast, like
the football game, was "new fashion." Arriving at midafternoon, entering the brilliant street through a grove of dark pandanus palms, I
suddenly seemed confronted with my own past. In the center of the
village, near the larger oval of a men's house, was a long pergola of
saplings, open at the sides, thinly roofed with boughs of casuarinas, a
temporary arbor that carried me back to my own childhood when
similar structures, fashioned from aromatic eucalyptus, provided shade
and a place to picnic at the annual Agricultural Shows. Confirming
these forgotten memories, under the arbor there was a long table
flanked by crude benches, the former covered with colored cloths and
laid with an assortment of tin and enamel plates in reasonable imitation of the white man's eating customs. Sticks of trade tobacco, rolled
sheets of newspaper, and several cakes of soap grimed with the dirt of
the houses where they had been stored hung on strings from the roof
of the shelter, suspended like party favors above the places where the
warriors would sit.

The teams were taking their places, crowding unceremoniously
along the benches and grabbing for their gifts, their eager hands dis-
lodging the boughs above their heads and shaking a rain of fine needles to the colored surface of the table. Most of them belonged to
Hunehune's generation, youths with close-cropped hair wearing clothes
appropriate for the style of the occasion, clean cotton lap-laps topped
with white or khaki shirts, but there were also older men the age of
Bihore and Namuri whose naked bodies sat awkwardly on the benches,
their plaits, their facial ornaments of bone and shell a startling, in-
congruous contrast with the younger sophisticates beside them. Serving

the players from behind, other men filled their plates with a stew of chicken and vegetables, following this with rice and canned meat, each course, down to the mugs of tea that ended the meal, an imitation of the dinners eaten in the wooden bungalows at Humeleveka.

I had been given a place at the table but could not eat the food placed before me. I was more uncomfortable, more embarrassed than when I sat on the ground at other feasts surrounded by noise and refuse. Outside the shelter the old men sat under the protecting eaves of the houses, silently sucking at their bamboo pipes and watching us from the distance of another generation. I was suddenly ashamed for this travesty of my own culture and drained by its larger implications, by the imperious passage of time and the inevitable discrepancy between reality and aspiration. I could not look at these youths in their semi-European clothes, sitting to table in this alien manner, for I knew the things they emulated and the impediments that faced them.

Often thereafter my mind returned to this celebration as I talked to Hunehune or Lotuwa in my house. Remembering the naked men who had sat so awkwardly beside the shirted boys, I realized how swiftly time was separating the youths in front of me from their elder brothers and from men like Makis.

Yet thinking of the age mates now, I realized that I knew very little about their ambitions in my own world, the world symbolized by the boxy houses, the grimy trade stores, and the regularly intersecting streets of the new township rising at the site called Goroka. I took it for granted that like others of their generation they had ambitions there. All of them sought the new experiences and the money that white demands for their labor offered; it was the thing to do, the hallmark of the sophisticate, even, perhaps, a necessary qualification for prestige and reputation in later life, as their cropped hair and their lap-laps eventually separated them from more "backward" people farther from the centers of civilization, the despised *bush kanakas*. At that time they were content with unskilled or semiskilled jobs, though there was already a scale of preferences reflecting the prestige attached to different occupations. *Cargo boys*, unskilled laborers, the men who carried, who worked on the plantations and the government roads, had less prestige than house servants who, in turn, were a notch below the mere handful of natives employed as drivers of trucks or jeeps. This last occupation was possibly the height of ambition for youths of Hunehune's generation. Realistically, they could not expect to achieve much more in economic status, but their sights were not set much higher than this. None of them had had any formal schooling; it was too late now for them to obtain it, nor did they seem to resent what they had missed. The opportunities available presented, for the time being, a sufficient variety of experience. They were not motivated by the largely inarticulate desire for abstract knowledge that I recognized in Asemo. Perhaps, almost certainly, their future contained a measure of disillusionment, but this was not apparent in their present circumstances. The problems that exercised them most, those with which I was most familiar, did not stem from the interplay of the two cultures, white and black, but were grounded in the traditional institutions and relationships of their own society.

The dominant value instilled in the youths was maleness, and women at best were second-class citizens. The ideal woman was sexually passive and socially submissive, subordinating her own individuality to that of her husband. She had no voice in public affairs, little, indeed, in the way of a public personality though certainly women were individuals, differing in temperament, in appearance, and in desirability. Men recognized that women had their own interests, even a subculture of knowledge and values of which they, the men, were not aware, but they did not consider it important, anything that a man would bother with or try to understand. It was the same with women's contribution to the group's needs. Their labor was necessary in the gardens; they performed important services in caring for livestock; they produced the children necessary to maintain the group's strength. Yet all this was taken for granted; it was nothing remarkable, simply the apportioned lot of women and, in the end, a contribution that did not compare with the more varied, more exciting, and more valuable roles of men. Ultimately, it was male knowledge, their command of lore and ritual, male skills, male dash and bravery on which the welfare of the group depended.

Yet the relationships between the sexes were not as clear-cut as the ideal seemed to suggest. Notions of ritual pollution threatening male strength and health surrounded the sexual functions of women and pointed to an ambivalence that qualified the ideal image of the superior, independent, largely self-sufficient male. Women were Circes, enticing men to casual dalliance, initiating affairs to satisfy their own desires or, perhaps, to accommodate a sorcerer who had designs on the life of their partner.

Some of the male notions of women received support from the low birth rate, even in polygynous families, though surely other factors were involved besides the infrequent practice of abortion. A high divorce rate lent currency to the idea of women's irresponsible sexuality and, incidentally, provided a rationale for the early marriage of young girls. Yet men were not by any means the innocent, largely unwilling partners in extramarital sex they publicly protested to be. The instructions novices received in the men's house included methods of enticing women to succumb to their charms. This was also one of the objectives of male dancing, and the soaring painted frames the dancer wore on his back, the pendulous and tossing plumes had fairly obvious erotic implications. Every youth went to courting parties armed with magically treated cigarettes and unguents that, hopefully, would break a girl's resistance as the couples lay together in the shadows at the rear of the house. Yet if the facts were a little different from the publicly promulgated version, the official male picture served the ends of intrasex solidarity, transferring the blame for sexual misdemeanors to women. In cases of discovered adultery, a wife might be killed, but anger with the adulterer was generally satisfied by shooting him in the thigh with the three-pronged *nagisa* arrow, a punishment he was expected to accept when faced with his crime.

Men undoubtedly exaggerated their importance, and women, though subservient, were not devoid of independence nor lacking in the means to express it. Indeed, there was some basis to the men's belief that women were prepared to challenge their hegemony; there was some foundation for the sexual anxiety experienced particularly by the youths of Hunehune's age group. Their most immediate personal problems were fundamentally sexual, generated by the ideas and patterns of behavior of Gahuku culture.

Each of the age mates had been married at the time of his initiation, or, rather, betrothed, for although a bride price had been paid, they had not received permission to live with the girls. But when I first met them only one, Hasu, was still joined to the wife his relatives had provided. Lotuwa's wife Kamahoe had left his father's house some weeks previously, returning to her own parents in a Gama village. It was generally assumed that her departure, taking her personal possessions with her, signified that she had broken with Lotuwa. Hunehune and Hutorno had been unattached for a number of years; indeed, two girls to whom Hunehune had been betrothed had left him since his initiation.

This pattern of events was not in the least unusual. Very few arranged "first" marriages survived to the point where the couple began cohabitation. Asked to comment, men tended to shrug the repeated failures aside, explaining that girls, who matured more quickly than men, became dissatisfied with waiting, saying that their "husbands" were "too small" for them. Characteristically, the woman was blamed, and the common explanation not only lent credence to notions of female fickleness but also pointed to a significant chink in the armor of male superiority, the implicit envy of biological womanhood. It was said—indeed Makis professed to have done it to one of his "wives"—that on reaching maturity a man might avenge this insult to his maleness by killing a girl who had branded him inadequate.

If these arranged marriages failed, it was usually left to a boy's initiative to find a second wife. Though his kinsmen sometimes arranged another match for him, they were not obliged to do so. As he grew older he was expected to look around for himself, using the courting parties that took place on moonlit nights in every village where there were marriageable girls. It was not a random search. Girls of his own clan and his mother's clan were usually not eligible wives, but members of almost any other friendly group were likely possibilities. His choice fell usually on a village where a woman of his own clan, a "father's sister" or a "sister," had married, for there he was assured of her support. She would make him welcome at her house, provide him with food and a place to rest, and the members of her husband's clan would not regard him as a stranger. The girls he met there were eligible, and if he succeeded in persuading one of them to be his wife, the marriage effected an exchange of women between two clans, an end of some importance to Gahuku.

At the courting parties a boy hoped to impress a girl so favorably that she would ask him to visit her again. If he received such encouragement, he continued to return to her, not only when she and her age mates received suitors in the courting house but also meeting her at her mother's house or at the dwellings of her other relatives. As a rule, he pressed his suit over many weeks, even many months, carrying gifts to her on almost every visit, hoping to persuade her to return with him to his village. If she agreed, they eloped together at night. Bringing her back with him, he installed her in the house of one of his relatives where she was found on the following morning when the villagers rose to commence the day's work. Thereafter, the young couple's elder kinsmen took over. The girl's relatives soon learned where she had gone and sent a deputation to demand an explanation from the boy's group, commonly accusing him of having removed her by force. At the gathering where both sides met to determine the issue, the girl was asked if she had left her parents of her own choice. If she replied that this was so, her kinsmen usually went home without her, but not without a show of opposition, for though she remained, technically betrothed to her lover, the matter of her bride price had to be determined.

If this courting pattern seems relatively uncomplicated, even slightly familiar, it was not necessarily so to the young Gahuku who, once they were seriously involved in it, were faced with major contradictions with the ideal of maleness. When a girl left a boy to whom she had been married by her relatives, the proper, the only manly attitude was unconcern. She was behaving according to her nature, showing the irresponsibility characteristic of the sex. Men had better things to do than to take such actions as a personal slight or to try to find a reason for them. Moreover, there were many more women naturally attracted to men who had to resist their appetites rather than seek women's favors. A woman was nothing to "cry about," as Makis said. Yet the deserted youth found that the facts did not match the picture of careless superiority. His absconding wife threatened his equality with his age mates if their first marriages had not ended in the same manner, and while his more fortunate fellows might be attending courting parties simply for diversion, his objectives were serious. Nor did his elders forget to remind him that his situation ought to be remedied. The older men inferred, even stated directly, that the unmarried state of the boys reflected discredit on their group. In the manner of the mature and the relatively secure, they implied that things had been different in their time when they had been sought by women and no one had been wifeless. "What is wrong with the present generation?" they asked. "What has happened to the strength of the group?" For their part, the boys were aware that a wife was necessary to achieve the privileges of adult status. They were held to account for no fault of their own, taken to task for something that everyone recognized as simply a female aberration, their masculinity questioned, their reputations at stake.

The elder men did more than hint that the boys were slow in remedying their single state. Often in the afternoon, waiting to open the ovens in some garden settlement where they had gathered to discuss a group activity, the men encouraged the youths to stronger efforts in their courting, and if their words were flavored with a sexual banter common to many all-male gatherings, their seriousness could not be questioned. The message was clear; the youths could not mistake their obligations.

Yet when they joined the courting parties with the goal of marriage, they found that the way toward it was more tortuous than they had been led to believe. True, there were some dramatically easy conquests. After any major festival several women in the watching crowds were sure to indicate desire for a dancer who had excited them. But these encounters were probably less frequent than the men liked to imply, and the youth who was trying to persuade a girl to elope with him found it was a long and tedious game. Even with the assistance of magic, often supplied him by older men, he had to press his suit continuously. An invitation to visit the girl at the house of a go-between increased his hopes enormously, but as meeting followed meeting he often doubted whether her intentions went beyond the presents she demanded. She seemed to prolong her decision unconscionably, demurring to set a date for the elopement, setting it, and then retracting; and if his persistence met with success, there was always the possibility that she might desert him later. This was impressed on him too when older males cautioned him against allowing a young wife to visit her parents too frequently, claiming that such visits were reason to suspect her loyalty. His personal experience probably gave him no grounds to question these insinuations: like Hunehune, many young men had been deserted more than once.

With the exception of Hasu, each of the boys in my house was trying to cope with this situation, and I knew at first hand the pressures that were placed upon them—the chiding of the men as they sat around my floor at night, the contained, expressionless faces of the youths who left as soon as the opportunity arrived, shouting then outside in the darkness to release their frustration. Their situation was aggravated by the apparently exemplary character of Hasu's wife. In showing them what was expected their elders did not lose the opportunity of comparing their single state unfavorably with that of Hasu, and his virtue in this respect may well have been an element in their evident dislike of him. Certainly, it qualified the ideal of equality. They could not be equal with Hasu while he alone was married. He was "one up," ahead of them in Gahuku gamesmanship, making it imperative for them to "even" with him for the sake of their own self-images. Yet Hasu's position was not an easy one. Each of the boys was old enough to receive permission to establish his own household, and Hasu would have been living with his wife but for the fact that his age mates were single. According to the rules, he was still required to avoid his wife, prevented from knowing her sexually until his friends had caught up with him. Probably, then, the disaffection and constraint was mutual. In the long-run, however, Hasu would have been permitted to establish his wife in her own house even if his age mates had not succeeded in obtaining women. Gahuku rules were not inflexible, and for this reason he was not criticized when it became apparent that his wife was pregnant.

It is difficult to say how often the rules of avoidance were violated. Surely it was more frequently than most men admitted, for the injunction covered the years when males are most active sexually, and there were not many alternative avenues for gratification. Casual liaisons with older, married women occurred; the gardens, enclosed by their concealing fences, provided places for hasty, furtive encounters in the deep furrows between the vines. And at the courting parties there was always the possibility that in the deeper shadows of the house, when the fire died and protestations were covered by the sound of singing, a girl would give her partner license to proceed. But during these years desire was also contained by the notion that sex was harmful to men. Young males were told that this was the critical period of their lives, that their maturity, their strength could be jeopardized by their associations with women. Continence was not enjoined, yet intercourse was discouraged.

In these circumstances it is possible that the girl a youth was supposed to avoid seemed to be the most suitable sexual partner. His relatives had chosen her for him; therefore, he might perhaps discount some of the cautionary tales concerning women and sorcery. Moreover, he saw her almost daily. She lived with his parents, and though her presence at their house precluded his visiting it freely, he could watch her as he sat with the men at feasts, his eyes following her as she took her place among the women, smoothing her apron as she sat down, lifting her head to laugh with his sisters. In the crowd he could catch her eye and arrange an assignation, or he might meet her alone, uncontrived, on one of the garden paths as she returned from work. Loyalty to his age mates probably did not prevent him from making the most of these opportunities. He was surely aware that they were equally prepared to bend the rules, and no harm was done unless discovery followed.

Hasu was probably no more guilty in this respect than his age mates had been in the past and would have been again in similar circumstances, yet his success rankled. The days when they might have shown their dislike for him in direct action had passed. They could not protest his breach of equality by venting their disaffections on the girl, instructing him in the canons of obligation under the cloak of solidarity, and furthermore, their elders accepted what had happened. Hasu, independent, not overly concerned with the niceties of public opinion, had made them even more aware of their vulnerable position.

Lotuwa's position was different from that of any of the other boys. Technically, he was still married to Kamahoe, though everyone was certain she had no intention of returning to her father's village. His elder relatives had not attempted to test this assumption by demanding that her kinsmen send her back, but they were watching her, waiting for evidence that would justify a visit to Gama to request an explanation. If she confirmed their suspicions, her bride price would have to be refunded. No one seemed interested in Lotuwa's feelings. Since he had not been living with the girl, the whole affair was handled by his elders. As a minor, he was expected to accept their decision, meanwhile behaving as though he was not affected. Clearly, however, he had an opinion of his own, and his age mates knew where he stood, informing me that he had no liking for the girl and did not want her back. If this was his attitude it could explain the waiting game of his relatives, for although he could not express his feelings publicly, his elders, knowing them, were unlikely to insist on the girl's return.

While the matter rested, another girl from Asarodzuha named Lotuwa responsible for her pregnancy. Since she was single, the girl's group demanded a meeting to determine the truth of her accusation. It was held at Susuroka, Lotuwa's relatives coming there from Meniharove to support him.

By ten in the morning everyone concerned had assembled in the street near my house. The tone was friendly but careful, the demonstrative greetings restrained, satisfying convention but with no unnecessary effusiveness, and after they were over the two parties faced each other, separated by twenty paces. Some of the Susuroka women sat apart against their houses, nursing children or twisting bark fibers on their bare thighs, curious but circumspect, not presuming to be anything but interested spectators. The girl was the only woman in the party from Asarodzuha, sitting with modest embarrassment among the men, her hair wrapped in a bilum, her head lowered, and her face invisible. It was also evident that Lotuwa was suffering; his brash demeanor had deserted him; his eyes were fixed on his hands as he shredded a stick of tobacco, clearly not intending to do anything so unconcerned as smoking it but needing something to cover his confusion. His age mates watched from behind my fence, separated from the proceedings by their status as minors.

The pattern of debate was so familiar that I did not try to follow it in detail, listening without much interest as the Asarodzuha spokesman opened with the usual oblique oration. Lotuwa's father followed in kind. The sun, diamond bright, began to hurt my eyes, and I thought of the shade inside my house. One speaker followed another interminably. The purpose of the gathering, which everyone had known from the start, had been mentioned by now and the crucial point was at hand. On his feet again, the Asarodzuha spokesman turned to the girl and asked her directly if she had had sex with Lotuwa. I strained to hear her reply and missed it, her voice was so lowered by embarrassment. Bihore, sitting next to me, answered my question with the information that she had accused Lotuwa, replying that she had met him by pre-arrangement beside the road to Humeleveka. Leading her again, the Asarodzuha spokesman asked if she liked Lotuwa, his question implying did she wish to marry him. This time her almost inaudible, affirmative response could be heard, the hesitant phrases competing and barely prevailing against the modesty of her lowered head. There was a moment's pause. Lotuwa's father rose. Addressing him directly for the first time, he asked his son if the girl was telling the truth. Lotuwa replied that it was so, adding, predictably, that he had not initiated the act; the girl had persuaded him to it. Clinching his claim to innocence, he said he could not be the father of her child since they had had sex only once. If this was true, the whole Asarodzuha case collapsed and there was no need for Lotuwa to add gratuitously that he did not like the girl, for Gahuku believe that conception cannot result from a single act of intercourse; the foetus has to be "made" over a period of time.

There is no way of knowing what would have happened if the girl had contradicted Lotuwa. Possibly her denial would not have hurt his defense, for his word meant more than that of a woman, and he had invoked a stereotyped excuse: the male beset by the sexual aggressiveness of the opposite sex. Indeed, the girl was not asked to confirm or deny his statement. The Asarodzuha, not completely satisfied perhaps, left with polite farewells, and Lotuwa, evidently relieved, thankful to be anonymous again, returned to my kitchen, where he soon gave orders with his customary self-assurance.

The episode had no appreciable effect on Lotuwa's relationships with his age mates. Their equality was not threatened by it, and Hunehune and Hutorno reserved their private criticism for Hasu. Their public attitude toward him was proper, but the feelings they expressed to me in private reflected an animus that showed in a slight reluctance to grant a request they could not refuse, their tendency to jostle him roughly as they ran in the street in the late afternoon. None of this affected me personally, but my life was constantly interrupted by the single-minded concentration of Hunehune and Hutorno on their own sexual difficulties.

For some time I could find no satisfactory explanation for Hutorno's constant tardiness. When he was needed during the day he was always asleep in Helekohe's empty house across the street, and when he eventually appeared his face was morosely heavy with fatigue. He was never very communicative, and now his listlessness, the wide, sullen mouth, the dull, resentful eyes often tried me to the limit of endurance, though eventually I developed some sympathy for him when I learned that his sorry state was due to the trials of courtship.

Hutorno was trying to win a girl in a Gama village and going about it in the stolidly determined, humorless fashion typical of his attitude to everything he did. He was unable to stand aside and view his trials objectively; he was deadly, doggedly serious. Perhaps he cannot be blamed for this, considering the attitude of his elders toward his single state, but others, particularly Hunehune, were able to extract some self-critical amusement from identical situations. Quite often the boys gathered in my house before they set out for a courting party. While they prepared the cigarettes that would undo the sexually aggressive girls, Hunehune and Lotuwa explained their properties and their uses in vivid detail, pantomiming their supposed effects: the swimming senses, the rolling and desirous eyes, the helpless, pressing abandon they would bring about; their deliberately exaggerated descriptions doubled them over with laughter. But Hutorno rolled his ammunition without a smile, with a puritanical disapproval of their levity and its implications of skepticism.

When he passed from the stage of group courtship to steadily visiting a particular girl, his pursuit seemed to acquire additional intensity, even an overtone of desperation. The girl's village was quite a distance from Susuroka, but he made the journey almost every night, leaving after dark and returning shortly after dawn. Though he knew I was aware of his activities, he would not discuss them with me, the shutter of sullenness falling over his face as soon as they were mentioned. Apparently he was just as uncommunicative with his age mates, keeping his own confidence rather than sharing it in the approved manner. Gradually, I began to feel that any hope of making something out of Hutorno, of keeping him in my employ, depended on a rapid termination of the affair. The longer it persisted, the more unsatisfactory he became, and my irritation spilled over to the unknown girl who refused to reach a decision. I tried to learn his progress from Hunehune and Lotuwa, but they possessed very little information and were entirely skeptical of the outcome. They did not think the girl intended to elope with Hutorno, supporting their conclusion with the opinion that the longer a woman delayed the greater the reason to doubt her intentions. If she really wanted Hutorno, they said, she would have come to him at once. Judging from their own difficulties, this seemed like another male shibboleth, yet the girl's continued procrastination began to persuade me to their view. Eventually, my patience with Hutorno ended. Whatever the outcome of his affair, I had to dismiss him.

The end was abrupt. One morning when he brought me my breakfast, Hunehune announced that Hutorno had brought the girl to Gohajaka. Later in the day, when I asked him if he was married, Hutorno smiled for the first time since I had known him.

Two days after this, the Gama came to Gohajaka to demand the customary explanation. Hutorno was not present, but I suspect his feelings echoed my own anxiety as I waited to learn if they would demand the girl's return. However, her confession that she had chosen to elope satisfied her kinsmen for the time being; besides, it is probable that they were planning to ask for his sister, Tarova, and saw that they could use her brother's marriage to a Gama girl as a threat to stifle possible opposition.

Discounting Lotuwa, Hutorno's success meant that Hunehune was now the only unmarried member of the group, a position he soon proceeded to rectify. Once again there were repeated absences, eyes dull from lack of sleep, an exasperating inattention to anything I said, but this time there was also a difference.

At the beginning, I had accepted Hunehune into my household because Lotuwa brought him to me. He had had no previous experience, but then I was not intending to run the kind of house found at Humeleveka, and Hunehune seemed to be willing and pleasant, considerations more important to me than efficiency. In the first few weeks I had little time for him or any of his age mates. I was away from the house most of the day, and except at meal times I hardly noticed their presence. At night they usually joined the crowd of visitors who cluttered my floor, acting as interpreters. When my novelty wore off and the visitors thinned, I began to give the boys more attention, enjoying both their company and their gossip. Gradually, I began to look to Hunehune whenever something had to be done. He often came to sit with me while I worked, and when I went out to the ridge it was usually he, until Asemo joined the house, who jumped up from the kitchen fire to accompany me.

Favoring him began as an unconscious form of self-protection to insulate me from the dourness of Hutorno, the slickness of Lotuwa, and the bully I saw in Hasu. Hunehune was slow, his curious, naturally gregarious nature unable to concentrate on a task if something was happening elsewhere. At the slightest provocation, the sound of voices in the street, for example, he would drop what he was doing to call out a question or a greeting, and the next moment, work forgotten, he could be found gossiping outside as though there was nothing else to do. In fact, the boys had a great deal of spare time. They were too many for the existing duties, and their idleness, their absences were only an inconvenience when I needed them in a hurry. Yet even when he exasperated me most, Hunehune was able to disarm me. I was not the only one on whom he had this effect; most people seemed to respond to him indulgently. Even when they were irritated with him, the anger in their voices generally died in a laugh, just as it was impossible to be severe when he faced me apologetically after some inexcusable lapse. He was full of protestations and shame, but even while accepting his excuses, I knew it was asking too much to expect him to change. He probably meant what he said, but he was too alive, too easily distracted to concentrate for long. He enjoyed tasks in which he dealt with people, buying from the women or giving first aid to the sick, where he could flourish the rudimentary skills required and indulge his fondness for talking. Though often wishing he would give as much concentration to his work, I silently shared the laughter that sometimes interrupted him, remembering my own amusement when I entered the kitchen unexpectedly and found him sitting against the wall, his legs straight in front of him, and his eyes closed, completely engrossed in his voice, oblivious to everything.

In many ways he became as open with me as he was with others, or, if that was not quite possible, at least he was more relaxed with me than any of his age mates were. Perhaps his own curiousity was complemented by my interest in the lives of the villagers, for he was always willing to talk and to part with information. He was by no means the best of informants on many subjects. Youths of his age had no public voice and were ignorant of a great deal that affected their elders, but within these limits, Hunehune seemed to appreciate my interests as only a few others did. Most people were unaccustomed to explaining themselves and to looking at their practices objectively. They became bored with my questioning, irritated by my apparent obtuseness, and to save themselvses further effort often disclaimed any knowledge of a subject. But Hunehune gave me the impression that he wanted to help, even regretting it when his own ignorance became a barrier to my enlightenment. Days after such an impasse, he would reopen the matter we had had to drop, informing me that in the interim he had asked around among the "big men," who had explained to him the things I wanted to know. He was inordinately pleased when I was able to surprise strangers with my familiarity with local custom. When I was more practised in the language, I often heard him exaggerating my knowledge and, meeting his eyes, could read his asking me not to deny it. What was learned from him was not gained in formal interviews; rather, it was given as we rested in a patch of shade on the ridge or when he entered my room unannounced in the afternoon and silently watched me until I was ready to talk. It was naturally entailed in the relationship we developed.

He was not seriously involved in the courting pastimes until a month or so after Tarova's marriage. By that time both Lotuwa and Hutorno had left me, Lotuwa of his own choosing, to find work at the government station, Hutorno because he had finally been dismissed. Hasu was still with me, though he was soon to go too, and Asemo had joined the household. I saw very little of Hasu and did not care to see him so long as he did his work. Hunehune was in charge of everything, and though there was some loss in efficiency, my personal life was more comfortable with him and Asemo than at any time since my arrival. When his involvement came, therefore, it disrupted my routine more than it would have done in the previous months.

Most of my knowledge of the courting institutions had been gathered from Hunehune. During Hutorno's crisis he had kept me informed of the progress of the affair as far as he knew it. Hutorno would not talk, but Hunehune did not allow embarrassment to inhibit his descriptions of what went on in the courting houses. It was he who told me about his two abortive betrothals, describing their lack of success without apparent rancor. Yet his attitude was not entirely frank; it was the stereotyped male response rather than an expression of his true feelings. He was no more immune to the pressures of his situation than any of his fellows; certainly, he did not escape them. Makis, backed up by the older men, constantly chided him with his single state. His comments were tempered by a bantering man-to-man jocularity, by advice on how to succeed, and offers to lend Hunehune the magical ingredients that would guarantee his suit. But the lesson was plain enough.

Hunehune sat impassively through these sessions. No other course was possible given the respect the young owed to their elders. There was no detectable difference between his attitude and that of Hutorno, though later, when the older men had left, I often wondered if he took them to heart as much as his age mate. Seriousness was not foreign to his nature. Indeed, he was no buffoon, and his characteristic expression was one of thoughtful inquiry, but this was tempered by a lightness Hutorno did not possess, a tendency, which I recognized in myself, to temporarily dismiss a problem rather than worrying it through to exhaustion, convinced that by the next day the situation may have changed so much that the cause of the trouble will have ceased to matter.

Everything Hunehune did seemed to confirm that this was what he felt. He went to courting parties as frequently as any of his age mates, more often in fact than Hutorno. But I felt that he did so more from joy, from his pleasure in company, rather than from any serious intent, from any compulsion to prove himself to his elders or to his age mates.

Yet I was probably wrong. Now, it seems that he was not so unaffected by the pressure of his elders, not so unconcerned by the failure of his previous betrothals, not so untouched by the pressures to justify his elders' expectations. His self-criticism and his objectivity, the ability to turn defeat to personal advantage by making himself ridiculous, this did not mean that he felt no anxiety. On the contrary, it might indicate that he was more aware of the inconsistencies and contradictions in his tradition and therefore felt them more keenly. Indeed, it is precisely this kind of sensitivity that seems to have elevated some Gahuku to positions of influence—the ability to see a little more objectively than others, to experience more deeply the often conflicting demands and expectations of their culture. It is entirely possible that neither Hasu nor Hutorno was as deeply involved as Hunehune in these sexual matters; they were protected by the very qualities that they lacked and he possessed. To Hutorno there was only one course open, and it did not consciously occur to him that its demands were inconsistent with other values (what it meant unconsciously is an entirely different matter), but Hunehune was endowed with a greater measure of intuition. Because of it, he was more vulnerable.

A change in his objectives became noticeable when Asemo, who had no skill, began to bring me my breakfast, his attitude an ample apology for the burnt piece of tomato and the broken egg that he presented to me on a not too clean plate. He was judiciously ignorant when asked the whereabouts of Hunehune, and I was not inclined to press him, recognizing his right to cover up for his elder clan brother. Appearing later, Hunehune was overcome with shame but not unwilling to explain himself. He had been to a Gama village where a girl had indicated her willingness to see him again. Obviously pleased, he reminded me of the potency of the cigarettes he had shown me recently, reporting that the girl was quite helpless, unable to resist him. This seemed no different from the many previous occasions when he had spent the night out, yet perhaps I underestimated the effect Hutorno's success had had on him. Now Hunehune was the only one of his age group who did not have a wife, though Lotuwa's position had yet to be determined. The pressures on him had increased, and though he was not as single-mindedly concerned about equality, there was no other satisfactory alternative.

His absences became more frequent. Gradually Asemo began to take over his chores, though he continued to appear at midmorning and remained until after dark. I gave up taxing him with his neglect, and for a while we never mentioned the cause. I was not anxious to make any changes just then, though it appeared that they might have to be made eventually. But before it was necessary to come to a decision Hunehune confided his hopes that the girl would elope with him.

Now he became even more dilatory in his duties, but it was impossible for me to complain. His confidences made me almost a party to the affair, as though I had a personal stake in it, and the girl's delays began to make me almost as anxious as he was. Many months before he had asked permission to keep his personal belongings in one of my trunks. Now, every day, he opened it with the key I had given him and sorted through the pile, deciding what he would take to the girl on his next visit. It was a meager and affecting collection, some lengths of colored cloth, sticks of trade tobacco saved from his weekly rations, some cakes of soap, dye for the hair and face, an envelope of beads, one bottle of cheap cologne I had given him, a small amount of cash in a tobacco tin. As he went through the things, he discussed what he ought to take. Sometimes the girl had made a definite request, asking as a rule for small amounts of money, a sixpence or a shilling, which she always said were not for herself but to honor some obligation to a brother or a sister. I began to feel unreasonably annoyed by her demands, foreseeing possible bankruptcy for Hunehune if she kept them up. It appeared that he also thought them excessive, but he had gone so far now that it was more prudent to continue. Nothing he had given her could be reclaimed, and she kept protesting her intention to elope. I was skeptical myself and felt he was not quite as certain as he wanted to believe. When asked a direct question, he always replied that she would come, but now and then as he weighed one of his possessions in his hands, his expression was anything but confident. At those moments it seemed as though he was about to put the article back and give up his suit, but he always had second thoughts, repeating his conviction and closing the trunk as though, surely, that evening would bring a decision.

Unlike Hutorno, he was always ready to talk about the girl and twice he pointed her out to me. The first occasion was at Meniharove where most of the men of Susuroka and Gohajaka had gone to discuss Gapiriha's charge that Helekohe had committed adultery with his wife. The charge was serious, for the two men were clan brothers, but the situation was exacerbated by Gapiriha's nature. Because of his hardness, everyone expected the worst, possibly an attempt to kill the adulterer. They had hurried from the ridge, collecting other people from the gardens on the way. Possibly their sympathies lay with Helekohe and the woman; Gapiriha was notorious for mistreatmenting his wives. But at all costs it was necessary to prevent an open, permanent split in the clan. The debate had gone on all morning, the invective and anger unparallelled by anything I had seen before. Gapiriha paced the ground in the center of the gathering, his naked chest and abdomen visibly heaving with the stress of his anger. He was in no mood for conciliation, repeating again and again his intention to take an axe to his brother. Each time Helekohe began to speak, Gapiriha shouted him down, moving toward him in a manner that brought the whole company to their feet. After several of these threatening exchanges, Helekohe was advised to leave. It was clear that Gapiriha was not going to be moved by reason, but given time, he might simmer down and realize the consequences of carrying out his threats.

The men were still talking when a party of women entered the street and walked to a house about a dozen yards from where I sat. There was nothing at all remarkable about them. They were simply visiting a female relative, bending down to rub their hands along the shoulders of women whom they knew, lowering their laden bilums to the ground and tucking their legs beneath them as they settled down. I took no further notice of them until Hunehune moved to my side, where he could speak into my ear without being overheard. He told me that his girl was one of the party that had just entered. The woman he indicated was his own age or a little younger; she was peeling a piece of sugar cane with her teeth and did not look directly at any of the men, least of all at Hunehune, though she must have been aware of his presence. She was not unattractive, I thought, feeling pleased for him and telling him so, which ended our exchange. Hunehune moved away to prevent any public notice of his interest.

Several days later, there was a new development. Hunehune came into my room; he clearly had something on his mind and stood against my table with a slight air of apology until I looked up to ask what he wanted. With some difficulty, moving his bare feet self-consciously on the floor, he said that his girl wanted me to give her some cigarettes. I did not refuse; the request was simple enough to fill. But it occurred to me that my role in the affair was becoming too active; I did not want to replace him as the supplier of favors. I was considering how to tell him this when he let slip that he had told the girl about my interest in their affair, allowing me little room to doubt that he had also done more. In fact, he had said I was angry with her, very displeased by her delays. His ruse was apparent at once. It was not very different from the jocular threats of my displeasure, the white man's anger, with which the boys teased the village girls who poked their heads inside my door. Yet, as his employer there was also some reason to assume that I supported him, some reason to assume, too, that because he was close to my ear I might be persuaded to act on his behalf. The proclivity and the power of whites to interfere was taken for granted. The pressure Hunehune had invoked could not be discounted entirely. However, I let it pass, having no intention of doing anything to force the girl to a decision.

Two mornings later he came to me, very pleased with himself. The girl had decided at last. He was not to go to her that night, but the following evening he was to bring her back to his brother's house at Gohajaka.

On the morning when she should have been safely installed with his relatives, I realized something was wrong as soon as I saw him. He was completely dejected. When he had gone to her house the previous evening, she had not allowed him through the door. Speaking through the wall while he crouched outside fearful of being observed, she had told him she was menstruating. Now they would have to wait until the end of her period.

In the following days Hunehune became increasingly morose, deserted by the buoyancy that had tempered his serious and protracted suit. The girl might have lied to him, choosing this way to break their relationship. I did not like to ask him directly but felt that the possibility had occurred to him also. One week later, however, he came to me with a face once again bright with self-assurance. A clan sister of the girl had brought him a message from her: he was to go to her village the following night; she was ready to come to his brother's house at Gahajaka.

This time, everything went according to plan. The girl eloped with him, was discovered at Gohajaka, and Hunehune walked about the village with a noticeable air of satisfaction. There was no other hitch. His future wife's relatives arrived for the customary investigation, received the assurances they sought, and gave their consent to the marriage. Then a month or so passed while the girl remained at his brother's house, working each day with his sister-in-law and his other female relatives. During this time they avoided each other, never coming closer than twenty yards as they sat on opposite sides of the street. But the final marriage arrangements were hastened. Because of the pregnancy of Hasu's wife there was no reason to delay them, and Hunehune was actually living with his wife before Hutorno had achieved the same privilege. Though his elopement had preceded Hunehune's, his kinsmen delayed paying the bride price for his girl, waiting to see if Tarova remained dutifully with her Gama husband's parents.

The kinsmen of Hunehune and his wife constructed a "marriage garden" for the young couple. When the first harvest was gathered from this garden, the produce would be given to the girl's relatives and to those of his kinsmen who had helped to provide the bride price. Subsequent harvests would help to support the new household.

Hunehune built a house for his wife inside my compound, and following the new custom, he slept there with her almost every night. Their relationship appeared to be perfectly amicable. Yet at first imperceptibly, later far more openly, it became clear that everything was not well. The girl began to make visits to her parents at Gama. This was her right. Gahuku, as I have said, recognized that a young wife, a stranger in her husband's village, would want to go back to her people from time to time, but visits that were too frequent or too protracted began to arouse suspicions. Now the older men began to voice their disapproval of Hunehune's wife. Sitting in my room at night, they remarked that she was gone too often, warning Hunehune that her elder female relatives would teach her methods of contraception and abortion or, because of their affection, would persuade her not to return to him. It was impossible to miss what they were doing—gradually sowing suspicions, fertilizing them with examples from their wider experience, confirming the male view of female irresponsibility, fostering the insecurity all men felt in their relationships with women, the insecurity that bred resentment and found expression in violence. Hunehune was learning that his troubles were by no means over. The long uncertainty of his courtship had been replaced by other uncertainties. His wife was potentially his enemy until she had proved herself otherwise. She could still withhold from him the rights to which he was entitled as a man.

Almost my last glimpse of them together showed that the old men's suspicions had taken root. Their house was less than fifty yards from mine and usually silent, closed during the day while the wife went to the gardens and Hunehune attended to my needs. But this particular afternoon as I prepared to put my work aside the sounds of violent altercation interrupted me. It was not an unusual occurrence, yet this time it came from my own compound and lifted me to my feet immediately. Reaching the door, I saw Asemo watching with the characteristic expression of people observing domestic quarrels, immobile, apart, neither approving nor condemning. There was Hunehune, clutching his wife's hair in one hand and wielding a stick in the other, his imprecations lost under her own screams and tears. Twisting and turning, she escaped his grasp, her hair loose, the string bag tossed aside in their struggle; running until she saw me, she darted behind me for protection, her arms around my waist while the blow intended for her glanced off the side of my head.

▲▲

CHAPTER FIVE

TAROVA

I saw Tarova first when she came to my door with a load of paw-paw, entering at Hunehune's invitation with the frightened, wide-eyed hesitancy typical of small girls. She had brought far too many for my needs and earned a rebuke from Hunehune. Tarova began returning the fruit to her bag until I stopped her and told her I would take the lot. The villagers had little use for them, and she had tried to please me by bringing so many, for I had spread word that they were among the things I wanted to buy. Hoping to secure my source of supply, I told Hunehune to explain that she ought to bring no more than two or three at a time but did not expect her to take the advice. Offering less food more often did not seem particularly efficient to the villagers, who expected me to scale my wants to their needs, but from then onward, until she was married, Tarova became my pawpaw vendor, always enquiring how my supply stood before she appeared with more to sell.

I did not find many Gahuku children attractive. Their perpetually runny noses blocked any desire for close contact, and the permissiveness of their parents often produced a definite physical revulsion. Children who soiled an adult's bare legs at meals were wiped casually with a bundle of leaves. There was no haste to train them; until they were four or five they simply micturated in the street against the walls or on the dirt floor of the house. But although they often appeared to be neglected, they were showered with demonstrative affection.

Adults held that no child should be allowed to cry until the fontanelle had closed, because the effort might prove too much and split the baby's head. Mothers became solicitous and offered their breasts at almost the first sign of a whimper. They were proud of their supply of milk, often demonstrating their capacity for my benefit by squeezing the breasts to show the generous stream they produced. Children were weaned only at the birth of subsequent babies; usually, the older sibling was near three, for parents were expected not to have intercourse until the baby was able to walk. Each succeeding stage in physical growth was marked by a ceremonial, commencing with magic to help the baby walk (its legs were rubbed with ash and gently stretched), and leading on through the violent events of male initiation or the celebration of menstruation to marriage. Along the way there was at least one other mandatory occasion to show both boys and girls to their maternal kinsmen, a formal duty no father could ignore without risking criticism and the possibility of some future questioning of his parental rights. This arose from the child's slightly equivocal position in a patrilineal society with strong matrilineal interests. Each person belonged to and had his civil rights located in his father's group, but his welfare was almost equally the concern of his mother's patrilineal kinsmen. His maternal uncles referred to him as their "given child," someone they had "provided" to another group through one of their own women and over whom they had residual claims. They expected a father to recognize such rights when his children were eight or nine years old, forcing his hand if he seemed unduly tardy by suggestions that his wealth was insufficient for the ritual outlay of food and valuables. Perhaps the relatives were most interested in the gifts they received: the joints of raw and cooked pig, the cowrie shells, and the lengths of cheap, bright cloth from the trade stores at Humeleveka, but the highlight of the feast occurred when the children were led down the village street for presentation to the gathering. For once they were clean, their bodies freshly oiled, shining with an unexpected brightness, their hair dressed with multicolored plumage, and their small chests hung with plates of mother-of-pearl, so bright against dark skins that the reflected light flashed like the sun on mirrors as they moved between their escort of armed adults. There were shouted greetings, exaggerated and affectionately joking praise, all of it borne solemnly and self-consciously by the children, who sat in the center of the gathering while the gifts were made in their names and escaped as soon as possible to run like birds through the shadows of the trees.

Tarova had been through these ceremonies when I met her. She might have been nearly thirteen; it was difficult to tell precisely. She had reached the age, however, when it was easier to find the children attractive. If they tended to be thin, they had also lost their round distended stomachs, and from frequent play in the water they were often clean. There was a glow to Tarova, a shine I noticed even before she came into my house, seeing her in the sun through the open door, standing to the rear of the older people who had come to me with vegetables to sell. It was not only that the light found coppery hues in her arms and her naked chest where her breasts were just beginning to form. There was also an unusual shine in her eyes, a gleam that flickered and varied in intensity with every change of expression—bright and open when she laughed, becoming subdued, reduced to a watchful softness when she was puzzled or uncertain—matching every mood and altering as rapidly as the movements of her body. She was not a beauty, nor would she have become one, but her face was arresting, making you want to smile with her at the flash of her even white teeth and to feel an echoing concern when she was serious.

Others too seemed eager to show her the intuitive affection that I felt on seeing her. The older boys were teasing her, trying to search her bilum and joking with the friendly, laughing protectiveness suitable for younger sisters. As she twisted and turned to face one way and then another, the long plaits attached to her hair flew in and out of their hands. There was no strength in their fingers, no intention to hurt when they grabbed at the streamers, releasing them almost at once and doubling up with mirth at her retaliating kicks and sallies, repeating her name with a long terminal "a" whose obvious warmth took all the sting from their chiding. She was out of breath when Hunehune called her into the house, the movement of her chest lifting the plate of mother-of-pearl she wore round her neck. She was never without some ornament: strands of colored beads to join the front and rear sections of her fringe skirt across her thighs, plaited bands on her upper arms, and bangles fashioned from the scrotum and testicles of a pig. Such finery was a typical indication of the pride parents took in their children, and Tarova received as much of this as anyone, even though her father's attitude set the whole community in an uproar at a later date.

I have always had trouble in recognizing people on a second meeting, and it was no easier for me at Susuroka. Not only were there many strangers, but their uniform coloring and their facial ornaments (the bone nose rings that hid their lips) also obscured their individuality. Painted for some special event they became just so many animated but abstract masks. But I recognized Tarova as soon as I saw her again, this time at Gohajaka where her father lived.

I was on my way along the ridge to Ekuhakuka, and as I was late in starting out the path between Susuroka and Gohajaka was deserted. Gohuse, Bihore's oldest son was with me, carrying my camera with the self-important and proprietary air he affected whenever he was permitted to accompany me. The screen of trees across the entrance to Gohajaka moved gently, almost imperceptibly in a breeze that was barely sufficient to keep the heat of the sun at a reasonably pleasant level. It was a long village, following the contour of the ridge in the approximate shape of an "s," the exit at the far end completely invisible as one entered. This and a dense grove of casuarinas and bamboos intensified my feeling of expectancy. The sudden change from open light to shadow set the mood at once, and walking over the damp covering of fallen needles, with the gardens lifting like a remote golden wave beyond the houses, I always became alert and watchful.

On this occasion the village street was empty. There was not even a sign of Meletuhu, who was too old to work and spent his days crouched over a fire outside the third house from the entrance. From the heap of ashes and the broken sticks of dry crotolaria it was apparent that he had not long gone, perhaps to exchange the shadows for the sun in a nearby garden, where he would sit with his head sunk between his knees and his hands aimlessly scrabbling in the dust. I was ashamed of my aversion for the aged. They lacked clothes or any other artifice and had nothing to cushion the shock of their pitiful condition. I took their hands when they held them out to me and looked back into their eyes, expressionless behind the milky film of cataracts, and I inwardly turned away from them, not daring to face the evidence of their decaying flesh that was so much truer than the comfortable image of the end of life encouraged by my own culture. There was no subterfuge here. Neither birth nor death were made more palatable by concealment, and the matter-of-fact acceptance of the infirmities of the old often struck me as a kinder, ultimately a more generous recognition of human dignity than the constant insult of trying to ignore the inevitable. But the open parade of decrepitude was never less than distressing.

My mind registered the ashes and the deserted houses with an uneasy sense of haste. All at once the dappled shadows were cold and a sudden pain struck my chest, a need to break loose from some intangible confinement. Anxious to put the empty street behind me, I quickened my pace and rounded the bend into the lower section of the village.

For a moment I did not see the two figures seated at the base of a clump of bamboo. My eyes were fixed on a point beyond them where the sun burned on the grasses of the open ridge. Then something

moved in the deeper shadows under the shrubs; it was no more than a
pale flash of light on a shell ornament, but enough to catch my attention.

They were two children, obviously a number of years apart in age.
The younger, a boy, was a little over three. He was facing the other
child, whose back was hidden under an array of long plaits. Whatever
they were doing, they were unaware of my presence. The older of the
two murmured indistinctly, a sound matched by the almost inaudible
movement of the trees and the pulsing color of the gardens walling
the settlement. Suddenly the voice rose in quick expostulation, and a
hand flashed out to prevent some interference from the younger child.
Startled, the small boy lifted his head, saw me across his companion's
shoulder, and immediately screamed with fright, staggering forward to
bury his contorted face in the protection of her long hair. Almost
knocked to the ground by his rush, the other recovered quickly,
clutched the baby with one arm under his buttocks, rose, and turned in
a single movement to face the threatened danger.

I recognized Tarova at once. Her eyes were wide with fear, and
the muscles of her legs were taut, poised and ready for flight. It took a
moment for her mind to register my identity and then she relaxed. Her
face broke into a smile, and laughing with embarrassment she turned to
the child in her arms, comforting and chiding as she tried to shift the
blame for her own frightened confusion. Reassured, the boy lifted his
head from her hair and turned uncertainly toward the hand I offered,
only to clutch her neck the more tightly and scream in panic as he
found my strange pale face so close to him.

We kept at the game a minute or so, Gohuse and Tarova speaking
my name again and again as they tried to make the baby look at me.
It was no use. Each time he lifted his head his face crumpled and his
struggles almost tore him from her arms. I told Gohuse to come, and
near the exit to the ridge took a final glance across my shoulder. Tarova
was standing in the same spot, leaning slightly to one side on firmly
planted feet to make the child a secure perch at her hip. Her plaits
fell in straight lines down her back leaving her arms and shoulders
bare as she pointed after me with her free hand.

During the following months I saw as much of Tarova as of any
other girl her age. Because she was little more than a child it was
relatively easy for me to speak to her; at least the difficulties were less
than those with girls of the slightly older age group, who affected by
turns coyness, a giggling embarrassment, or a determined boldness

(which they were unable to sustain for more than a minute). Yet I was never really close to her. Even at her age the fact that I was male, and also white, meant that we stood on opposite sides of the basic division in Gahuku life.

At thirteen she already had less freedom, less spare time than the boys who crowded into my kitchen or followed me about on my walks along the ridge. The little asked of them they did reluctantly with rather poor grace. Yet when they returned to the villages in the afternoon there were usually a number of relatives who were willing to feed them. At the houses where the boys were called to eat, girls like Tarova shouldered long sections of bamboo to fill them with water from a spring lower down the hill. They helped in every stage of the meal's preparation, leaving the settlements in the morning and working beside the women in the gardens, coming back along the paths with laden bilums that looked too heavy for their slender necks. There were always children for them to mind, younger brothers and sisters, numerous cousins, who had been replaced at their mothers' breasts by a newer baby. The Tarovas of Susuroka cared for them all, scolding and disciplining, comforting them when they cried, hugging them, planting resounding kisses on every inch of their bodies. If they had another freer life it was hidden away in places where I never saw it. Their carefree childhood seemed to have ended by the time they were ten, for the groups that splashed about in the streams and filled the cool taro patches with the sound of their rough and tumble games seldom contained a girl above that age. They were more likely to pass by under a load of firewood or garden produce, turning their heads at the sound of their shouted names, ready to run or retaliate at the first sign of teasing interference.

This was the Tarova whom I knew for more than a year and a half. Our acquaintance grew slowly. At first we met at infrequent intervals, by chance along a path, or she stood behind a garden fence, rising out of the vines with the open but uncertain smile that always made me want to call her name in the affectionate tone with which others hailed her. Later on, we met more often at Gohajaka, where I knew her father Gihigute.

His was not a friendship I had sought; in fact he was rather distasteful to me. But our relationship had quite a unique flavor.

Gihigute was past middle age. His hair was turning grey under its coating of grease, and his face was heavily lined, two especially deep

furrows extending from either side of a broad, flaring nose to the corners
of his mouth. When he smiled (which was nearly all the time when I
was with him), his eyes almost disappeared in a mass of quizzical
wrinkles, and his lips parted to show a remarkably fine set of teeth.
His build was slender, less well developed than that of many Gahuku
men, with little spare flesh on his frame. From a distance, however, he
was easily mistaken for a much younger person. His back was straight
and he walked with an important, jaunty swagger. His speech was
faster than anyone else's, and he had a disconcerting habit of standing
as close as possible when he addressed me, holding my hands and
breaking the flow of words to smack his lips together in an unmistakable, highly descriptive kiss. I understood little of what he said, but
from the manner in which his audience reacted, bending over and
shaking their heads with laughter, he must have had a talent for
embellishing the customarily outspoken greetings with a wealth of original obscenities.

He always played to the gallery when I was around. I did not care
for the embraces that came whenever I joined a group of men, but
their restrained handling was preferable to Gihigute's uninhibited demonstrations of affection; the first time it was a complete surprise. He
folded his arms around my legs, lifted me off the ground, and began to
carry me along the street. His head came to the level of my chest and
over his matted hair I could see the villagers of Gohajaka waving their
hands and thoroughly enjoying this new display of his originality. Having scored one success, he tried to repeat it every time we met. It
became a minor battle of wits in which I tried to beat him by sitting
down before he had time to scramble to his feet. Others soon saw what
we were doing, and my efforts to avoid him caused almost as much
merriment as the occasions when he won. Much of his behavior was an
attempt to test me, to see how far he could go and how much I was
willing to take. I put up with his embraces when necessary, but it was
less easy to go along with another of his favorite gambits.

There was nothing appetizing about Gahuku food. Most of it was
tasteless, far too dry and starchy for my palate, and usually coated with
dirt when it came out of the ovens. As a change from my own canned
meat the pig that appeared at every feast might have been welcome,
but since it was only partially cooked I never risked taking more than
a little out of politeness. I took home the joints that were presented to
me as gifts (explaining that it was my custom to eat later in the eve-

ning) and satisfied appearances by chewing on a piece of taro or a sweet potato. At least this excuse usually worked. But when Gihigute was present he did not let me off so easily. Sitting opposite me and giving a knowing look, he would reach out and select a particularly objectionable morsel from a heap of entrails, bite off a portion, turn it round and offer me the end that had been in his mouth. I could have refused the food, but the first time it happened I had a stubborn desire not to let him best me. I took the proffered piece of intestine, bit where he indicated, and tucked it into my cheek, keeping it there for the rest of the afternoon. After this we went through the same procedure every time we met where food was being served. Once or twice I wondered if he thought he was doing me a favor. Then I remembered that the other villagers never offered me anything more exotic than the liver, which they thought appealed because I had once accepted some lamb liver from a white settler, and to still any lingering doubts he always watched me carefully, waiting to see what I would do, seeming faintly disappointed when I accepted without apparent distaste.

Gihigute's effusiveness moderated in time. He was an inveterate actor, always seeking to make an impression and keeping his more original demonstrations until he had an audience. I came across him quite often when I passed through Gohajaka and usually accepted his invitation to join him where he sat with Tarova or one of his small grandchildren. He had his likeable qualities. He was relaxed and friendly when we were alone, perhaps inclined to ask too much of someone with my own cultural background, but hardly more demanding than other Gahuku whose requests, lacking any equivalent for "please" in their language, were always phrased in the imperative. When I lit his cigarette and noticed the quizzical expression in his eyes, he appeared to be trying to tell me that he meant no offense in his public behavior. It was as though he wanted me to recognize a gentleman's agreement in which I accepted the role of straight man for the benefit of his gallery.

These casual meetings gave me many opportunities to observe him with Tarova. He seemed genuinely attached to his daughter and for her benefit sometimes tried to engage me in one of our comedy routines, sending her into fits of laughter while he sat back on his hands smiling with obvious satisfaction. Then he would lie down with his head in her lap, asking her to delouse his hair. Father and daughter were physically much alike. Both had the same rather large teeth and the broad smile that seemed to come from deep inside them. Even in their more serious moments, when Gihigute often appeared as tired and as old as his years, there was a subdued shine of joy in their eyes, Tarova's younger and more fragile but plainly kin to the restrained delight in Gihigute's face when others responded to his antics. Their movements also had a similar quality, Tarova's quickness, her twists and turns, showing an unschooled awareness of self, was a reflection of the more contrived or self-conscious straight and jaunty walk of Gihigute, the slightly arrogant lift to his head, and the vocal manipulation of his rapid-fire phrases.

My liking for Tarova grew throughout my months at Susuroka. Even though I never broke completely through her shyness we managed to establish a relationship that set her apart from the other young children of the village. It found expression in nothing more personal than a mutual exchange of names when I passed by a garden where she was working or in my sudden pleasure when she appeared at my house with fruit for my table, but out of these small things I developed such feeling for her that I was deeply moved by the circumstances that led to her departure from the village.

Its beginning is quite clear in my memory. I had awakened later than usual and while dressing glanced toward the open door of the house. Outside I saw Hutorno standing at the fence with his back toward me, looking into the street. He should have been helping to prepare the breakfast I had ordered, but he moved with obvious reluctance when I called a second time, reappearing several minutes later with an enamel plate containing a piece of pawpaw, which he studied with a very dirty thumb.

Other people were moving about in the street, stopping to look in the same direction as Hutorno, exchanging a word or two and disappearing below the level of the fence as they took up positions on the ground. When Hunehune appeared with my coffee I asked him what was happening outside, for there was every indication that something untoward was taking place. Looking preoccupied, he replied that some men of Gama had arrived with a bride price to "buy" a woman. He shrugged, disclaiming any knowledge when I asked whom they wanted, remarking that they had "planted" it outside Namuri's house. Taking my coffee with me I went to join Hutorno at the fence.

Since I had watched marriages arranged on previous occasions, some of the activity in the street was immediately meaningful. A dozen or so of the villagers of Susuroka were gathered outside my compound. The women, who must have been setting out for work when the Gama party arrived, sat a little apart from the men and filled the delay with the never-ending task of rolling bark fibers on their bare thighs for making bilums and other articles of apparel. On the opposite side of the street were six strangers, all male, clearly the visitors from Gama. Makis had just offered them tobacco, placing a bundle of native leaves in front of a man of about his own age who acted as their spokesman. The two of them were talking in a friendly fashion, but the other five were silent, sitting close together with an air of strained formality. The object that indicated the purpose of their visit had been placed in the ground a few feet from Namuri's house. It was a wooden staff approximately seven feet high surmounted by two necklaces of large white cowrie shells centered on a piece of red cloth. Six plates of gold-lipped mother-of-pearl were arranged in a horizontal row within the double circle.

There was no sign of Namuri; he had left for his gardens before the arrival of his visitors. The news had been sent to him, and now they waited his return. In the meantime I filled the interval by speculating about which of the village girls had been chosen by the Gama men.

Namuri had no daughter, but even if he had possessed one of marriageable age it was not customary to negotiate directly with a girl's father. Overtures were made to male relatives of her subclan. They formed, in effect, a "corporation" whose "estate" included land, sacred symbols, and women; for theoretically all the men had rights of disposal over all the female members of the group. This meant that a woman's subclan "brothers" were as interested in her marriage as her own father, even though his wishes carried the greatest weight. Indeed, they were the more appropriate relatives to approach in seeking wives for young men. Being less closely connected with the chosen girl, they took a more objective view of the matter, were less swayed by emotion and affection than a parent, who was expected to show reluctance at parting with a daughter.

Thus, anyone passing through Susuroka could have gathered that the Gama men had come to ask for a woman of Namuri's subclan. I knew as much as this in a single glance, and possibly the villagers had narrowed the field still further. Hutorno said not, but I suspected his denial. The people in the street knew better than I the names and status of the possible candidates as well as other considerations that might affect the choice. It was highly likely that one particular girl was already favored, but they never offered a premature judgment.

As soon as he returned Namuri went to his visitors and rubbed his hands along each man's shoulders. It was a formal and rather stately performance; the exchange of phrases and the reciprocating caresses on his bare thighs varied from a politely perfunctory gesture to a sustained embrace as one was better known to him than another. At the end of the line he retired a few paces and sat down to talk with the Gama spokesman. As usual, the proceedings seemed painfully protracted. No one was anxious to approach the subject. There were smiles, snatches of conversation thrown from side to side, and now and then a burst of quick laughter. It required the closest attention to detect the transition from informal pleasantries to serious business. There was no noticeable break, and to someone like myself the only clues were a subtle increase in the attentiveness of the audience and a slightly more sustained flow of words from the Gama spokesman. Instead of the preliminary unstructured chatter, he was speaking and they were listening.

In most Gahuku discussions I missed many of the clues—changes in expression or vocal tone, a gesture or a seemingly extraneous reference to some past event—all of which helped to guide the villagers through apparently interminable exchanges of opinion. The most skilled orators treated their audiences to virtuoso performances, delivering long harangues in which they mingled unstinting self-praise with moralistic homilies and accounts of the heroic past and present grandeur of their tribe or clan. The appreciative "ahs" they drew from their listeners often echoed my own response; it was impossible to remain completely detached from the drama of their voice and movements. Yet after a while the speeches began to pall, to seem brash, conceited, and unnecessarily long-winded. At the end of a morning of such proceedings the men appeared to be no nearer to reaching a decision than when they began, when suddenly the meeting dissolved, the issue settled and everyone aware of what he had to do.

This gathering outside Namuri's house was no exception. There was no specific reference to the purpose of the visit (perhaps none was needed with the explicit evidence of the bride price displayed on the staff). Instead, the Gama spokesman expounded on their long-standing friendship with Nagamidzuha and joint exploits against common enemies. There was answering assent from the Susuroka people. The atmosphere was one of mutual accord and goodwill. Perhaps I lost the thread of the exchanges. In any case, it was a surprise when the youngest of the Gama party lifted the staff from the ground placing it against the wall of Namuri's house, and the remainder of the group rose to take their leave.

Namuri sat watching them until they disappeared. He seemed a little disturbed and less than pleased at the visit. There was also a noticeable change in the other villagers. Their polite attention vanished. They moved about impatiently and uneasily; a number of complaining and dissenting voices began to speak at once. In the middle of the hubbub Bihore went to the house, shouldered the bride price, and followed after the Gama party.

Moving across to Makis, I learned that Namuri had returned the bride price, an action signifying his rejection of the offer but not an end to the negotiations. This was customary procedure. It was proper for a girl's relatives to meet initial overtures with a show of reluctance and to take time to bargain for more than had been offered. Those seeking their consent would have to approach them at least a second time, returning a day later to "try" another of her kinsmen. After several days of negotiations at as many different houses they might yet fail, but there were risks in holding out for too long. Gahuku did not offer valuables or make gifts indiscriminately any more than we do ourselves. Such transactions were a necessary and expected expression of already existing obligations or they were undertaken from a desire to establish new connections. They were clearly double-edged, and a refusal to accept the proffered objects permitted several interpretations. It might indicate an intention to break an established relationship or hostility toward those who hoped to make a new accommodation. It could also be an insult, a way of belittling the resources of a group or an individual, and finally, it might backfire, allowing the conclusion that one's own wealth was insufficient to meet the duty of making an equivalent return at some future date. Thus, a continued unwillingness to accept a marriage offer might generate suspicions that one group harbored ill-will for another and might lead to aggressive retaliation in such forms as feuding or sorcery.

There were also other reasons promoting agreement in most instances. Since ideally, those who belonged to the same clan could not marry, women married outside their clan and went from its locality to their husbands' settlement. With one or two exceptions, all the married women at Susuroka were there as the wives of Nagamidzuha men and not by any right of birth.

Although men had to seek their wives (and through them provide new members for their own group) from among the women of other clans, it was not a random search: their own daughters and sisters could be used to obtain what they wanted. In most circumstances a party setting out to negotiate a marriage for a fellow clansman would settle upon a group for which their own clan had provided a wife, in effect expecting to accomplish an exchange. Even in the absence of any formal agreement at the time of the first marriage, there existed an implicit obligation to make the return when requested. A refusal to do so not only aroused justifiable hostility but might also mean closing off an avenue that could be used again in the future.

There was no doubt in the villagers' minds that the Gama men would return. Makis said as much when he explained that Bihore had given the bride price back to them. I still had no idea of the identity of the girl involved and thought that if anyone could give me an unequivocal answer it would be Makis. He hesitated when asked, then remarked in a casual, off-hand manner that he thought it was Tarova. That was difficult to believe. She had not yet celebrated her first menstruation, and Gahuku girls were not considered ready for marriage until after this event. Like initiation for boys, it marked a change in their status, the assumption of a new role. Ceremonies performed at the time emphasized this transition. The girl was confined to her mother's house until a day or so after the termination of her period, when she was formally introduced to the assembled kinsmen of her subclan. As she stepped through the door, freshly oiled and dressed in a new string apron, an elder male took her by the hand and, turning to the four points of the compass, gave notice "to men of distant places" that "our daughter is ready for marriage." Someone handed her a platter of cooked pork, which she accepted self-consciously, offering it to each of her kinsmen in turn. This was the normal procedure. Yet if the Gama were asking for Tarova it seemed that other arrangements were possible. When I expressed my doubts to Makis his reply failed to satisfy me completely. It seemed too much like a rationalization, something that he wanted to believe himself, to excuse an act that did not have his inner assent.

He agreed that I was right in principle. It had never been the custom to send a girl away before her blood had come down, but times were changing and there was talk of new ways. In the past, girls had been reconciled to the several years they spent with their parents-in-law before they were allowed to have intercourse with the men to whom they had been betrothed. But nowadays girls had become promiscuous, and their kinsmen were unable to control them. Because of this, some of the elders thought they ought to try a new practice, sending the girls away when they were no older, perhaps even younger than Tarova. At that age they were too young for intercourse. Their parents-in-law would care for them like their own children; there would be time, many years in fact, for affection to develop, for the girl to identify with her new group and be content to remain there as a dutiful wife.

I asked if Tarova's relatives were prepared to make such an arrangement. Makis disclaimed any knowledge of their intentions. So far, he said, there was simply talk. The Gama would return tomorrow; then we would hear what people thought.

I was not present when the Gama offered the bride price for a second time. They took it to the house of Helekazu in Gohajaka, and when I arrived it had already been returned to them. There was unmistakable tension in the attitudes of the villagers sitting in the shadows of the trees. No one spoke. I wanted to know what had happened but felt excluded by the silence and too self-conscious to ask the necessary questions. Makis gave me a brief glance and a single word of greeting, merely my name, spoken in a tone that barely acknowledged my presence. He was whittling a piece of bamboo with his bush knife, holding it between his knees and cutting into it with slow, deliberate strokes, each deep slice of the blade expressing his anger and resentment. Some distance away Gihigute was offering his head to the ministrations of Giza, Namuri's son, who squatted on thin haunches at the old man's back, one hand parting the matted hair while the other carried the lice to his mouth, a practice only slightly more revolting than killing the creatures with an expert crack between the nails of finger and thumb. Awkward moments passed. I waited for something to happen, but no one seemed inclined to act. At last Namuri uttered a phrase of curt dismissal. Makis dropped the bamboo at his feet, tucked the knife into his belt, and, ordering me to follow with a brief "we go," set out for the path to Susuroka.

The anger in him was apparent, and the other villagers watched closely as we walked away. Not knowing if the meeting would continue

in his absence, I wanted to stay behind, but his manner had left me
little choice. I was at his heels when we left the trees at the entrance
of Gohajaka. He had not addressed another word to me, but out on
the ridge he squared his shoulders in a gesture that seemed to dissociate
him from anything that had taken place in the village. Feeling him relax, I asked what had happened. His replies were vague, but apparently
this time some of Tarova's kinsmen had been inclined to accept the
Gama offer. One consideration was the fact that Hutorno had recently
acquired a Gama bride. I had forgotten this, though I should have remembered the trouble I had with him while he was courting the girl.
No bride price had changed hands yet, and according to Makis the
girl's relatives were stipulating the betrothal of Tarova to one of their
clansmen as one of the conditions for giving their consent. He was
against acceptance, not because he doubted the validity of the pro-
posed exchange, but simply because he felt that Tarova was too young
to be sent away. He gave the impression that he alone was moved by
her interests, that others, including Gihigute, were motivated by cupidity, wanting the money that had become a necessary part of any bride
price along with pigs and traditional valuables. Speaking with feeling,
he said they could do as they pleased when the Gama returned a third
time; he would have nothing more to do with it.

The following day, however, he made a final attempt to obtain the
decision he wanted. I was at Gohajaka when the Gama party arrived,
precisely the same men, as far as I could judge, as the group that had
come before to Susuroka. They were obviously expected, for none of
the Gohajaka people had left for work and many others had arrived
from Susuroka and Ekuhakuka. Morning mists billowed through the
trees at the entrance to the settlement, and the fire burning outside the
house where I joined Helekazu and Bihore gave off a welcome heat.

Shortly after sitting down I heard Bihore announce the appearance
of the visitors. They entered the settlement from a point midway down
the street, coming up the eastern side of the ridge along a garden path
that cut several miles from the normal route to Gama and brought
them suddenly among us. Their entrance could not have been more
effective if it had been purposely contrived. The mists were thickest
there with the sun behind them, an opaque white shot through with
intermittent flashes of color—the emerald of banana leaves, the yellow of
crotalaria flowers, and once in a while the bright blue of a patch of sky.
The men materialized silently and slowly, uncertain and illusory

shadows that acquired dramatic form as they emerged from the background one by one and proceeded down the street in single file, the last two carrying the bride price on their shoulders. The chatter of the villagers subsided like a wave retreating from the margin of the shore. Careful eyes watched their progress, following them until they reached the house of Kimitohe, where they raised the staff with its emblem of red cloth and white shells. I felt a sudden drop in the level of attention, an almost audible release that seemed to signify the end of an opening scene and the start of less essential connecting action. Here and there along the street voices quickened into life, lifted in sudden flurries of sound, held with a sustained note, then faltered and died to be answered like an echo from somewhere else in the row of houses. Men rose to follow Kimitohe, who had greeted the visitors in the customary way. Sugar cane and tobacco were placed before them, and the whole company settled back to wait.

The demeanor of the Gama party seemed different compared with my recollection of their first visit. The Gama, had an added wariness, accentuated by their isolation, for the men of Gohajaka had retired to leave them alone beside the staff. They were not long in coming to the point. The man who led them began to speak in an even and controlled tone that masked the perceptible vibration, the slightest hint of anger in his voice. He referred again to the friendship between Gama and Nagamidzuha, mentioning occasions when they had fought side by side against such tribes as the Uheto and the Notohana. On the surface it was an ordinary recitation of common events, but he managed to give it a subtle note of didacticism, an arrogant twist implying that his audience owed their present existence to the strength and prowess of the Gama who had come to their assistance. His intention was clearly twofold, to indicate the indebtedness of Nagamidzuha and to suggest the risk of failing to honor the obligation. His veiled aspersions were not likely to pass unnoticed. Helekohe, sitting two houses to my left, answered him with a quick rebuttal and immediately encountered several sharp injunctions to keep quiet. The voice of the Gama spokesman rose above the outburst, quivering with open anger. Dropping all pretense, he reminded his listeners that Gama had given many women to Nagamidzuha. Without mentioning names, he cited the most recent instance of Hutorno, making it clear that they would force their own girl to return unless their offer for Tarova met with acceptance. At his command, the two youngest members of the party lifted the staff from the ground and placed it against the wall of Kimitohe's house.

After the Gama had departed I waited for the villagers to reach a decision. Helekohe began almost at once, speaking with the belligerance that had created the outburst several minutes previously. His scornful belittling of the Gama amounted to a rejection of their offer, an attitude implying that the Nagamidzuha had nothing to fear and need not be coerced into acceptance. He received surprising support from a number of other men who sharply reminded everyone that they were not dependent upon the good will of Gama to obtain their wives. The strength of Nagamidzuha was such that women came from everywhere to marry them.

At this point Kimitohe spoke. He did not deny the highly exaggerated appraisals of Nagamidzuha's power and position nor counsel directly for acceptance, but his reasonable recital of the ties that linked the two groups suggested that Tarova's closest relatives favored the exchange. As he concluded a woman's voice from the sidelines shouted an angry criticism of men who had no feeling for their daughters. This was enough to draw the wrath of even those who may have agreed with her. Amid a clamor of voices calling on her to keep quiet, Kimitohe turned in a fury toward the source of the interruption. He had a long cane in his hand, and in one stride he reached the woman and lashed her bare shoulders repeatedly, telling her to keep her place while men were talking. Mutterings of dissent and resentment among the other women were quickly silenced as he wheeled to face them with the cane ready to descend.

At this point Helekazu seized the opportunity to capitalize on the common interests that had caused the men momentarily to close ranks. Pointing out that Hutorno was past the age when most youths had acquired women, he implied that it was the duty of his elder kinsmen to provide for him. He also cited the number of other youths of marriageable age who were in a similar situation, reminding the gathering that Nagamidzuha did not have many girls to give to other people. Far from being an expression of weakness, his last remark was intended to boost the pride of the members of the group: they were stronger than others because their men outnumbered their women; at the same time it suggested that they should stand together, that their interests and needs took precedence over any other consideration in matters affecting women.

It was becoming increasingly clear that those whose rights were most involved had reached a decision to agree to the Gama conditions. Theoretically all the men of Tarova's clan were entitled to speak on her bestowal, but the more distantly related were unlikely to hold out against the determined commitment of her closest kinsmen. They might not approve, but the meeting would end with the appearance of consensus.

Makis knew this too and chose that moment to speak. Sitting alone on a block of wood, he had been silent throughout the whole discussion. When he joined it now, it was not with any hope of changing the course of events. In some ways it was an uncharacteristic performance. He spoke from a seated position, omitting any gestures and most of the time looking at the ground, but his voice retained its peculiar power to hold an audience in silence. Deep in quality, it flowed as though he was listening inwardly to its sound, altering its pace and pitch to fit some intuitive conception of what the whole should be, orchestrating the pauses and bringing the speech along so that at the end it was complete and one was left with the feeling that he had listened to a work of art. He spoke about the relationship between parents and children of Tarova's age, developing a picture of someone who was too young to be sent to strangers. The life of a child, he said, was simply play; she knew nothing else and could not be expected to grasp the duties that would be required of her. Certainly marry girls off, but later, when they were older and they no longer thought of their parents and their brothers. This was the customary and proper thing, for a girl like Tarova needed her brothers, her father, and her mother. She knew no one else. If she went now, what would she do but think of them all the time, and they also would feel their loss more keenly. Marry Tarova if her father and her brothers wanted it that way, but remember that she belonged to Nagamidzuha. Tell her she need not stay at Gama if she was lonely for her own people, and keep her if she came back. Return whatever the Gama gave for her and let her remain. His words had no immediate effect; they did not alter anything, but he had stated what many others felt, and during the following weeks there were times when everyone involved appeared to remember them.

The acceptance of the bride price that morning was only the beginning. Gahuku marriages were not concluded in haste. The wealth displayed on the staff was only a token payment. Protracted discussions were necessary to determine the amount that was finally acceptable to a girl's kinsmen, and many events of different scope and quality led up to the day when they handed her to her husband's people. When I had seen them before, there had never been the same feeling of personal involvement. It was not only my liking for Tarova that brought them so much closer to me this time; they appeared to have a similar effect upon the villagers, and I was caught up and carried along with their emotions. At all the other marriages the girls had been much older; there was no questioning the rightness or the necessity of what was being done, and those concerned were clearly out to enjoy the feasts and ceremonials, making each one an occasion to indulge their fondness for movement and color and self-display. This kind of pleasure was also present at the marriage rites of Tarova, but there was something unique as well, a feeling that the symbolism of the events had suddenly come alive, that something had been touched in each of the participants, penetrating the unconscious levels beneath tradition and sharply illuminating the motives, values, and divisions of their lives.

This became apparent on the afternoon of that third day. It was nearing five o'clock. The sun was still bright, but the shadows of the houses had begun to reach toward the center of the street at Susuroka. I had been working ever since leaving Gohajaka in the morning and had stepped outside to rest my mind and eyes before it was time to light the tilley lamp and to settle down for the night. There were a number of people about, tending their fires and preparing their evening meals. My boys and several of the village children formed a circle outside my kitchen, their heads bent in concentration over a game. Wanting to be alone, I walked away from them to the far corner of the fence where the path to Gohajaka left the settlement. Angled into the grasses of the uncultivated hillside, it was several yards beyond the last house in the row, so remote that the sounds of the street were barely audible beneath the rustling of the kunai. The breeze was like the touch of mountain water to cupped hands following a long walk in the sun. It spread through my body slowly, releasing the tiredness and replacing the worry with a lightness and confidence that came to me so rarely that, wanting to keep it, I breathed deeply and then held my breath. Across the valley, lifting from ribbons of azure haze, the peaks of the mountains were indigo against the paling sky. Smoke rose from a distant ridge, mounting in a slender column to the upper air where it turned and drifted down toward the river.

Standing there, I suddenly heard the sound of girls' voices approaching along the path. There were several talking at once, too far away for me to distinguish any words although I could tell they were speaking with the low-toned urgency of a hurried consultation, ending on a note of laughter. Several moments passed. They were not visible through the grass, but they must have been no more than a yard or so from my position when one of them spoke again. Evidently they stopped, for I heard them whispering together, and then another voice, older than the rest, told them to hurry. Almost at once they began to sing, uncertainly at first but quickly gaining strength and confidence. As a rule, Gahuku music failed to impress me, but there were times such as this when its quality seemed entirely right for the occasion. The rather thin and high-pitched voices had a slightly keening sound, the faintest hint of questioning, which seemed to express a universal awareness of the poignancy of evening, to match the lightly colored air, the movement of grass, and the slow withdrawal of the sky toward the far reaches of the night. I felt an answering ache in my own mind. The wind chilled me, blowing more strongly now as I stood transfixed beside the fence, vaguely aware of shouting farther down the street and of bare feet running to join me where the singers presently appeared.

There were six of them, including old Alum of Gohajaka, who was several yards ahead of the rest, conducting them into the village with all the proprietary pride of a showman displaying an attraction to the public. The staff in her left hand struck the ground with a flourish, and her eyes, alive in the wrinkled face, darted from side to side with a glint that matched her garrulous obscenities. She seemed the very picture of an ancient drum majorette trying to recapture the times when she had strutted at the head of her band. Four of the girls behind her were over fifteen years of age, with full, firm breasts, their thighs smooth and shiny as dark-hued silk. The open boldness of their walk matched the extra care they had taken with their dress, the freshly oiled plaits and the jaunty bustles of colored leaves caught at the waist by clean string aprons. Everything about them spoke the language of invitation, their arms linking them together hip-to-hip, the bent heads, and the hands that flew to their lips to stifle the bursts of giggles leading from one song to another.

Knowing the fifth girl had to be Tarova, I felt a sharp reaction of protest on finding her in the center of the group. Her head barely reached the shoulders of her companions whose added height and obvious ripe development accentuated her childish immaturity. It was the first time I had seen her since the Gama had appeared at Namuri's house. I wanted to ask her what she thought of the events that had occurred since then, but knowing the opportunity would never come, I studied her face for some clue to her feelings. She was singing with the others, holding her head high and throwing laughing glances to the side. At one point, when the group halted at the end of a song, she covered her face with her hands, swung suddenly about, and tried to hide among the other girls. The completely uncalculated movement, a mixture of embarrassment and self-conscious confusion, did more than anything else to remind me of the opposition to her marriage. She was a child caught up and swept along by the currents of adult life, enjoying the attention of the present moment, taking a young and fresh delight in the things it offered—the close companionship of older girls and the eyes that turned to watch their progress down the street—but unaware of its larger implications, incapable of comprehending where it led. It was all wrong, a reversal of standards made more obvious by the contrast between her slight figure and the other members of the group, the girls so obviously pushing their sex and the knowing old woman who led them like a salacious wink.

This was the first of many afternoons when the girls paraded singing through the countryside. I did not see them often, for they took the paths to Meniharove, Gorohadzuha, and Gama, even traveling as far as Masilakidzuha, which lay on the northern side of the main road to the government station. But after dark they returned to Susuroka to a vacant house belonging to Helekohe, where they waited in what was now a courting house to receive the eligible youths or any married man who was willing to risk his wife's displeasure. During the day they gave up their normal work, spending their time in the cool green light of the taro gardens, cooking for themselves at some isolated homestead, bathing in the streams, and resting before they set out with old Alum to advertise their readiness to accept the men who wanted to court them.

To the promised bride these activities marked the end of girlhood, formally closing a period in which she had been relatively free to bestow her favors on any young man who took her fancy.

On the few occasions when I visited courting houses I did not stay very long. The heat was intolerable, and the stuffy atmosphere, reeking of body odors and the rather sickly, aromatic smell of unguents, sent me hastily in search of the fresh night air. I was also embarrassed and self-conscious in my role of objective observer, made uncomfortable by a reticence that was quite unwarranted, for none of the lovers, usually ten or fifteen couples, seemed the least concerned at my presence. In any case, it was difficult to see. The small fire in the hearth produced more smoke than light, only crackling into flames whenever someone thought to feed it with a branch of dry crotalaria wood. Then for a brief instant figures materialized dramatically against the darkness to lend some substance to the singing and the laughter: a row of faces decorated with red and yellow pigments, more like masks than recognizably human features; breasts suddenly projected from the shadowed areas of upper chest and throat; a knee or muscled calf caught in the bright illumination, black flesh dusted with a bloom of light.

There was no adult supervision of these gatherings. Conventionally, the courting was confined to singing and to petting, where a couple faced each other lying on their sides, the girl's head pillowed on the boy's forearm while they rubbed their chins and lips together aggressively. Girls were supposed to reject any closer intimacy than this, loudly publicizing any attempt at penetration and thereby shaming an overeager partner. But the boys hoped to prevail.

For a whole week I went to sleep to the sound of young people singing at the house of Helekohe. For although their meeting place was only a short distance from my compound, the voices did not intrude and keep me awake; their sound was simply one of the many expressions of the night outside my room. It was the time of the month when the moon was extraordinarily bright, silvering the street and the thatched houses and flooding the immense sky with a pearly radiance that filtered through the plaited walls at myriad points, pricking the blackness like the stars of some unknown firmament. Lying on my bed, I seemed to be cradled in the core of darkness, detached and swinging gently at the center of a private universe. I felt the life in my extended limbs as one recognizes the presence of the sea long before it has appeared on the horizon, hearing it upon the air, faint but unmistakeable.

I often wondered what these nightly gatherings meant to Tarova. Of all the rites of marriage they seemed to be most symbolic of the change it effected in a girl's life, for they ended, closed to her forever, on the day she joined her husband's people. From then on, she would only listen to the singing as the sound of a past that had retreated a little farther with every afternoon she had taken to the paths along the ridge. But was Tarova aware of this? She was still too young to have had much of the experience of her more mature sisters. Could she feel the drama of inevitable closure as she took her place among the other girls and followed behind Alum? I saw her only once more, when I went with Hunehune to the house of Helekohe, a child's face lifted toward me as the fire spurted into sudden flame, projected on a background of shadows and indistinct figures, enormous dark eyes picking up the light and flashing it back. Her voice emerged silently, lost in the shrilling that beat against my inner ear, only the movement of her narrow chest locating it among the others.

All this time there was hardly any mention of Tarova's impending marriage. The opposition that had appeared at Gohajaka seemed to have crystallized into silence; no one wished to talk, for talking would only reopen a breach that was best forgotten. My questions elicited only the noncommittal statement that it was "all right for her to marry," and the closest thing to an expression of feeling was Zaho's remark that Gihigute's avarice was wholly to blame for the course events had taken. The days went by and even the gatherings of young people began to seem like a normal routine, losing any relationship to the decision that had set them in motion. But matters had not stood still. One week from the last visit of the Gama I learned that the men of Susuroka and Gohajaka were going to their village on the following day to bargain for the pigs that were part of Tarova's bride price.

I remember the details of the walk to Gama very well and, more vividly, the highly dramatic character of the return journey, when the whole valley seemed to flare with passions that were as intense as the metallic light that bowed the plumed heads of the grass. It was early morning when we left the trees of Gohajaka and set out for the Gama village, which lay an hour's walk to the west. The mists had gone from the ridge and the floor of the valley below us, but the steep path through the gardens was slippery with moisture where they had lain all night. Drops of water clung magically to the curved surface of banana leaves, glittering crystals containing rainbows of refracted light, magnifying the veins of the jade-green surface where they rested, splashing down to the low-growing vines, and seeping through the fabric of my shirt like the touch of cold lips. The air had the softness of recent rain when scents blend, no longer identifiable with their separate origins but thinned to a single tender and ecstatic essence. The men said little as we filed through narrow corridors of grass that parted abruptly at the edge of cliffs where, thirty feet below, a stream coursed over stones and greyish sand, its surface untouched by light, visible only as a pale reflection at the bottom of the angled shadows of its banks. The coldness rose as we descended the track into the ravine. The moving air above the water had the chilly touch of a dawn that seemed to lie above us once again, burnishing the summit of the ascent on the far side where we presently emerged to continue through the sodden grasses for two more miles.

We approached the village from the bottom of a gentle rise, entering it from the rear of the houses and sitting down at the base of a castor-oil tree, which provided the only patch of shade in the street. The Gama met us politely, rubbing our shoulders, murmuring the stock phrases of welcome, and bringing us sugar cane and tobacco leaf. As was often my custom during the lengthy exchange of pleasantries, my mind followed an orbit where I was only half-aware of other people; I looked over their heads to the row of houses whose thatched roofs marched over a rise in the ground like the diagrams of ships that depict the curvature of the earth in children's books. This habit was partly to avoid the discomfort of the curious glances and the questioning my presence always provoked, but it also expressed the natural inclination of a mind that operates pictorially rather than in abstractions—impelled to register the deckle edge of shadows under thatched eaves, the silkiness of morning light on chickens scratching in the dust, the spiny brilliance of the castor-oil fruit hung like vermillion sea urchins on the infinite depths of the blue sky.

My attention returned to the purpose of our visit when the Gama began to parade their pigs for our inspection, bringing them one at a time from the rear of a house where they had been tethered to await our arrival. It was a slow and largely uneventful process. The men beside me sucked noisily on their bamboo pipes, saying little, their eyes narrowly focused on the animals, appraising their qualities and judging points quite beyond my range of appreciation. At the end of an hour four out of the six pigs offered had been selected. The Gama indicated that this was their limit but under pressure produced two more that they had clearly held in reserve for such a contingency. Satisfied, the villagers rose to help in trussing the animals for the return journey to Gohajaka.

As happened so often that by then I should have learned to anticipate it, there was a sudden change in the tempo of the gathering.

Where there had been a quiet concentration that failed to hold my interest, there was now movement and noise, the squealing of pigs thrown to the ground as their legs were bound, dust rising to obscure the half-naked figures straddling the writhing animals, voices raised in a rapid fire of urgent directions. I was pushed to one side, thrust to the perimeter of activity and completely forgotten until the moment of departure when the men who were ready to shoulder the pigs assembled at the entrance of the path by which we had arrived, looking excitedly across the grasslands and taking stock of the route to Gohajaka. I knew what they sought; somewhere out there the women of Tarova's clan were waiting to waylay them, armed with anything at hand, eager to kill the pigs before the men reached the safety of the settlement. I had watched this ritual of opposition on several other occasions, moved by its graphic symbolism of the cleavage between the sexes. It belonged to that broader category of custom in which the subjects of a sacred king engage in ritual rebellion—a license granted on one day of the year—abusing and insulting an office beyond the reach of normal criticism. Like all ritual, the catharsis usually was managed with a tacit recognition of prescribed limits of expression, the women satisfied with and the men allowing the capture and death of one of the smaller pigs.

But this occasion seemed different from all the others. There was concern in the voices of the men who were planning to split up and return to Gohajaka by different routes, a staccato urgency in their phrases that appeared to presage the approach of untoward events. The air of expectancy coursed through my body and pulsed with barely perceptible insistency in some chamber of my mind. Or was it simply the noon sun? For the morning had gone in the negotiations, and below the rise the whole valley was prostrate in a colorless heat, the mountains indistinct, an image on the far horizon that exhausts the will in the futile effort to give it form. Miles away the casuarines on the ridge of Gohajaka were a blur, an illusory island quivering in the reflected light of the vast sea of grass, a mirage upon mirage.

Remembering me as he was about to shoulder one end of a pole on which a trussed pig swung like a grotesque charm, Helekohe told me to return with him and Helekazu. The others had already gone, disappearing in several directions among the grasses that closed over my own head as I stumbled down the path clutching at cutting leaves to maintain my footing. The uncertainty of my progress contrasted with the sureness of the two men ahead, the pole with its burden secure

on their shoulders as their feet unerringly found the different levels of
the uneven track. Even unencumbered I could not maintain their pace,
and they had soon left me behind. Alone, the only sound in the whole
valley seemed to be the abrasive rustle of the kunai against my
clothes. My throat became parched as my heart pounded against the
sticky wetness of my shirt. It was difficult to breathe, as though all the
air was being forced from the valley by the weight of grass closing
in on either side of the track.

I cannot recall how long it took to reach the stream we had crossed
that morning. The muscles of my legs trembled from the exertion of
keeping my balance along the route, and I felt an extraordinary relief
on coming into the open and standing at the edge of the cliffs. For a
moment I was fully occupied with my body's straining efforts to recover
its normal equilibrium; then moving into the center of my consciousness
came a medley of sounds, something of which I had been vaguely
aware many minutes before, even hastening toward them without fully
realizing what I was doing. Now they drew my eyes down to the stream
below me.

Its aspect was entirely different from the one it had presented in
the early morning. Jagged shadows sliced into the ochre face of the
cliffs, darkness alternating with light in a hallucinatory succession of
accordian pleats. The stretch of grayish sand seemed to have shrunk
in size, withdrawing from the edge of the water whose surface shattered in glassy, coruscating fragments on the stones, its sound a turbulent background to the shrill cries of the foreshortened figures struggling at the bottom of the ravine. Helekazu was picking himself up
from the sand spit on the opposite side; Helekohe, on his knees in
the water, looked up in a movement of graphic anger at the indignity
of his position. The pig lay abandoned between them, its trussed legs
kicking ineffectually in the sand. A woman I could not recognize darted
toward it with a raised length of wood to be intercepted by Helekazu
who had regained his feet and knocked her to the ground. At once it
was clear that the men were outmatched, taken aback by the venom
of the women's attack, retreating to stand defensively above their
charge, their voices expostulating in a tone that lies between disbelief
and anger, needing only the evidence of some equivocal act to tip the
balance one way or the other. It came when another of the five women
hurled a stone that caught Helekohe on the shoulder. The muscles of his
neck tightened with rage as his shouts of unintelligible abuse were lost

in the scuffle erupting around his effort to grab the assailant. Even with their greater numbers the women might not have prevailed, but the men were handicapped by the need to stay near the struggling pig, prevented by their concern for the animal from following up their advantage of strength. They could not guard it and themselves as well. The women broke through their defenses and the anguished squeals of the bludgeoned pig penetrated my ears like a needle.

The women withdrew when they had accomplished their end, putting a safe distance between themselves and the men who stood over the dead animal shouting their outrage at the enormity of the act. Later the women might also have misgivings about what they had done, but now they were too overwrought to measure it against the objective perspective of established custom. Listening to their unrepentant replies, I became aware of other sounds that had been held back as I concentrated on the scene immediately below me; cries rose from a dozen places in the valley, lifting from the grasslands on the opposite side of the ravine, from the barred shadow of the trees at Gohajaka, echoing back and forth until the whole landscape seemed to be afire with anger. The women also seemed to hear it. Still hurling invective, they took to the path that mounted to the top of the cliffs, halted for a moment in quick consultation, and then disappeared among the grass.

Later that afternoon at Gohajaka I learned that in several running fights the women had managed to kill three pigs, two mature and valuable animals as well as the small one intended to fall into their hands. There was a feeling of sullen anger and resentment in the settlement while the men prepared the carcasses for cooking, hostility for something to which they had acceded, knowing it wrong but caught up in a pattern of loyalties and interests that bound them to its course. Makis and a number of others refused their share in the meat when the joints were taken from the ovens.

These events had left an indelible stamp upon the village. Outwardly, life resumed its normal routines, but all around me was a feeling of impending climax, of events moving forward to an appointed end that nothing could prevent. It was not simply my imagination. As I watched the villagers going about their tasks, they seemed like people recovering from a recent shock, outwardly carrying on in the ways expected of them but consumed by an endless interior questioning that rejected the conventional forms of justification. The singing resumed in the house of Helekohe, but on two successive nights Makis took the unusual step of stopping it and sending the young people away.

It was against this background that four nights later I went to Gihigute's house for the celebration of the rite that ushered in the day of Tarova's departure. I had seen it all before, the bride and kinsmen gathered in her father's house, the songs that lasted through the night, the farewell speeches and the advice on the duties of her new station, the moving little ceremony as dawn arrived in the street outside the doorway; but this time the heart of the whole village seemed to be beating in the hut, and the poignancy of the last act was like the final cry that recognizes life is a necessary turning away, a series of points connected by the inevitability of prescribed patterns.

It was late, near midnight, when I set out for Gihigute's house at Gohajaka. The villagers had long since gone from Susuroka, and for once I was completely alone as I followed the path along the ridge. Long grass threw a filigree of shadows across the track. At the entrance to the village the spired blackness of trees stood in monumental silence, a dream of ruins clutching at the heart with an inexplicable sense of loss, and on the other side the round dwellings watched over the empty street. I had approached within a dozen yards of Gihigute's house before hearing the low, ruminative voices that conjured a vision of people leaning against the wooden walls and singing with their eyes closed against the darkness. Feeling a sudden throb of loneliness, I sat down on a log near the ashes of Gihigute's fire, unaware of time passing. A pearly haze dusted the trees, rode between the branches on a colonnade of moon beams, and splashed the shadowed ground with marbled whiteness. Every once in a while the singing stopped and a single voice spoke quietly for several minutes, its tone tender, the even flow of words suggesting the protective but didactic quality of explanations with which an adult hopes to draw the curtains of security around the sudden, swinging visions of the world that open to a child's eyes.

Several hours must have passed before Bihore, coming from Gihigute's house, noticed me sitting on the log. The sound of my name, spoken with a gentle questioning inflection, penetrated slowly to the place where I had retreated. Squatting on his heels he transferred a cigarette from behind his ear to his mouth and asked me for a match. I complied mechanically, cupping the flame in my hands and listening to the sound of his sucked in breath. I was suddenly aware that the singing had increased in volume. Women's voices rode in a shrilling descant against the deeper throaty tones of men. The moonlight on the thatched roof quivered with a new intensity, a final flood of brilliance counterpointing the sounds of climax in the house. Bihore rose and hesitated impatiently, gesturing toward the doorway with an imperative thrust of his chin. He stood aside while I entered ahead of him, going through the narrow opening on my knees.

Inside it was darker than the deepest shadows under the trees. I found a place close to the doorway, where on past occasions it had been possible, by bending sideways, to breath the cold night air. With one knee jammed against my neighbor's leg I fixed my eyes on the fire, now no more than a rosy glow under a veil of ashes.

The extraordinary effect of the next half hour is difficult to describe. The house was packed to its capacity, but in the blackness I was unable to discover so much as a single feature of the man who sat beside me. Almost immediately, enveloped in disembodied voices, I felt the first stirrings of a curious panic, a fear that if I relaxed my objectivity for so much as a moment I would lose my identity. At the same time the possibility that this could happen seemed immensely attractive. The air was thick with pungent odors, with the smell of unwashed bodies and stranger aromatic overtones that pricked my nostrils and my eyes. But it was the singing, reverberating in the confined space and pounding incessantly against my ears that rose to cloud my mind with the fumes of a collective emotion almost too powerful for my independent will. Momentarily the night vanished, and my purpose, even the circumstances of my presence in the village were no longer important. I stood poised at a threshold promising a release from the doubts and anxieties that separate us from one another, offering, if one took the step demanded, a surety, a comforting acceptance such as those who share an ultimate commitment may experience. Even though the words were unintelligible, the massed voices were like a hand held toward me, a proffered embrace.

It was this thought, or, rather, this intuition, for it was hardly a conscious reaction, that held in check my feeling of suffocation. The songs followed one another without a perceptible break, a single shrill and keening voice lifting now and then to point the way to a new set. As the others joined in strongly, I felt close to the very things that eluded me in my day-to-day investigations, brought into physical confrontation with the intangible realm of hopes and shared ideas for which words and actions, though they are all we have, are quite inadequate expressions. In analytic language, the situation could be accommodated under the rubric of a rite of separation—an event by which a young girl in her father's house, surrounded by her kinsmen, was brought to the morning of the day on which she must assume a new status and be transferred to her husband's people, but its quality could not be conveyed in any professional terms. While the voices swelled inside the house, mounting to a climax, the barriers of my alien life dissolved. The sound engulfed me, bearing me with it beyond the house and into the empty spaces of the revolving universe. Thus sustained, I was one of the innumerable companies of men who, back to the shrouded entrance of the human race, have sat at night by fires and filled the forest clearings and the wilderness with recitals of their own uniqueness.

I was aware of a flurry of movement in the doorway, and I remember turning my head and noticing in the greying light the woman who knelt outside and handed through the entry several bundles of familiar garden produce, pit-pit and numerous varieties of aromatic greens and relishes that had been picked from gardens where Tarova worked. They passed from hand to hand along the hearth where the fire glowed like a jewel at the bottom of a well. From close beside me, underneath the singing, came the sharp crack of crotolaria wood as my neighbor leaned forward to rake the ashes from the live coals. The red glow increased, only to be extinguished a moment later as fuel was heaped upon it. Darkness descended on the house again as the singing leaped toward a new intensity. At its peak, when it seemed impossible to sustain the shrillness any longer, a shower of golden sparks was tossed toward the roof and seconds later the fire blazed in the hearth like some extraordinary flower brought magically to full bloom.

In the leaping flames the polished planes of faces made bizarre cubistic compositions; the shadows decorating the circular walls seemed to totter wildly in the changing light. As the singing stopped my eyes found faces I knew, the lines around their eyes and the corners of their mouths witness of the strain of the long night of wakefulness. Somewhere in the rear division of the house, where a plaited bamboo screen hid them from sight, Tarova sat among her age mates. From time to time in the preceding hours, during the intervals between songs, she had been addressed by her elder kinsmen and instructed in her duties as a wife and the proper manner to conduct herself among her future husband's people. There was frequent reassurance, I learned later, that she need not remain if she was harshly treated, such explicit consideration showing the continuing doubts that many shared concerning the propriety of her marriage. But for the time being a prescribed pattern of events had taken over and after a moment or two, at some undiscovered signal, the voices rose in song again. This time the sound was hushed, containing in its alien scale a lingering sweetness. I recognized in the words an implication of closure, the heart-clutching evocation of the moment of departure when a necessary end is stated. The volume increased slightly, and as the last note thinned to a vibration someone near the hearth extinguished the fire with the prepared bundles of garden produce. At that moment, as the blaze dissolved in total darkness, I could see the street beyond the doorway lit by the pale light that holds the world suspended in the brief pause before dawn.

Somewhat later as I walked back to Susuroka the path was a bridge between the ghost of night in the valley and a sky already painted with the unfolding colors of day. I was unutterably tired, chilled by the wind and vaguely disturbed by the inexplicable unease with which, reversing the accustomed order, we meet a morning ready to go to bed as the rest of the world awakes.

It was midafternoon before I returned to Gohajaka once again, and by then the preparations for the concluding events were already well advanced. The area near Gihigute's house was crowded with women who sat in chatting groups busy with the tasks with which they occupied the long periods of waiting at every ceremony. Sweet potato peelings and other refuse littered the ground around them, tempting the village pigs to come forward with a greedy wariness, their snouts snuffling at the piles of garbage, but ready to back off with indignant squeals at the first angry word or sign of an upraised hand. Tall cones of earth sealed the ovens where food for a feast cooked slowly over hot stones.

The men were congregated at a spot considerably farther down the street, a crowd containing well over fifty individuals many of whom I did not know. These plumed strangers wrapped in cloaks of bright red cloth were explained to me later as the descendants of Ozahadzuha men who during that clan's most recent eclipse of power had taken refuge with allies on the southern side of the Asaro River. Though their children (the present visitors) had never returned to its territory to live, they were regarded as members of the Ozahadzuha clan, to which group Gihigute, and therefore Tarova belonged, and like any of her other clansmen they could expect to receive a share of her bride price.

Joining the crowd, I was accosted immediately by Bihore, who asked me to take out my notebook and record each transaction. The Gahuku always impressed me with their phenomenal memory for debts, an acquired aptitude reflecting the fact that every gift made or received required a future return, possibly as much as several years hence. But perhaps because it was difficult to keep track of every outstanding commitment when each man had so many, I was often pressed into service as bookkeeper for important transactions. None of the men could read the slips of paper on which such details were recorded, but they said that my notes could be useful if the debts were ever disputed and it became necessary to settle the matter before a white official. Sitting down to write as Bihore instructed, I thought that this was his present purpose. There was sufficient opposition to Tarova's marriage to suggest considerable support for her if she ran away at a later date and refused to return to her husband, and if this happened, those who had received any of her bride price would have to return it. Bihore was preparing, perhaps hopefully, for this eventuality.

At this time only the money portion of the bride price was being distributed. Twenty-five Australian pounds in silver (about $56.00) had been collected by the Gama. It lay in a cracked enamel dish on the ground beside Makis who, as the clan's official spokesman, doled it out to everyone entitled to a share. Even boys such as Gohuse, no more than twelve years old, received a shilling, answering to their names reluctantly and self-consciously. As custom required, many of those present would provide as a return gift to the Gama a sum precisely equivalent to their allocated share, but at the end of the transaction there were some obvious discrepancies in my tally sheet. No one would tell me how much had been kept by Gihigute and Tarova's elder brothers. Even Makis, who had refused to accept anything for himself, feigned ignorance when he was asked, and Bihore acted as though it was no concern of anyone present.

For the next hour or so the whole company feasted at Gihigute's house. While I toyed with the food that had been offered to me I noticed a staff, set upright in the ground, to which had been tied a newly made grass skirt and a necklace of shell. At its base two bilums bulged with assorted cooked joints and entrails, and several feet away, out of reach of the marauding pigs, three stretchers fashioned from saplings each held a whole carcass. Everything was in readiness for the appearance of Tarova, but the company finished eating and still she did not come.

It was growing late. Above the trees the sky was clear and blue, but the sun had retreated from the street, drawing back to the outskirts of the settlement where it burnished the garden fences with the intense and pulsing colors of evening. There was a good deal of noise around me, the chatter and laughter and the complaining cries of children that provided the undifferentiated background to all such gatherings, but there was something else as well, a growing impatience and an air of irritation, unvoiced yet plainly visible in a rapidly turned head and the quick glances directed to the entrance to the village. Even the children chasing through the trees appeared to be only half attending to their game while they listened and waited for something more important.

It came quite suddenly, with startling and dramatic effect: first the sound of massed girls' voices, then with hardly any pause the singers themselves, perhaps as many as a score, entered the village where a clump of bamboo stood like a lacquered screen against the darker foliage of the casuarinas. Shoulder to shoulder, holding each other at the waist, they formed a tight protecting circle that moved forward slowly, a pace at a time, as they sang. Somewhere in their ranks Tarova was hidden, borne reluctantly toward us by her age mates.

I stood quickly when the girls appeared, lifted to my feet by the sheer theatricality of their entrance and moved by the expectation of seeing Tarova. The light glowing among the bamboo leaves illuminated their figures with a touching radiance as they faced the shadowed street, adding its measure to their air of youthful and uncertain fragility. Almost at once there was a general drop in the level of noise around me, a hush that seemed to foreshadow something yet to come. No one turned in the girls' direction, yet beneath their apparent disinterest they were aware of the group's precise position, even measuring its progress toward them by the volume of the singing.

As the minutes passed it became evident that the girls were genuinely reluctant to cover the intervening fifty yards that would bring them to Gihigute's house. The slowness of their pace went far beyond the requirements of custom, which demanded only a formal show of unwillingness and hesitation as the bride was brought to the spot where the men would separate her by force from her companions, carrying her off against a merely technical resistance. On this occasion I felt that the symbolic elements had come alive again, brushing the heart of everyone present and quickening the conflicting emotions that had been held in check since the violence of the return journey from Gama.

An almost complete silence had descended on the company. The younger children stood immobile under the trees, their games forgotten. Once or twice a man's voice commanded the girls to hurry, the careful casualness of his tone screening an impatient readiness for action. Out of such small details the atmosphere of climax built toward a peak where it was almost a physical presence in the street. Even so, I was completely unprepared for the violence into which it erupted.

The girls had approached within ten yards of Gihigute's house when Helekohe rose with a sudden unintelligible expostulation and ran towards them. Momentarily they sustained their singing, falling back as they absorbed the shock of his rush against their linked bodies. Their ranks reeled and reformed, lurching forward several paces under the momentum of recovery. Almost at once their song ended in a distressed cry that mobilized the whole company. Men ran to the assistance of Helekohe, to be met, quite unbelievably, by others who interposed themselves in front of the girls and struck back to protect the threatened circle. More than a dozen fights broke out before my eyes, the embattled men shouting their outrage at this challenge to an established right. There was no concern to cushion the blows that sent them sprawling to the ground, but the anger on their faces indicated a deeper perplexity and hurt, a mutual questioning of what was happening to the formally prescribed limits of expression and of the conditions under which it had occurred. I felt that the antagonists recognized that their behavior was wrong. Each knew intuitively that custom is an arbitrary boundary that, while it cannot define all that an individual feels nor everything he may wish to express, it is the best available definition, the only safe route to take. Each knew that any departure from it ought to be resisted, for then the way is opened to questions that are too troublesome to answer, requiring, as they do, a reappraisal of motives that have become so fixed that they are accepted as an inevitable part of nature.

The struggle lasted only a few minutes, but during that period its intensity became the catalyst that resolved the ambiguity of my own position. At the first onslaught I had been pushed unceremoniously to the edge of the street, where I stood physically apart from the action and completely disregarded. Like the contagion spread by panic, the violence of the emotions in the struggling throng swept over me, drawing me to the point where my own fear was indistinguishable from the distraught expressions of the girls whose circle of linked bodies rocked and staggered under the buffeting of the men. It was quite unthinkable that they could win. Not only were they badly outmatched, but also no one in the crowd intended a conscious repudiation of the impersonal order that shaped their lives. The girls' challenge was not deliberate, not undertaken from any rational objective that they hoped to gain. Yet for a brief moment I hoped for the impossible, and when the end came as Helekohe, breaking through the circle, grabbed Tarova by the arm and dragged her to the base of the wooden staff, I felt so helpless, so emptied by distress that my eyes filled with unashamed tears.

All around me others found the same relief as they crowded to the staff to dress Tarova in her new skirt and shell necklace. The men worked swiftly, almost as though they regretted the consequences of their actions and feared that they might relent if they looked at her. For the first time in many days I could see her plainly above their bowed heads and once again wanted to protest the contrast between her child's face and figure and the events in which she was involved. Nothing could have prepared her for the tempest of the past few minutes. The uncomprehending terror that must have gripped her as she was caught in the struggle and threatened by trampling feet was evident now in her broken face and the rushing tears with which children protest a world that has suddenly come too close to them. Watching her hands push ineffectually at the naked shoulders of the men, I remembered that the end of childhood is not a matter of age alone. It is simply the culminating point in a slow but inevitable process of attrition where innocence is lost as step by step, without warning, some defense is breached by a demand to which we must respond, knowing that nothing will ever be the same again. This is a child's vulnerability, the defenselessness that out of our own past sweeps up the heart in a rush of tenderness.

Now this knowledge seemed to touch the whole company as the men hurried through the final preparations, shouldering the litters and distributing the bags of entrails, Tarova's gifts to her new relatives, to the women. Several feet away Hasu was crying silently, completely unaware of anyone but Tarova as his eyes·enfolded her with a glance in which I read my own deep wish to reassure her. Watching him I felt that with everyone present he wanted her to understand his helplessness to change the course of events and also to give her the comfort and protection whose need showed so clearly on her face. She had ceased resisting the administering hands and stood in her new clothes with her back to the wooden staff, a small figure conveying the essence of abandonment. Anointed with a new coating of grease, her skin and hair shining like dark water were perfect foils for the multiple strands of red and yellow beads looped at her loins and embroidered on bands that clasped her upper arms. Over her brow a circlet of emerald beetles held two soaring plumes of the magnificent bird of paradise, golden showers of incredible delicacy that seemed to light the air around them. At other times I had noticed her delight in less rich adornments, when her quick but unschooled movements asked one not only to admire the finery, but also to share the affection they represented; now, however, their air of flaunting celebration jarred against her frightened eyes and her obvious distress. The invitingly oiled skin and the brazen plumes were so opposed to her in mood, so unnatural an affront, that she seemed to stand for all the hurt children suffer in their long chronicle of subjugation to adult ends.

I realized suddenly that there is no final absolution for what we do to them. The guilt we subdue with the false assurance that age brings understanding rises to possess us when we least expect it, turning our hearts in upon ourselves with a flooding need for expiation. Sitting near Tarova, Guma'e spoke for everyone when she rose swiftly and in a single, sweeping movement of concern, tore the shell pendent from her neck and placed it over the child's head.

At that precise moment someone in the crowd lifted Tarova to the shoulders of Namuri. Clutching his hair for support as he rose from his knees, she was lifted into the evening light, poised unsteadily above the throng with the splendid plumes fluttering like heraldic birds around her head. There was no more than a second or two to absorb the rending beauty of the image. Almost at once he moved off at a loping gait, disappearing into the darkness of the trees to a full and penetrating chorus of broken cries.

The sound of these voices in the grove of Gahajaka accompanied us on every step along the route to Gama. It was a swift and almost silent procession under a sky withdrawing visibly toward the night. In the ravines it was already so dark that in order to prevent a fall I had to concentrate completely on my footing. Once or twice as the cold waters of a stream rushed into my boots I looked up to the opposite side to see the figures of those ahead of me moving in black relief across the pale green air before they disappeared among the grasses.

The vanguard of our procession halted at the entrance to the Gama village, and Namuri set Tarova to the ground. The women fussed around her arranging the bags of entrails on her slender shoulders. Makis caught my eye and gestured imperiously with his chin, directing me to a place beside him in the front rank of the men who were forming up to escort the bride across the last few yards. Joining him there I looked down the avenue of trees to the village street. Beyond the two round houses flanking the entrannce the light danced on the open ground in a warm and golden contrast to the shadows where we stood. I do not remember hearing any sounds, though the Gama waited for us just ahead, out of sight around a bend where a faint haze of wood smoke billowed like blue gauze curtains through the upper branches of the trees. My body tensed, and a nerve at the back of my head quivered involuntarily as I drew myself together and waited, like an actor in the wings, for a cue to step across the threshold into the bright illumination. By now the men with the litters had arrived and had taken places near me. The alert voices, speaking in low tones, and the jangling response of a shell ornament to a hurried movement increased my feeling of anticipation. I did not look behind me and yet was vividly aware of massed red cloaks falling in loose, dramatic lines from the shoulders of half-naked bodies. The preparations were completed quickly. Standing beside me Makis glanced across his shoulder, spoke a brief command and we moved forward into the street.

At the very edge of my line of sight three old women bobbed forward to receive us, flapping mats of dry pandanus leaf in front of their bent bodies and emitting shrill cries of welcome. As we slowly rounded the bend in the street, we came face to face with the assembled Gama sitting on the ground. The crowd was much larger than I had expected—over a hundred people—and almost completely silent. Every head was turned toward us but I could not read the expressions on the faces my eyes met in the crowd. Obscured by paint and decked in feathers, they flowed together, a gaudy panel that flickered like the thought of violence whenever someone moved or changed position. Responding to their close scrutiny, I felt a perceptible rise in the contained alertness of the men around me. The pace of our procession slowed and became more mannered. On either side of us the old women bobbed and turned like tops that had almost exhausted their momentum. As we came closer, the light burnished the painted faces of the seated figures. Red and yellow daubs were punctuated here and there by the stark white of a bone ornament, an effect of such barbaric splendor that, entranced, I felt impelled involuntarily toward them.

For a moment, the only sound seemed to be the level breathing of the men beside me. Then the Gama spokesman rose and advanced about five yards toward us, followed immediately by perhaps a score of Tarova's new relatives. At the same time, Makis and Namuri took her by the hands and led her out to face them. The brief concluding ceremonies, conducted with a solemn, quiet dignity, seemed even then a perfect expression of the Gahuku talent for establishing the right mood for each occasion. There were no unnecessary embellishments nor any attempt to extract from the situation more than it held. Holding Tarova's hand Makis addressed the Gama in a tone that omitted the grandoise flourishes of conventional oratory and substituted a direct eloquence to make the points he had stated many days previously at Gohajaka. It was usual at this stage of the proceedings to remind a bridegroom and his kinsmen of their duties, but on past occasions the exhortations to treat the new wife with kindness and consideration had failed to arouse in me any answering concern. I did not deny that they were expressions of genuine attachment, but they also impressed me as formally required statements lacking the conviction with which Makis drew attention to Tarova's age and the additional need for tenderness and understanding that it imposed on the Gama.

Listening to his measured flow of words I felt myself again possessed by the strong currents of a common emotion. The light had faded rapidly, and the gathering dusk increased the distance that separated us from the three figures standing with their backs toward us. The top of Tarova's head was several inches lower than the shoulders of the two men who held her hands. She was perfectly still but once while Makis spoke I saw her knees tremble and the muscles of her calves tense under the weight of the laden string bags. I wanted to reach out to her, to gather her up, remembering the same affectionate anxiety that she had aroused so often as she rose from among the vines to greet me from the opposite side of a garden fence. Almost unaware of what I was doing I found myself mentally calling her name, forming it with the lengthened and enfolding ending the older boys had used as they chased her in the sunlight outside my house.

Makis stopped speaking, and the Gama spokesman stepped forward to reply. There were none of the usual overtones of belligerency in his voice. Instead, he spoke with a persuasive seriousness, answering not only the content of what Makis had said but also testing his words against the invisible currents that held Tarova firmly to the men behind her. Ending his speech, he approached the three figures and held out his hand to Tarova. For a suspended moment no one in the whole street moved. The silence was so complete that I could hear the blood throbbing in my ears, a sound like the distant sea, as I wondered what would happen if now, at the final minute, Makis and Namuri refused to relinquish Tarova. Disaster was as close as the Gama spokesman's outstretched hand that wavered uncertainly while he waited for the next move, eyes alert and ready for the unexpected even as they seemed to be prompting Makis to remember his assigned duties. When the move came I knew it could not have been anything else. Loosing the child's hand Makis changed his grip to her elbow and raised her arm toward the man in front of him. Their fingers met and the currents that had held her tugged at her legs, weakening slowly at her first unsteady steps, then releasing her as the Gama spokesman led her away from us and the ranks of her new kinsmen closed around her.

There was only one more duty to perform. It had grown so dark that now and then as an unattended fire came suddenly alive a spurt of flame throbbed like a signal in the smoke outside the houses, The paint and feathers that had lit the faces had faded to the point where they were barely recognizable as colors, their violence washed away by the absence of reflected light. My mind went back to the ridge of Gohajaka, so recently torn by deep emotions and now, like the street in which I stood, settling down for the night among the spired and murmuring darkness of its trees. The loss I felt at that moment went far beyond the recent events, though my eyes focused on the girl who had been their central figure, holding her with a glance that summed up more than I was able to admit at that time. I have felt deeply, even if the knowledge came to me rather late, that we live only through other lives that touch us and that to live in this way at all requires more care than most people are prepared to give. For ultimately there is nothing more astonishing, more fraught with mystery, than the mutual response that occurs across so many obstacles of time, of place, of background, and of the events that form us. When I have experienced it, it has seemed like the only security I have known, and perhaps because I can number such times on my fingers I have tried harder to resist change. I cannot move around the world on a string of acquaintances, and the something more that I need ties me more closely to the places and the people where I find it.

I watched the indistinct figures of the Gama at the far end of the street, where Tarova now sat cross-legged behind a large wooden bowl. My mind was filled by this revelation of nearness and my heart cried because of the things I could not say—even less to the men who stood beside me than to people of my own kind, for there were no words that I could use to explain to them my intuition of their worth.

At that moment, walking toward Tarova and feeling the watching eyes of the Gama who were ranged behind her, I looked ahead to the time when I would have to go, and Tarova, lifting her face uncertainly toward me, stood for the enduring debt that I would take away, the knowledge, which was so impossible to share, that between these mountains, among the grasses of the valley, and under the bright envelopment of this sky I had felt a sudden and interior flowering like the compensation of grace, absolving me of my inadequacies and renewing my own existence in the lives of others. Following the example of Makis, I bent down before the girl and placed my gift of money in her bowl.

We walked back to Susuroka in silence and in darkness. The street was quite deserted, and although it was early the doors of most of the houses were already fastened. Hunehune brought the lamp into my room, but I turned it down and went to bed. For a while I lay and listened to the immense stillness of the night, sleeping at last with the vaguely troubled feeling that one more step had been taken that could never be retraced.

▲▲▲

CHAPTER SIX

ZAHO AND GOLUWAIZO

Makis had been unable to alter the course of events that led to Tarova's marriage. It was also apparent that his influence was waning in other areas of life, but his ultimate eclipse was not the result of any personal flaw. It came about because time was moving too rapidly for anyone of his generation to keep pace with it. His skills were inadequate for the future; age prevented him from learning what he had to know. But Goluwaizo was flawed, flawed for his time or any time before it, a man ambitious but lacking the qualities that would secure his ambitions for him.

Zaho had introduced me to Goluwaizo while I was staying temporarily with Young-Whitforde at Humeleveka. He was not very prepossessing then, though later I discovered elements of genuine beauty. When Zaho's hair was caught back with bands of shell and colored beetles, surmounted by nodding plumes, his whole face altered dramatically. Then one could see the fine line of his lips and the sweep of eyelids that were curiously Eastern in their suggestion of strength and languor, an effect heightened by the high cheeks emphasized with paint, the long nose and the neck that seemed to be a supple extension of his shoulders. He was quite tall, about five feet nine, and slim, well made but not exaggerated in his physical development, his movements marked by the grace that sat so easily on all Gahuku men.

None of this, nor any of the other qualities that endeared him to me later, were visible to me at that first meeting, but his appearance made no difference to my response. At that time, I was permanently elated. I was back in New Guinea, in that part of the country where I had wanted to go for so long, and Makis' warm reception seemed to speak well for the work that lay ahead of me. And when I was new to the valley everything was a revelation, so important that I felt compelled to record even the close-packed blades of grass on which I walked, as though the smallest detail added an essential measure to the whole. Indeed, it is entirely possible that my preoccupation with the physical setting has inadvertently colored my perception of the human life within it. It was the first thing I knew, and even before going to live at Susuroka I may have begun to impose my own terms on the villagers, looking at them through the refracting lens of this light, of the sea colors of grass and mountains, of dissolving distances and splendid, bravely moving clouds, wanting to see only that which echoed the vast spectacle of the country.

Certainly, each detail of the setting in which I first met Zaho is filed in my mind with our words. We sat in an arbor of shadow formed by the interlacing branches of the casuarinas, a thin shade deepened by contrast with the dazzling, emerald brilliance of the grass beyond the limits of the trees. To one side, water coursed through a wide ditch, part of an irrigation system introduced by Europeans that tapped the high mountain streams and carried them to the thirsty roots of roses in the gardens of the government houses. The water's sound was lost under the movement of the branches whose needles shook continuously in the wind that filled the white socks at the edge of the airstrip, but the coldness of the damp earth spoke of its source in the silent forests where there was no sun and mosses fed on the moist nourishment of perpetual clouds. Delicate cosmos, also of European introduction but naturalized now, burgeoning wherever their seeds fell, lifted their pink and white flowers on slender stems, spangling the grass like the desert blooms that light the landscape in a Persian miniature. Bamboo framed the portion of the valley visible from the plateau's elevation—the wide sweep of green, the myriad spired groves, the cloud reflections, the nets of blue that fastened the distant ranges. I was atonished by the landscape's power to hold me, even romantically obsessed by the accidents that bring us to places we know we were meant to find.

This was my mood when we sat beneath the trees. Everything was just beginning, and whatever Zaho had to say to me, I was anxious to listen. He was then little more than an extension of his setting, and I looked at him with eyes brimming with air and sky, my mind filled with the heady clarity of light and its precise, revealing definitions.

He mentioned Susuroka and also the name of Makis, and I assumed that he lived there and had seen me two days before, one of the crowd who had stood behind Makis when I selected the site for my house. He mentioned other names as well—Nagamidzuha, Gehamo, Anupadzuha, Meniharove, and Gorohadzuha—all of which were meaningless to me then. I realized they were local names, connected in some way with the village and the people among whom I had chosen to live; I decided to follow this line of questioning. Zaho leaned forward cooperatively, arms resting on his knees while I wrote down the names that he enunciated carefully. Slowly, I began to perceive a pattern in his information. Though I could not yet identify them with any anthropological label, I realized that there were at least two major named groups of people in the locality of Makis' settlement, Nagamidzuha and Gehamo, that Makis belonged to the first and Zaho to the second. More importantly, the white government evidently regarded them as one and had confirmed Makis as luluai of both of them. This was the injustice that Zaho wanted me to understand. The reasons were not clear, but Zaho told me that Gehamo resented the titular ascendancy of Makis and Nagamidzuha. I began to see his purpose. He hoped to persuade me to throw my weight on the side of the Gehamo, using my influence at Humeleveka to help them acquire their own luluai.

I was interested in these hints of local factions and their implications for the broader structure of relationships, but I did not want to be identified with any group or to give the impression that I had connections with the official world at the government station. I became more wary, and Zaho began to appear in a new unsympathetic light. He began to remind me of men I had known at Tofmora, those who had been most willing to talk to me but who had never seen me as anything but the representative of a power they hoped to manipulate to their own benefit. I saw echoes of this attitude in Zaho, and though such people could be used if they were handled carefully, my attitude toward him was a little less than liking when we parted.

He was outside the house again the following morning, accompanied by a man named Goluwaizo. Having nothing in particular to do, I sat with them under the trees at the edge of the airstrip. Almost immediately I learned that Goluwaizo was the *tul-tul* of Nagamidzuha, an official administrative office created by the whites and subordinate to that of luluai, a sort of second-in-command position intended originally for a younger man familiar with pidjin English who could interpret for his older, less sophisticated but more important colleague. After finding out that Goluwaizo was a Gehamo man, the reason for his presence was obvious, though Zaho did not mention it at once. He referred to our conversation of the previous morning, and, drawing Goluwaizo in for corroboration, began to fill me in with further details of the relationships between Nagamidzuha and Gehamo. Makis' position rankled because until the whites arrived Gehamo had been ascendant over Nagamidzuha. His rise to prominence under the white man and the prestige his group had acquired had virtually reversed the previous standing of the two tribes. Disparagingly, the two men pointed out that Nagamidzuha was small, its numbers certainly insufficient for protection if warfare had not been proscribed. At any earlier time it would have had to depend on the superior strength of allies, such as Gehamo, or suffer complete annihilation. The Gehamo grudge was not simply that Makis had achieved an enviable reputation throughout the valley, but that the whites had confirmed him in a position of authority over his benefactors, who were not "Makis' men." It was an unfair slight, an unjustified advantage to Nagamidzuha, and equity demanded the official separation of the two groups by the appointment of a luluai for Gehamo. Who was the man, I asked? Zaho looked at Goluwaizo, who answered, however, on his own account.

I was wary of Goluwaizo from the beginning, though this may have been prompted by his association with Zaho. Yet I had watched Goluwaizo closely during the present discussion, and felt there was something about him I did not like. The qualities that signified strength to Gahuku were then unknown to me, otherwise he might have been assigned immediately to that type, and thereby I might have oversimplified his personality. He appeared to be several inches shorter than Zaho, though the difference in height was mostly accounted for by their hair, for Goluwaizo wore his in the new close-cropped fashion. A young man in his early thirties, he was not precisely handsome but certainly not unattractive. His dark brown skin shone with satiny lights that were generally dulled by dirt on other men. Goluwaizo was clean, his neat khaki lap-lap held at his waist by a leather belt with a brass buckle. Though he knew more pidjin English, he allowed Zaho to do most of the talking, sitting on his crossed legs and watching me from the distance of a few feet, his back straight, rather stiff, his face expressionless. The rigidity of his pose disturbed me, indicating an arrogance also visible in his eyes that held me steadily under their long lids. They were curiously contradictory: dark brown and fringed with long black lashes, they should have been soft; instead, they were hard, their shine an echo of the will that drew his lips together in a firm demanding line. Now and then the muscles of his cheeks moved almost imperceptibly, involuntarily, flicking with an inner tension. His hands, however, were relaxed, hanging loosely between his knees, the only part of him that did not seem to be on edge, though they, too, might suddenly stiffen at the threat of opposition that he seemed so ready to anticipate. He gave the impression of proud willfulness, not the kind of person to cross, for if his expression was not exactly cruel, one sensed that he might be brutal when aroused.

This was the candidate, on his own admission, for the position of luluai of Gehamo, and clearly, both he and Zaho, possibly many others as well, were hopeful that I might be enlisted to his side. The intrigue was moving much too rapidly for me. Their allegations might have been entirely false, but irrespective of their truth, I wanted nothing to do with this design. I had no wish to antagonize them; indeed, that they had come to me might be useful when I went to live permanently at Susuroka. I tried to explain that there was no connection between me and the white "government," but they were unconvinced when we parted a few minutes later.

I did not see Zaho again until my house was finished and I went to Susuroka to live. He was among the crowd who gathered to watch my arrival on that first afternoon, stepping forward to offer his hand. I met him warmly, pleased to find a familiar face in the crowd of strangers. It helped to cover my uncertainty, and later, as my things were unpacked in the house, my eyes sought him repeatedly, looking for some relief from the strain of the incomprehensible chatter, the gestures of astonishment and appreciation, the overheated smell of the eager, pressing bodies. Even on that first day it was noticeable that his handshake, so different from the close embraces and the questing hands that followed my progress around the room, was complemented by a quietness, a lack of display and demonstrativeness. He sat or stood at the back of the throng, watching everything that came from my boxes and trunks, but showing his interest only in his eyes. He was no more familiar with the marvels of my belongings than any others present, but his attitude was different from the uninhibited enthusiasm of the villagers. It was not supercilious; it carried no overtones of superior sophistication. He did not want to leave, yet there was a dignity to his interest that was striking in that noisy curiosity.

Every time we were alone together, his attitude reflected what it had been that day when his eyes, meeting mine, seemed to apologize for invading my privacy. Zaho was one of the few people who never asked me for anything. He had no more than others, was no less in need, yet he never took advantage of me. Indeed, he granted me an equality that I did not perceive until much later.

It was probably some inkling of this that led me to seek him out again. The meeting in his garden on the hillside between my house and Asarodzuha did not begin auspiciously. I was on the point of going when Zaho rose from the garden furrow and asked me to go with him to his house, his chin peremptorily indicating the crest of the hill where a clump of castor-oil trees lifted above the garden fence. Not knowing how to refuse and thankful for any diversion, I followed where he led. This was my first visit to his house, a place I returned to often in later months.

We entered a small clearing where two houses faced each other at a distance of a dozen yards. Both were relatively new, the thatch neatly trimmed at the eaves, the rough planks that formed the circular walls still showing the clean gashes of the axe. Zaho left me to enter the nearest house, returning almost immediately with a piece of wood, which he placed for me to sit on, settling himself in front of me on the ground. I gave him a cigarette and waited for him to speak, expecting him, now that we were alone, to return to the subject he had broached at Humeleveka. Instead, he remained silent, looking beyond my shoulder to the place where we had entered. Curiously, his lack of interest did not bother me. The clearing was extraordinarily peaceful, separate and self-contained, cut off from the world by the fence, the tall grass, and scattered casuarina seedlings. The tallest trees were the castor oils behind me, which Gahuku regarded as weeds and usually destroyed as soon as they appeared, caring nothing for their decorative qualities, for the large, red-veined palmate leaves, or for the spiny fruit. Their form was too open to provide a dense shade, but I welcomed the protection they gave. The sun was high, for it was not long past noon, the heat intense outside this frail shadow.

For the first time in many days I relaxed. The small clearing, the two silent houses placed like an echo of our own position, the dark stain of ashes where someone had sat beside a fire in the early morning, the bright leaves above my head, perfectly still but bent by the weight of light, the russet walls of grass, all these combined to produce an atmosphere entirely different from the long, bare village street where I was so exposed, so set apart from the noisy course of an alien life. Here I began to have some feeling for the quieter places that lay beneath the visible surface of the stream.

I fell easily into the pattern of all our subsequent exchanges. Zaho's quietness was not peculiar to his relationship with me. He lacked all the qualities identifiable with the Gahuku concept of strength. His fellow villagers were quite aware of his deficiencies and probably classed him as weak. He was not disliked or scorned (no Gahuku had to suffer the indignity of constant public ridicule), but lacking force or ambition, he was undistinguished, not precisely ignored, for he never asserted himself sufficiently to encounter opposition, but not consulted either, simply taken for granted. Perhaps his kind possessed a worth that was recognized by the others; they were never a cause of trouble and could be relied upon to do their duty in the areas of life suited to their temperament; but this reliability, this unspectacular virtue meant that the stronger, the more competitive did not have to account for them in their calculations. The attitude of Makis was typical. He never questioned my friendship with Zaho nor ever openly disparaged him, but whenever I mentioned him or repeated information he had given me, Makis' eyes seemed to dismiss it as inconsequential, listening politely yet implying I would be better served by cultivating people whose opinions carried more weight.

But it was the qualities that cost him the admiration of others that attracted me to Zaho. I was hardly even aware of him in a group, never went to sit beside him upon arriving at a gathering, and there were days, even weeks at a time when I never saw him, until, suddenly, I would think of him and try to find him. He provided me with a refuge from other people. I could sit with him at his garden house without having to endure the attention of the people who gathered around me at Susuroka. We talked easily, but when I wanted to be silent, he did not intrude nor seem to think it odd, and having him near helped me to relax and to sort out the ideas in my mind, as though his quiet, undemanding presence gave me a needed assurance that I could find the order underneath the vastly unfamiliar pattern of events. Even Ilato and Helazu took their cue from Zaho. After their first effusive greeting in his garden, there were no more demonstrations from them. They smiled and touched me lightly if they were present when I came to Zaho, then they left us alone, each occupied with her woman's work as they sat outside their respective houses.

On my first visit he told me that he was married to a Nagamidzuha woman of the same clan (Ozahadzuha) as Makis. Since the Gehamo had invited the Nagamidzuha back to their ridge, there had been many marriages between the two tribes, though, as usual, this did little to reduce traditional suspicions, but it explained why Zaho had a garden on Nagamidzuha land. Its site belonged to Ilato's subclan brothers and would eventually revert to them or their descendants, but meanwhile Ilato and her husband could make use of it. Women retained these residual rights in the resources of their patrilineal group, though it was only when they married close at hand that they were able to exercise them effectively.

From his own background, I passed to the events that he had broached to me at Humeleveka, skirting the edges of the design he had revealed to me then, but fully expecting him to take advantage of the direction of my questions to bring it up again. He did not do so, either at that time or at any of our subsequent meetings, and his silence was never reconcilable with the pressure he had tried to exert near Young-Whitforde's house. The more I knew him, the more his behavior on those two days seemed to be out of character. It was entirely unlike him to act so positively, with such unmistakeable overtones of intrigue. Perhaps the simplest explanation for his later reticence is that he accepted my disclaimer of any influence that might be helpful to the Gehamo's cause, for there was real substance to his complaint. The Gehamo were not happy with their official subordination to the Nagamidzuha, wanting the independent identity of their own luluai, though I do not believe that their hopes were centered on Goluwaizo. Zaho's reasons for backing him escape me, but the opposition of his own group is the essential core of Goluwaizo's tragedy.

I saw Goluwaizo again at Gorohadzuha, quite some time after settling down at Susuroka. Our meeting occurred in Zaho's company once more, at the house he maintained in the village situated on the lower ground to the west of Susuroka.

Zaho's presence provided me with the necessary reason to go there, but though it was usually the intention of finding him that took me back on subsequent occasions, the short walk from my house also had a deep attraction. Leaving Susuroka by the track that connected with the government road to Humeleveka, the path to Gorohadzuha turned abruptly through the kunai, winding down the ridge toward the stream. It was marvelously open, turning in unobstructed air, flanked by yellow crotolaria whose scent drifted above it like a thin, invisible veil. I never failed to stop for a moment at a point halfway down the descent, an exposed bend that seemed to catch whatever breezes coursed around the ridge, so that even in the early afternoon, when Susuroka had been crushed breathless in the heat, the grasses moved a little in the wind here. The village on the heights behind me was quite invisible. There was nothing but the outline of the ridge, a long, suspended curve cresting at the distant grove of Gohajaka. Fifty feet below, in the trough separating one ridge from another, the flat terraces were a darker green, a patchwork of garden fences enclosing rows of vines. The path entered this depression where a grove of pandanus palms cut the sun to an enclosed and silent shade. Here, the ground was always damp. Even at noon a distinct chill brushed the exposed portion of my body like some wayward strand of hair, its touch drawing my eyes apprehensively to the palms, which seemed to have halted on their stiltlike roots, engaged in debating whether or not to block the passage to the stream. The crossing was made on a moss-covered log, the path on the other side mounting almost immediately through trees that continued to a few yards below the next terrace—once more the dazzle of light, then, as one's feet touched level ground, the village street, longer and wider than Susuroka, older too, many of its flanking houses untidily tilted, their thatch disheveled and streaked with the charcoal signs of age.

The walk to Zaho's village house carried me the whole length of the street. Other people invariably joined me on the way, so that by the time I reached him there was no longer any possibility of having a private meeting.

Goluwaizo was among the crowd who gathered there at my first visit. Like Zaho on an earlier occasion at Susuroka, he was not effusive, yet there was a world of difference in their attitudes. His eyes seldom moved from my face, holding me as steadily as the straight line of his back. Surely, anyone who saw him would have described his expression as sullen, and would have been right, for he certainly lacked lightness and never showed a sign of the casual animation that moved so rapidly, with endless changes, over the faces of other Gahuku. He looked like a man who feels he is worthy of more than he has been given, though perhaps because of his age his face had not yet settled into lines of resentful disappointment; rather, he was still hopeful, still anticipating what his talents owed him. He seemed to dissociate himself from the other men, listening to them with only the periphery of his mind, not uninterested or openly scornful, but inwardly critical, reserving his right to dissent, looking for something that lay beyond the limited range of their vision. He did not give the impression that he had viewed what others failed to see, only that he knew it was there and felt himself better qualified to find it. The slight tic in his cheek could have been impatience, not only for those who wasted time on inconsequentials, but also with the conditions preventing him from gaining what he wanted, with constrictions he felt but could not understand. For there was uncertainty in Goluwaizo, not, however, the uncertainty that leads to vacillation, but something deeper, something far more costly to the personality. He was sure of his superiority, sure of his deserts but not sure of what they were or of how to set about attaining them. He was not immobilized by a multiplicity of choices and the difficulty of deciding among them; rather, he suspected there was only one choice that had not yet been revealed to him. If it was known, he would go to it by the most direct route. Meanwhile, he merely marked time, growing more impatient with an obtuseness that would not recognize his worth, with the conventions relegating him to a subordinate position.

Setting these words down now, I am analyzing him by hindsight. All the elements of my description were there, but it was not until much later, in the light of future events, that I was able to put them together. He was puzzling at the time, but my dominant impression was one of rather sullen arrogance containing a continuing possibility of violence. His attitude confirmed the antipathy I had felt for him at our first meeting at Humeleveka.

Weeks passed without any further contact with Goluwaizo. He came into my thoughts from time to time, principally in connection with the rivalry between Nagamidzuha and Gehamo, since I knew by then that the feelings expressed by Zaho also colored the attitudes of the Nagamidzuha. There were many personal ties between individual members of the two tribes, and overt relationships were entirely friendly, but the old suspicions were still strong. The Nagmidzuha knew the source of Gehamo dissatisfaction, and if they had been taxed with it, most of the people of Susuroka and Gohajaka would have agreed that the Gehamo had a valid complaint. But legitimacy was not very important in the endless competition for prestige. The Nagmidzuha were well aware that their position had been delicate until the arrival of the whites. They pointed out that they were numerically inferior to their neighbors, and virtually surrounded by enemies they had indeed faced the possibility of extinction. The white proscription of warfare had been a distinct advantage to them, an advantage crowned eventually by the favor Makis found with the newest power in the valley.

The Nagamidzuha had risen on this favor to a position incommensurate with their numbers and achievements in the brave days of fighting. When strangers, foreigners from the far side of the Asaro River who spoke a different language, stopped at Susuroka to consult with Makis before they walked the last few miles to the government station, it reflected credit on his people as a whole. His name had spread to areas where no member of his group had ever been, could not have gone only a short time ago, and through him Nagamidzuha's reputation stood high among the tribes. The fortunate conjunction of white power and his personal vision had placed his group several places ahead in the competition for prestige, and none of his followers was prepared to forego the intangible rewards of their ascendancy for anything as unimportant as the legitimacy of Gehamo's grounds for complaint. Indeed, they were prepared to use any means available to keep the status quo. These attitudes were known to me when I had my next meeting with Goluwaizo. They did not color my own part in what transpired, though they may have contributed to his attitude and, almost certainly, did affect the attitude of the villagers of Susuroka.

I was working in the house recording the activities of the day and anxious to finish before the sun went down, looking forward to a short break outside away from the stuffy disarray of my room. It was after four o'clock and the light beyond the narrow door had begun to fade, the heat departing with the advent of a mellowing glow. Though it was much too early to call for the lamp, the light inside the house had grown perceptibly dimmer, drawing my head closer to the pages on which I wrote, increasing the urgency that knotted my mind. After the long silence of the early afternoon came the sound of voices as people returned to the village from work. The closer chatter and laughter, interrupted by the importunate wails of infants, arose from the assembled vendors of sweet potatoes, corn, and pawpaw who waited patiently outside the house. They came regularly at this hour, so routinely that I did not raise my head when Hunehune appeared to tell me they were waiting. I was in no mood to be interrupted and so, knowing he enjoyed it, left the task to his discretion.

The buying was done inside the house, only a few feet from my table, those who had something to sell entering one at a time while Hunehune weighed their bilums and gave them what he thought the contents were worth in salt, beads, tobacco, or money. This afternoon I was not anticipating any trouble. The procedure was simple and the prices paid were generous. While I worked, I could hear Hunehune bantering with the women. This part of the transaction often amused me, but today the chatter and self-conscious giggles were irritating. I moved my legs impatiently at the table, keeping my head down and hoping that it would soon be over. Possibly fifteen minutes passed; the end of my work was in sight, and with it the opportunity to leave the oppressive atmosphere of the house. For a moment I did not realize that the tone of the exchanges had altered dramatically and only looked up when the unmistakable sound of anger pushed my own thoughts into the background. Startled, still not certain what had interrupted me, I looked at the two figures standing across the table from me.

Goluwaizo and Hunehune faced each other across a bilum filled with corn. Both were rigid, Hunehune's face unbelieving, recoiling from the anger flashing in Goluwaizo's eyes. In the background, other faces looked in through the doorway with white, astonished eyes, and even farther back conversations died in the village street as people turned with puzzled apprehension toward my house.

Lifted to my feet, I spoke to Hunehune in pidjin English, asking what was wrong. He turned his head as though he had difficulty in hearing me. Struggling for control, he told me Goluwaizo would not accept the price he had offered for the bag of corn at their feet. Relieved that this was all that exercised them, I was also unreasonably irritated by the pettiness of the squabble. Perhaps, too, something in Goluwaizo's behavior sparked a similar response in me; my dislike for him unconsciously hardened my attitude. Trying to keep my voice level, I asked Hunehune to weigh the corn again. When it was done, I asked him what he had offered and, turning to Goluwaizo, told him to accept it or go.

He faced me across the table, his chin arrogantly raised, his body stiff with defiance. The doorway behind him had filled with people pressing into the house. Namuri thrust his great bulk forward, shouldering Hutorno and Bihore aside, his rush of words questioning, warning, expostulating with Goluwaizo who turned toward him slowly, tightly controlled, moving only his shoulders and his head, his chin still high, his eyes adamant. I could not follow a word of what was said. Hunehune's voice was unnaturally high, almost breaking with righteous disbelief as his tongue ran through an explanation, stopping only when Namuri interposed a question or turned to silence the sudden explosions of hostility from the audience behind him. When Goluwaizo deigned to speak in his own defense, his voice was deep with scorn, wounding and inflaming with the cutting edge of insult, rising only to counter the angry fire of opposition. He was perfectly still, and his expression never changed, even when I fully expected that Namuri's hand would strike him. He was waiting, perhaps even hoping for the word or act that would touch off the pressure of his anger, provoking it with his eyes, challenging it with calculating words. My own hands tightened against the edges of the table. No one was really concerned with the cause of the argument, and suddenly I wanted nothing more to do with them. Momentarily, all my irritation centered on Goluwaizo, whose hard insolence released my anger. I cannot recall precisely what I said, but the words beat luxuriously in my throat, and the astonished silence, the eyes turning to stare with palpable shock rushed pleasurably to my mind, a flooding reward for all the times when I had disciplined myself to smile and to keep from showing my feelings.

I did not care that the people in the room were suddenly subdued, fearful because of my color. I was pleased that it was so, savoring the accident that gave me this power, wanting to press it. Goluwaizo turned to me. His hot eyes held me for a fraction of a second, then my hands relaxed, withdrawing from the table as he bent to retrieve his bag of corn. After he had gone, I sat down at the table, deliberately ignoring the silent crowd near the door, opening my notebook and picking up my pen, inwardly telling them to go. Unable to read the words on the page in front of me, I kept my head down, following Hunehune while he closed the trunks, listening unmoved to the cautious questions and answers in the crowd, thankful at last when Namuri's urgent whisper sent them away. Much later I left the house, crossed the street on a wary, following silence, and sat alone under the clump of bamboo. It was dark before I was ready to return. The small brushwood fires had died; the planks were fastened across the doors of the houses.

In the morning I was contrite, ashamed that the accumulation of petty irritations had overcome my self-control. My anger had been turned against myself as much as the villagers, expressing a growing doubt of my capacity to persevere with the plodding, wearing pace of working with them. But the villagers found nothing to criticize in my display of temper; rather, they seemed to interpret it to their own advantage. It had been directed at Goluwaizo, and they were not displeased by the public spectacle of his discomfort. On the contrary, they seemed to interpret my behavior as evidence of my identification with their own cause, as though I had helped them score a point in their rivalry with the Gehamo. The incident opened the flood gates of an animosity that was usually concealed under a thin veneer of cooperation and politeness. No one had a good word for Goluwaizo. Curling their lips, they dismissed him as an upstart, a person of no account who had grown too big for the reputation he deserved.

There was not much comfort in their approval. For one thing, I did not want to be identified with their cause, and for another, I was beginning to be sympathetically inclined toward Goluwaizo as I came to understand him. His behavior had been unjustified, possibly an expression of these very rivalries rather than the result of genuine disagreement with the price he had been offered for his corn. Indeed, the ostensible cause of the argument was incidental to much broader issues, merely a peg upon which he could hang the anger of thwarted ambitions. He had probably come to the house prepared for an argument, yet I had no wish to be the instrument of his discomfort. Those whom we have hurt often possess an advantage of which they are unaware, and after this incident I was more prepared to like Goluwaizo than at any previous time in our acquaintance, impelled toward him by shame for my own action, wanting to expiate it by a deliberate effort to understand him.

Yet we did not meet for some weeks. Though I wanted to indicate that I did not harbor any hostility for him, I did not know how to tell him. There were no guidelines in this unfamiliar situation, and reticence prevented me from taking the most direct course and seeking him out at Gehamo. He did not come to Susuroka, and, in time, the incident faded, only to be revived again in the circumstances of our next meeting.

Makis and I were walking to Uheto and already mounting the slopes a mile beyond the stream Galamuka when we learned that Goluwaizo had attacked Gameha with an axe. The word was passed from place to place along our route, shouted from Gehamo to Susuroka, traveling from there to Gohajaka, down to Namuri at work in his taro gardens and across to Mihore, whom we had passed ten minutes before. By the time his voice reached us there was hardly a person within several miles who did not know of the attack, and those who were involved directly through a relationship to Goluwaizo or Gameha had already gathered when we arrived at Gorohadzuha, sorted into opposing factions, filling the air with angry charges and heated imprecations.

The details of the quarrel echoed countless others. Goluwaizo had felled a pandanus palm that Gameha said belonged to her son, a young man presently absent from the village. Goluwaizo did not deny the charge but claimed that his action was justified, pointing out that one of Gameha's pigs had broken into his garden four times. He had warned her repeatedly, he said, and by rights she should have attempted to control the animal, perhaps removing it to a distance where Goluwaizo's garden would be safe from its depradations. Since she had ignored his warnings, he might have killed the pig; instead, he had taken the less costly course of teaching her responsibility by cutting down her palm. Gameha was an old and garrulous woman, and she had no liking for Goluwaizo. Ignoring his justification, she countered with the accusation that Goluwaizo had not yet repaid her son for his contribution to Goluwaizo's bride price. This calculated insult had so enraged him that he had struck at her with his axe, fortunately connecting with only the back of the blade. Evidently, they had been alone, but Gameha's wails and screams, her loud, self-righteous accusations had quickly gathered a crowd, resulting in the urgent call to Makis.

There was no doubt that the initial fault belonged to Gameha. Goluwaizo could have killed her pig, but he had retaliated in a manner that would cause less hardship, showing a worthy sense of restraint. However his virtue had been tarnished by his subsequent physical attack. Admittedly, there had been no serious injury, and, after all, Gameha was a woman and his provocation had been intense. In all likelihood nothing further would have happened, after the necessary discussion and time for tempers to cool, but it did not end this way.

The personalities of two protagonists contributed importantly to the outcome. Gameha was not only elderly, she had also achieved the highest status available to women: she was the mother of a Gehamo man. Members of the group to which she had contributed a male could not rightly regard her as a mere woman; she had demonstrated her worth, and if her own husband, had he been living, had wanted to put her aside, he would have met with criticism from other Gehamo men. Goluwaizo's action could not be properly excused even by invoking the paramount value of male solidarity. There is no doubt that the Gehamo men would have supported him, but not without reservations, not without indicating that he had acted too precipitately. Moreover, Gameha evidently felt she could count on this sympathy. Surely, she knew that admiration for the strong was tempered by caution, since it was they who were least amenable to persuasion, least careful for the equality of others. She impressed me, too, as a person of some determination, ready to insist upon her rights and to exploit the situation to her own advantage.

If this was so, she could also count on the support of her own people, the Nagamidzuha. She belonged to the clan of Makis, and by the time we arrived at the grove it was principally the Nagamidzuha who stood beside her, marshaled to support a sister and the absent sister's son. In different circumstances they might not have been so ready or open with their sympathy. Gameha was indeed old, virtually no longer a member of the tribe, incorporated as a Gehamo woman and protected by her status among her husband's people; she was surely not subject to the abuses that might have been encountered by a younger wife and also less in need of outside protection. But the rivalries of the two groups provided a reason, or an excuse, for the Nagamidzuha to take a more active part. In supporting Gameha they expressed their hostility to Goluwaizo and the Gehamo.

Makis behaved impeccably. He did not care for Goluwaizo, and he also knew the Gehamo's dissatisfaction with his own leadership, yet he seemed to be eminently fair, moderate in his whole approach, counseling an end to the matter, recognizing Goluwaizo's right to protest the devastation caused by Gameha's pig, as well as her right to object to her subsequent treatment. He did not condone Goluwaizo's resorting to physical force, but he also suggested that Gameha should have accepted her initial lesson in responsibility. If her reaction was not sufficient justification, at least it excused or reduced the seriousness of the attack upon her person. In any case, no harm had been done. It was proper to forget about it; the scores were even.

But for once I was hardly aware of Makis, looking beyond him to where Goluwaizo stood with some of the Gehamo ranged behind him. It was the first time I had seen him since the argument in my house, and except for the different setting—the thirty feet of dusty ground, the background of tilted houses, and the thin screen of trees—nothing seemed to have changed. He was as straight now as when he had faced Namuri, his features set in lines of scornful determination, his eyes denying anyone the right to judge him. Though he listened to the reasoned arguments of Makis, he seemed to be totally unmoved by them, rejecting their gentle criticism, standing firmly on the certainty that what he had done had been right. He did not care if others were prepared to counsel compromise, weighing one fault against an-

other, and, for the sake of peace, persuading that the injuries balanced
Such fine distinctions did not concern him. Gameha had provoked him
twice, excuse enough for his reaction even if the consequences had
proved to be more serious than the provocation warranted.

Had it been anyone other than Goluwaizo, nothing further would
probably have been heard of the incident. No one later questioned the
equity of Makis' counsel, but also, there was no one who attempted to
dissuade Gameha when she refused to be satisfied and carried her
complaint to the District Office at Humeleveka. She received no overt
encouragement from the Nagamidzuha. However, the puzzle lay in
the Gehamo's failure to persuade her to accept the objective consensus that Makis enunciated in the grove. Makis had a personal reason
for pressuring litigants to accept the decisions that grew out of the traditional form of debate: too frequent recourse to the alien authority at
Humeleveka cast doubt upon his qualities of leadership. But others
were generally no less anxious to avoid the white man's interference.
All too frequently, the magistrate's court at Humeleveka was used only
by opportunists who hoped to obtain a reversal of decisions that had
been reached in the villages. Indeed, the existence of this alien, superior
tribunal served more often to undermine the traditional basis of law
and order than to promote the ends of justice. Those who had recourse
to it were often not seeking equity as much as a decision favorable to
them, regardless of the merits of their case.

If Gameha refused to accept the counsels of reason that seemed to
express the objective and collective opinion of those who heard her
complaint in the grove, then there was no one who could prevent her
from carrying her appeal to Humeleveka, for no one commanded any
instruments to enforce the decisions reached in the give and take of
the debates. The authority of such decisions rested on the fact that they
expressed consensus; their sanctions were intrinsic to the system of
personal relationships in which the litigants were placed. At most, pressure could be brought to bear upon persons who were not disposed
to listen to reason. They could be reminded of obligations transcending the passions aroused by their present sense of injury, but there
was no explicitly coercive power to enforce what they refused to
accept.

Even now Goluwaizo dissociated himself from the debate, refusing
to acknowledge any fault, standing on his own internal sense of what
was due to him. He was impelled to impose himself on others, court-

ing opposition as proof of his superiority, ascribing each failure to the inadequacy of his fellows, to the clouded vision holding them to a too cautious past. His whole demeanor was critical, impatient of the niceties of reason and debate, questioning the grounds that required him to recognize others as his equals. Remembering my own blind reaction when I had faced him in anger, I could understand why no one, not even the Gehamo, seriously countered Gameha's determination to carry her case to Humeleveka. Her right to do so, or rather, their technical inability to prevent her, absolved them of responsibility, and, indirectly, provided the means of teaching Goluwaizo a needed lesson.

The meeting closed inconclusively, with Makis counseling an end to the incident and Gameha garrulously reiterating her sense of injury. Two days later, a member of the native police arrived at Susuroka with orders for Makis to report to the District Office with Goluwaizo on the following morning. Gameha had been as good as her word and taken her case to Humeleveka.

I set out with Makis for Humeleveka shortly after breakfast; Goluwaizo and half a dozen Gehamo men were waiting in the street. All of them except the accused greeted me cordially. It was the first time Goluwaizo had appeared at Susuroka since the afternoon he had left my room, the first time we had been face to face since then, for in the grove of Gehamo he had not looked at me. He was standing apart from the other men, leaning against the roof of Guma'e's house. His arm rested negligently along the thatch, yet, even so, there was nothing relaxed in his stance. Bending down to touch my hands to the shoulders of the Gehamo visitors, I realized that when my rounds were completed I would be separated from him by only a few feet, compelled to look at him to give some sign of recognition. Perhaps it would have been simplest to be direct, to have stepped across to him and offered my hand, but shyness constrained and confused me, and I had no plan when the inevitable moment arrived. I looked uncertainly toward him, able only to muster his name as a sign of recognition, hoping that its syllables would substitute for the more intimate and demonstrative gestures bestowed on the men who were with him. His lips moved as he replied briefly with my own name, but there was no invitation to come closer. I turned away, more aware of him in my discomfort than if he had smiled and offered me his hand, painfully reminded of my part in the argument over his corn, and liking him a little less because his attitude would not allow me to forget it.

This discomfort remained with me throughout the journey to Humeleveka. Makis led our group; he was dressed carefully because of his official role, his forehead banded with shell, his hair graced with fringed and nodding plumes, the brass badge of his office centered importantly in his decorations. Four of the Gehamo men walked behind him, then I, followed by two Gehamo with Goulwaizo in the rear. Makis and the Gehamo talked easily, but the silent presence of Goluwaizo was too much in my mind for me to have any interest in what they said. Normally, I enjoyed the hour or so the journey to Humeleveka occupied. Leaving Susuroka, the path, barely wide enough for a jeep, marched irregularly through an avenue of kunai. The road was less enjoyable later in the day when the tall grass turned it into an airless tunnel, but in the early morning it contrasted pleasantly with the village I had left behind. Usually, it was quite deserted. There were no gardens between here and the government road a mile and a half ahead, and few people came this way to Susuroka, preferring the shorter route through Asarodzuha. The grasses were diamond bright, washed clean by the mists that had left a largesse of irridescent drops. The freshness of the hour, the silence, the feeling of crystal space revived the enthusiasm with which my eyes had first beheld the valley, an elation often forgotten in the stress of closer contact with its life, but sharper by contrast when it returned, lightening my step, yard by yard increasing my pleasurable anticipation of the next stage of the journey.

My sense of drama always urged me to halt at the place where the track joined the government road. Perhaps no one else would have found it remarkable, for it was superficially a very ordinary junction with almost nothing to mark its existence to a stranger. The avenue of grasses thinned a little as they met the south bank of the government road, a wide thoroughfare that had been cut from the soil by men, mostly prisoners from the station compounds, wielding pointed sticks and shovels under the relaxed eyes of a native policeman. Standing at the top of the bank, the road ran east and west for miles. In the west it diminished in a long, straight perspective, the converging avenues of grass brightened by the curiously artificial formality of variegated croton, the mountains beyond the Asaro a wall of peacock blues and greens. To the east it turned round the hot, red face of a cliff, reappearing at a higher elevation, a white line bordered with clumps of bamboo, dropping steeply, dangerously, to the narrow bridge thrown precariously across a stream, mounting again in hair-pin bends until it gained the windy, open heights of Humeleveka. Very occasionally, a jeep went by, lurching on the uneven surface of the roadbed, followed by the curious eyes of the dark figures walking prudently close to the sides. Anyone with local knowledge could tell approximately from where they came, the style of headdress, the cut of bark-cloth vees, the width of a plaited belt, the drape of a bilum telling of homes in the valley— Kabidzuha, Kotuni, Uheto, more than a score of other names attached to the groves of casuarinas on every ridge, villages farther away on the slopes of the western mountains, Asaro, Heuve, and Gururumba; homesteads in valleys beyond the ranges, Chimbu and Tchuave; places to the east and south, Seuve and Bena-Bena, even distant Henganofi, their names a roll call of a multitude of peoples, each somewhat different from the other, separated by language, linked by friendship, opposed by enmity, differentiated by custom, but brought together on this highway whose existence could be measured in less than a decade of years. Standing at the place where the track from Susuroka met the road, my heart always beat a little faster before I took the three steps down the bank to join this stream of people. The syllables of the alien names sang inside me, and when the puzzled questions came, I answered briefly with the words for my own home, Susuroka and Nagamidzuha, or told them I belonged to Makis, watched the quick flash of recognition in their eyes and felt that I had found a place where I belonged.

But on this morning the presence of Goluwaizo completely changed my feeling for the road. My constraint at meeting him again checked my anticipation as I followed Makis down the bank. I did not look at him, yet I was aware of Goluwaizo's firm tread, able to distinguish the cushioned pressure of his bare feet from the other men, his own curious vibration registering a mental image of his erect carriage. His somber face betrayed not even a hint of interest, much less concern, when Makis responded casually to questions that we were on our way to court. His silent but pervading presence still pricked my mind with discomfort, yet the intuitive dislike was qualified by an unexplainable attraction, by a need to penetrate the arrogant, self-contained façade. The tension of this feeling—rejection tempered with sympathy and incipient understanding—walked with me all the way to Humeleveka, fending off the pleasures the road normally provided.

The court house at Humeleveka was simply the old District Office, which stood to one side of the disused air strip. It was a thatched, rectangular structure entered by a short flight of wooden steps. A pattern of angular flower beds outlined with white-washed stones led up to the door, a dispiriting combination of opposites, of frontier discipline and the aesthetics of Sunday gardening in the crowded, asphalt-bounded terraces of a distant homeland. These rectilinear borders, the clipped edgings of variegated plants, the rank cosmos and the impressed crotons, the imposed and cautious tidiness, spoke to me with the sad accent of decayed gentility, of houses that watched each other across macadamized streets, their life veiled behind lace curtains, its past and its hopes tied to the florid, faded patterns in threadbare carpets and the photographs in oak frames ranged precisely on flowered walls. They were sharply, incongruously at variance with the open sweep of green in front of them, with the spired trees whose thin needles murmured softly, invisibly vibrating to the movement of light and air.

Leaving Makis, I walked down the formal path to speak to Young-Whitforde, wanting his permission to be present at Goluwaizo's trial. On the way I passed Gameha and a second group of Gehamo men who had arrived ahead of our party and stopped briefly to speak to them, touching hands to shoulders and thighs, receiving an especially effusive welcome from Gameha whose wrinkled old face and bright, coal-black eyes met me without a hint of embarrassment or coyness. She knew that her age and her garrulous determination would meet with an amused tolerance helpful to her cause.

Several cases came up before our own was called by the court interpreter. Makis entered from the bright, green light of the airstrip, composed, assured as he halted in the center of the room, faced Young-Whitforde behind his desk, and brought his hand to his forehead in a smart salute. Young-Whitforde leaned back easily in his chair, listening while Makis explained that the case he had been asked to hear was not a "big trouble." He ran rapidly through the events, minimizing their importance, implying that the matter should have been dropped after Gameha had aired her grievance in the grove at Gehamo. He wanted to give the impression that it was only Gameha's obstinacy which had brought them to Humeleveka, hoping to forestall any criticism of his own authority, yet, it was also true that Goluwaizo had been provoked, and his assault had caused less physical damage than many men inflicted on their wives. Makis was justified in pleading that the case should be dismissed, handed back to the villagers for settlement according to their own custom.

When Makis finished, Young-Whitforde called for the litigants. Gameha entered first—bent, wizened, and voluble, extending her hand in the squeezing gestures of appreciation, her tongue unable to keep pace with the rush of expressive, highly descriptive endearments. Suddenly, she reminded me of Gihigute. There was the same shrewdness in her lively eyes, the same evident delight in creating an effect, a willingness to play humorously on her own infirmities, calculating the effect of her exaggeration, deliberately working for the tolerant, involuntary smiles that would gain her the sympathy she wanted. Goluwaizo had found a formidable adversary. She was shrewd enough to know that the dislike she harbored for him stood a better chance of satisfaction here than in the village, that in this room she possessed two enviable advantages: her age and her sex, and from the moment she entered the court she played them for all they were worth.

Separated from her by the width of the room, Goluwaizo made no attempt to counter her effect, even rejecting the sympathy to which he was entitled. He stood squarely on the rightness of his action, impervious to the possibility that it could have had more serious results. He probably was aware that Gameha's behavior was a calculated part of her defense, but he made no effort to rebut it or to cast himself in a light that would be more profitable to his cause. As I looked at him, I knew what Young-Whiteforde must be feeling. His straight figure, the hard, recalcitrant set of his features did not inspire liking; rather, they seemed to expect, even to want a similar response, as though they would not be satisfied by anything less than opposition. But there was much more to him than appeared on first acquaintance. He did not seek, nor necessarily want affection; at least he did not want it if it had to be bought by deliberate efforts to ingratiate. He was utterly impatient with the subtler, sometimes tedious methods of eliciting support. Indeed, this was his flaw. Given the character of the society in which he lived, position depended not only upon a demonstrated proficiency in some admired pursuits, but also upon a sensitivity to the claims of others, upon the rare and difficult ability to give without conceding. This Goluwaizo could not do. He could see things only in the sharpest contrasts, in the simplest, most direct terms. He was blind to all the intermediate positions, blind to the infinite shades of compromise.

All this was suddenly apparent to me as the case proceeded. There was Gameha, lifting her shriveled breasts to seek sympathy, showing her ancient back, and graphically moaning in recollection of the pain caused by Goluwaizo's axe. There she was, everybody's mother, in-finitely excusable, pointing to the belly that had given birth to sons, demanding recognition for her pain, asking a favor for the milk her breasts had once held and all the while concerned for the impression she made, concealing her dislike and her vindictiveness under a cloak of self-abasement. Oh, how her eyes rolled, how her tongue tripped through the wrongs she had had to bear, how her knees quaked and her poor back ached from the loads she had carried! She had no one to support her now; alone, she was only concerned with protecting the interests of her son. Had he been here, she would not have had to suffer this treatment. Well, when you are old, no one cares about you. What can an old woman do to protect herself?

And there on the opposite side of the room was Goluwaizo, impas-sive, standing on his right to teach her a lesson. Whatever the provoca-tion, he should have shown more self-control. He surely does not care that he might have killed this woman (the audience forgot that he may have used the back of his axe deliberately). He has to be taught that there is a law and an order to which he must subscribe. He must be dissuaded from a possible repetition. Three months in jail and removal from the tul-tul's office ought to impress on him that any form of violence is proscribed.

On our way back to Susuroka with Goluwaizo left at Humeleveka, the men had little to say. Makis held to his view that Goluwaizo should not have been punished, but he shrugged with philosophical resignation when asked why Gameha had been allowed to take her case to court. If someone determined to go to the white man, who could stop him? There were no explicit sanctions that could be invoked against a person who refused to accept the consensus opinion of his peers, yet, various forms of pressure, such as withholding assistance could be applied to him. They had not been applied to Gameha. No one had seemed sufficiently interested to support Goluwaizo, but that night, someone did come to his aid. I had gone outside to sit with Makis for a while before having dinner. The evening was well advanced. Makis and Gama'e had forgotten me temporarily, turning to the small brushwood fire in which they were roasting their meal of sweet potatoes. All along the street in front of every house there were similar groups of people sitting near fires that had begun to lick the coming night with bright, orange tongues. Boys still ran outside my compound, but their calls had lost the strident quality of an earlier hour. Underneath them could be heard a gentle, intermittent murmur, the sound of voices settling down to the quiet interior of life. I was content with everything as it was, neither expecting nor demanding more than the moment offered. It was enough to sit there, talking if I chose to Makis and his wife but also aware that they were willing to accept my silence, that they were not concerned about my presence.

Suddenly, a piercing cry shattered the privacy of the street, a single voice that was quickly joined by another, climbing and descending the peaks of anguish, keening, laden with grief, protesting a blow that was too sharp to bear in silence. Heads lifted all along the street. Boys ran to the edge of the ridge behind the houses and voices called questions from fire to fire. Now, in the grove of Gorohadzuha, where it was already dark, other sounds broke in upon the abandoned wailing, sharp commands, deep barks of rejection, a rush of words pulsing with anger, expostulating, cautioning, opposing the insistent cries. Every head was turned, listening, eyes searching for the boys, barely discernible against the sky. Meals were forgotten; the whole village was alive with interest, the sounds of query and debate imposing on the distant altercation. Now and then the rhythm of the ululating cries broke on a tearing note, an outraged shriek that traveled across the mind like a fingernail on glass, ritual sorrow suddenly thrust aside by physical pain, but resuming once again on a deeper, richer note, the stylized grief holding a new protest. Makis rose quickly to his feet, calling to Namuri who was also standing at his fire, his legs, outlined in orange flame, tensed with indecision. The voices of the boys collided with excitement, scrambling the information they tried to send back from the edge of the ridge. Moving at last, Namuri shouted the street to silence, disappearing behind the houses where he was joined by Makis. Now the sounds of distant argument rose above the murmured speculation in the village, charge and countercharge, imprecations, words demanding reason, balancing on the thin edge of patience, contending with the throbbing cries that were gradually responsive to the pressure of persuasion, trailing off against the night, which had reached the ridge of Susuroka.

It was quite dark when Makis returned. Stirring the fire to life, he reported laconically that the outcry had been raised by Goluwaizo's wife and mother protesting Gameha's action, which left them alone, temporarily without support. His tone was quite objective, but listening to the disembodied voices at the other fires, I could detect a current of sympathy and criticism. No one openly blamed Gameha. Even if they recognized her fault, the feelings of Nagamidzuha were too divided to admit it. They were not particularly concerned for Goluwaizo, yet it could not be denied that Gameha had been vindictive, allowing her sense of injury, perhaps her personal grudge, to aggravate a situation that should have been permitted to cool.

The voices worried the issue back and forth, tiring of it gradually, drawn back to more immediate concerns by food burning in the brushwood fires. My own meal had been delayed, for Hunehune's voice had been among those reporting from the ridge above Gehamo. Yet something else kept me from returning to my house. The cries at Gorohadzuha had not ended on a note of acceptance; rather, the silence seemed a temporary lull, the kind of pause in which events move closer.

No one else shared my premonition, a feeling difficult to explain, lacking definite shape, yet so sharp that I was short with Makis when he offered me a piece of charred sweet potato raked from the fire. I tried to still the feeling, pulling my mind away from the insistent presence of the path that twisted down the hillside to Gehamo. For some unexplained reason, I could see it as clearly as though I stood above it, its familiar turns cast, however, in a light different from any of the times when I had walked along it, deeply shadowed by the grasses that seemed to invest the entire ridge with a pale, faintly phosphorescent glow. Deliberately rejecting the play of my imagination, I had begun to rise when without warning the street was torn apart again by cries that left their faint vibration on the valley.

I turned abruptly toward the last house in the street, aware that Makis just as suddenly stopped eating the sweet potato in his hand. It was quite dark now. The row of fires were small, red eyes whose light was insufficient to illuminate the figures grouped around them. The pointed roofs of the nearest houses were barely visible against the sky, but farther out, where the night shuddered with the cries, there was only darkness and the intimation of grasses blowing along the ridge. Yet I also knew that this void was filled with movement. Invisible figures were rising, leaving their unfinished meals, closing around the sounds, which were coming closer, approaching from the far end of a long tunnel.

Then the darkness lightened, ejecting a white wraith, a formless, flapping object like a wounded bird helplessly flailing to its own calls of distress. As its flight carried it closer to me, it increased in size, gradually took shape, became, at last, a ghostlike figure, human in outline but terribly emaciated, stark white, and lacking any hands or feet, the eyes mere sightless sockets, the mouth a moving hole from which the anguished sounds fled like bats from a cave. The apparition passed Gotome's house, gathering attendants from the fires, reached Bihore's house, staggered the last few paces, and fell to the ground a few feet from where I stood.

It was only then that I realized there were two figures, not one, an older woman, almost completely covered with a thick coating of white clay, and a younger one daubed and streaked about the face and shoulders with the same material. The older woman raised her skeletal arms toward me, her death's head face rocking to the cries that beat down the hubbub of voices around her. As soon as her wails began to falter, the younger caught them at their highest note, sustaining the sound and rhythm while her hands convulsively opened and closed on her knees. Completely at a loss, I looked to Makis for guidance. He was standing now, facing the two figures, waiting, evidently aware that they would stop their crying when they were ready. Minutes passed, then the cries died, their place taken by the sympathetic sounds of the assembled villagers. Makis began to speak, carefully, persuasively questioning, nodding at the choked answers, turning quickly to silence an interjection of opinion from the crowd. The women were Goluwaizo's wife and mother, come to protest Gameha's action and to ask my intervention. While he spoke, the old woman lifted her clay-smeared breasts, begging understanding and mercy for her motherhood, asking recognition for her helplessness, just as Gameha, earlier in the day, had tried to influence Young-Whiteforde. Goluwaizo's sentence left them without support, two women who would have to struggle along alone until he returned. Surely I could make the government see that his imprisonment was wrong.

Now the recent commotion at Gorohadzuha was explained. The two women, learning the verdict when they returned from a distant garden, had dressed themselves in mourning to show Gameha what she had done to them. Gameha was not contrite; rather, she held to her view that Goluwaizo deserved his sentence, and the men had wanted nothing further to do with the case. Perhaps the ritual display of grief confronted them with their own guilt, which, in turn, led them to try to silence it, reacting violently to the insistent exhibition of distress. Goluwaizo's mother turned her shoulder to indicate where their blows had fallen, repeating that she expected me to aid her.

The women had my complete sympathy. I discounted their exaggerated descriptions of their suffering, knowing they would not starve while Goluwaizo was in jail, though, to hear them tell it, this was an imminent possibility. But even though the consequences were negligible, Goluwaizo had been badly treated, not by Young-Whitforde, who had acted from entirely different considerations, but by his own people, who had tacitly welcomed the opportunity to put him in his place. Admittedly, I had been happy to act in the same way, gaining unreasonable satisfaction from the burst of anger his attitude had sparked in my house. But my distance from him enabled me to see him in a slightly different light, to place him more clearly against his background, judging him less ambiguously than his fellows. I had begun to see his difficulties in a way that could not be appreciated or, at least, articulated by the Gahuku. The difference was almost entirely one of training, stemming from a heritage of inquiry into the relationship of man to his society, a perspective that fastened upon the inner working of the individual, his needs for self-expression, and the limitations placed upon them by the nature of reality. Reality, too, so my training informed me, is only the possibilities that are recognized and transmitted within a given group from generation to generation, but these are the possibilities within which men are compelled to operate, and those who find them too constricting are bound to suffer.

For all the sympathy I felt for Goluwaizo, there was nothing to change his situation. I would not lend myself to any appeal, not because it was doomed to failure, but because I wanted to dissociate myself from any notion that I could influence the members of my own "tribe" at Humeleveka. Makis knew this already, and he explained it. Finally the two women left, passing the row of fires and disappearing in the darkness of the ridge as they took the path to Gorohadzuha.

In the following months, I often thought of Goluwaizo, comparing him with the other men. There was nothing obsessive in this exercise. It was simply that from time to time I measured what I knew of him against these other personalities, trying to place him in the continuum of discernable types. Because of the manner in which we had met, he came to mind most often when I was alone with Zaho. There was only one resemblance between them, a tendency to avoid debate. Yet even the quality of their silent participation was vastly different, relaxed and comfortable in Zaho, the expression of a gentle self-effacement that lacked the watchful hardness visible on Goluwaizo's face. Zaho was content with his relative obscurity, interested certainly in issues of a public nature, but willing to accept decisions that were made by others, not driven to taking an active part in forming them. Goluwaizo's posture at the sidelines spoke of some basic disaffection rather than a quiet acceptance. As a youngish man, married only fairly recently and not yet a father, he was not entitled by traditional conventions to express himself as freely as the older men. Yet his attitude was different from the younger people who were subject to the same restrictions. He chafed against these limitations, but his resentment also transcended them; they were simply a small and temporary part of the opposition with which he felt compelled to contend.

As with Zaho, so Goluwaizo shared a trait with Makis. Here, it was self-awareness. When I watched Makis in his public role I was often convinced that a part of his mind remained uninvolved, listening with some inner ear to the flow and rhythm of his periods, watching his gestures with some inner eye, waiting for some sensitive antenna to receive, decode, and transmit the signals received from his audience. Goluwaizo was aware of himself too, but his feeling lacked self-knowledge. It was a dark, emotional involvement, much simpler than anything associated with Makis, not externalized, merely intuitive, and therefore both more dangerous and more vulnerable. Makis was willing to contend with the individuality of others. He was sensitive to their claims, knowing that his reputation depended upon his ability to manage rather than to decide, aware that the lead he gave had to be couched in a form others were willing to accept. Goluwaizo lacked this subtlety. No less sure of what he deserved, he wanted it without the wearing necessity of coping with the recognition that others also demanded. He was impatient of the finer shades of opinion that Makis knew he had to manipulate, and in his more direct pursuit of his ambitions, Goluwaizo also lacked the histrionic abilities that seemed to go hand in hand with the recognition to which he aspired. He could not bring himself to play to those whom he needed, giving them what they expected. The frills of oratory and debate did not satisfy him; his worth should have been recognized without them.

Superficially, but only superficially, Goluwaizo seemed to share most with Gapiriha. Both were consumed by the impatience of the strong. Even their facial expressions were similar—lowering, tense, superior. Yet Goluwaizo had a quality that Gapiriha lacked. The latter was transparent, wearing his aggressiveness as casually, as openly as Zaho wore his gentler disposition. Gapiriha was essentially uncomplicated, a close approximation to the hard precipitate man of action, with which the Gahuku were quite familiar. Such men knew that they were valued even though they lacked the qualities necessary to gather and maintain a following. Indeed, they may have had no aspirations for generalized leadership, finding a sufficient reward in the more limited pursuits for which their talents suited them. They were admired, even if admiration stopped a little short of trust. They had earned a reputation, and they knew that others would listen to them when they spoke. Subtlety was not a part of their nature, and while their attitude often exacerbated a difficult situation, their reactions were also predictable, allowing others to anticipate the measures necessary to contain them.

Goluwaizo had a noticeable measure of the aggressiveness characterizing this type. He had their directness, their sensitivity to opposition, their impatience with arguments or with reasons other than their own, but to these qualities he also added a deep, almost pathological sense of dissatisfaction. It is true that some of the more obvious avenues in which these temperaments expressed themselves were closed to him, proscribed by the new masters of the valley, compelling him to focus his ambitions on positions where his personality was a liability rather than an asset. Yet, I am not convinced that he would have been any more content, or any more successful in the less restricted past. Unlike Gapiriha or others of his kind, it is doubtful if Goluwaizo would have found the rewards of being strong sufficient for his needs. If he lacked the objective self-knowledge of Makis, he was also more self-conscious than Gapiriha, less easily satisfied by a limited reputation.

Piece by piece, during the months of Goluwaizo's imprisonment, I began to put the elements of his character together. Gradually, it was Makis rather than Zaho or Gapiriha who, by contrast, seemed to reveal his flaws. Makis' talents were limited. His vision was not sufficient to chart an acceptable course through the times that had already overtaken his people, but this was not because of any personal weakness. He knew that his influence would soon wane. Perhaps this is what he saw and expressed in his own way, that day when I followed him through the grass and watched him shoot his arrows at the empty air; almost certainly, it accounted for my own presence in his village. But no one could hold him responsible for the future; indeed, less than a decade previously no one could have foreseen the rapidity with which the future would overtake the past. In his time, Makis had seen farther than his fellows, taking the step Susuro had made much later, when, in his more distant home, the boundaries of traditional expectations had been breached so casually. Makis' future eclipse could not be held against him; it subtracted nothing from his stature. It was not this that made me compare him with Goluwaizo. Basically, the two men were similar in their ambitions, both seeking influence, both wanting reputation, but Makis knew and accepted the limits of self-assertion. Goluwaizo felt them too, but lacking the ability to cope with them, he was driven further toward resentment.

My sympathy for Goluwaizo commenced on the day following our argument. It increased with subsequent events, with the altercation in the grove at Gorohadzuha, with his trial, and with his imprisonment. By the time he was released from jail, I could see where his difficulties lay and wanted to help him. It is perfectly possible, highly probable, that by this time my warm response was inextricably linked to my feelings of guilt, that without this, the few remaining weeks of our acquaintance would have been quite different.

I was coming back to Susuroka from Gorohadzuha, taking a recently discovered path, a narrow track that reached the crest of the ridge midway between the village and the government road. Coming this way on previous occasions, I had noticed a new garden whose fence abutted on the path. It had always been deserted, and on stopping to look at it above the canes I often wondered why it seemed to have been abandoned. The fence was relatively new and strongly constructed. The ground inside had been cleared some time ago, and a few tentative furrows had been etched through the soil. But now it was rapidly reverting to weeds, empty and curiously desolate, as though whoever had been engaged in its construction had been interrupted suddenly, had left and would not return.

Alone on this morning, at the point where the path followed the garden fence it occurred to me that it was not as I remembered or expected it. It was past midday, for I was hurrying home, anxious to reach the shade of my house. The path was steeper than the normal route to Gorohadzuha and also more confined. My legs and arms brushed the grasses on either side; their tassels almost met above my head, the air so dense with heat that I could hear my own labored breathing. But this was the only sound in the whole valley, so it was something else, some intuition, that drew my eyes across the garden fence.

Three figures were working in the usually deserted rectangle, a man and two women, kneeling, methodically wielding digging sticks, loosening the weeds, and arranging them in neat piles as they moved slowly across the slope. Downhill, in the far corner of the garden, a rough shelter had been made, a place to retire to when the sun was high. A small fire burned in front of this refuge, sending out a thin, colorless plume of smoke.

I stood for an indefinite time beside the fence watching the automatic movements of these figures, the hands that thrust the sticks into the soil, the backward movement of an arm as the weeds were cast aside, a rhythm almost hypnotic in its concentrated regularity. From the first I knew they were Goluwaizo, his wife, and mother and was held firmly to my place beside the fence by a sudden flood of feelings reaching back to the time when we had met under the casuarinas at Humeleveka. No one had told me that he had served his sentence, yet at that moment I knew I had been expecting his return, trying to anticipate the circumstances in which we would meet again, worrying about the resumption of an acquaintance containing so much that I regretted, holding so much that I wanted to forget. Now he was here again, on the other side of the fence, the curve of his naked back answering to the rhythm of his arms as he moved on his knees across the patch of ground. No one had seen me; it was still possible to continue on my way. Only a few feet separated me from the corner of the garden where the grasses closed around the path again, concealing it until it gained the ridge. I was tempted to go on, justifying the choice by questioning the basis for my feelings, arguing that I had allowed my own part in recent events to assume inordinate significance, that Goluwaizo probably had not given them a second thought, certainly did not attach any lasting importance to them. But I countered these assurances with the knowledge that it did not matter what Goluwaizo thought, that I owed it to myself to do what I had wanted to do on the morning when I had faced him as he leaned negligently against the roof of Guma'e's house.

I climbed the fence and dropped down into the garden, stumbling a little on the soft, uneven soil. The three figures were less than thirty yards ahead of me and I had walked perhaps half the distance to them before the older woman saw me and warned the others with a startled exclamation. They sat back on their heels, the movement of their arms arrested, the digging sticks pointed across their shoulders, their heads raised, looking into the sun behind my back. The old woman recognized me first, spoke my name, and raised her hand toward me in a squeezing greeting, perhaps remembering the night when she had come to Susuroka to ask my help. Goluwaizo rose as I bent to touch the hands and shoulders of the women. He took a pace backward, stepping out of the shallow furrow, brushing his hands against his cotton lap-lap. I could read nothing on his face. It was as still, as self-contained, as somber as I remembered it, but he no longer wore the badge of his former office round his neck, and this, more than anything else, brought home to me the collapse of his ambitions. Without thinking, I arranged my arms to receive and give the customary embrace, speaking his name as my hands moved down his back and thighs. When we separated, the two women were smiling broadly, looking up with eyes half-closed against the light, muttering the polite but uninhibited phrases of welcome. Later, it came to me that Goluwaizo had been surprised, momentarily taken aback when I met him this way instead of shaking hands. There had been no time to plan it, but I was glad that I had fallen automatically into the local greeting, for it disarmed him, paving the way for the closeness between us that developed later.

This renewal of acquaintanceship was strained, not, perhaps, for Goluwaizo, but certainly for me. We sat together in the furrow while the women returned to their work, now and then looking across their shoulders to grin and repeat their earlier greetings. I was more aware of the intensity of light and heat, more discomforted by it, because I did not know what to say to Goluwaizo. His characteristic taciturnity did not help me. We smoked our cigarettes, and I asked him about the garden where we sat, receiving brief, laconic answers to my questions. It was always difficult to draw him out. He never communicated all he felt, but this occasion was also strained by the fact that my questions were not remotely related to the things I wanted to say. Goluwaizo showed no signs of similar distress, and when I rose to leave he embraced me naturally, the ease of his gestures going far to relieve me of the weight he had placed on my mind.

Perhaps a week or more passed before we saw each other again. A plan was forming in my mind, sparked by our most recent meeting, sown on my return along the road to Susuroka. I am not even sure of any determination to speak to him about it so soon, but I persuaded him to accept my idea as though it had already been thought through. We met in my house, at midafternoon. He had not come with anything to sell, and perhaps this accounted for my sense of warmth at his appearance, taking it as a sign that he wanted to accept the kind of relationship I offered him. It was not easy to talk to him, and as I tried to hold back the silence, I suddenly made the suggestion that had been maturing in my mind.

At that time the European community was impressed by the economic possibilities of passion fruit as a cash crop. The fruit, which had been introduced some time ago, had proved so suited to the valley that it was almost naturalized in some of the villages. My own house and fences were already covered with vines grown from casually scattered seed that had received no care or attention. The prolific character of the vine had aroused the interest of a mainland firm of cordial and jam manufacturers whose best-known products were made from the fruit. Subsequent investigations led the firm to establish a pulping and freezing plant on the coast at Lae with the intention, ultimately, of building another near Goroka. A white planter had been appointed the firm's representative in the valley, and efforts were being made to encourage natives as well as Europeans to grow the fruit for sale. The crop did not promise the spectacular returns expected from coffee, but it had some advantages. Coffee did not mature for a number of years, passion fruit did so in a matter of months; coffee needed considerable care and skill in its cultivation, passion fruit almost none. It seemed eminently suited to native agriculture, for it could be grown in the gardens along with traditional subsistence crops, and the price promised for the product offered a modest but reasonable cash income in return for a minimum of extra work.

I suggested to Goluwaizo that he ought to take advantage of this new opportunity, setting aside some of his garden for the vines. He was interested but skeptical, wanting a host of answers that I could not give him. How much money would he earn? Figures, even if I could have provided them, meant nothing to him, but he gave me his own standards. Would it be enough to buy a jeep? Would the money fill the room in which we sat? As the interrogation went on, I found myself persuading and encouraging, trying to counter his uncertainties. I promised to take him to the planter who would buy the fruit from him, committing myself to obtaining seedlings for him and to seeing that he received advice in planting and training the vines. An odd irritation and frustration began to build inside me. I had been urged to suggest the enterprise because it might be one way, an easy way, through which he could recover some of the things he had lost. I had banked on the materialism that is such a marked characteristic of Gahuku and knew it was this that he found attractive, turning the gains over in his mind, trying to assess my general assurances in concrete terms. Yet he seemed too cautious, too uncertain. Goluwaizo knew what a bilum of sweet potatoes would bring if his wife carried it to the government station, and, like his fellow villagers, he was accustomed to selling his small surplus when he had need for modest sums of money. He was not satisfied with what he was able to obtain in this way. His sights were set much higher, but how could he be sure that my plan would give him more than he already had?

The project I suggested that afternoon occupied most of my spare time from then onward. Perhaps if I had known that everything was going to end so suddenly and so soon, it would not have had so much of my attention, or, on the other hand, I might have tried more strenuously to move it forward. I saw Goluwaizo several times each week. As promised, we went together to the planter who could help him most. We received a promise of interest and assistance, and Goluwaizo appeared to be enthusiastic. But his resolve seemed to fade as soon as I left him.

We met most frequently in the garden where I had come upon him after his release from prison. By now I had a personal stake in persuading him to accept the plan. This was the only occasion on which I attempted to interfere in the lives of any of the villagers, and, whatever my unconscious motives were, what I had planned might prove to be a means of self-fulfillment for Goluwaizo, compensating for the other things he wanted but seemed unlikely to gain. Now he was almost continually on my mind, so that I was frequently moved to leave my work and to set out for his garden. We sat for hours at a time, discussing what he ought to do. His two women had become so used to me that on my appearance they merely lifted their heads and smilingly said my name, continuing their work without interruption. Goluwaizo always rose from his knees, waiting stiffly for me to reach him. His greeting was never effusive. He never again embraced me, yet in his own self-contained way he seemed to have made up his mind that he needed me.

I sat beside him and observed the progress of his work. Down the hillside, the women wielded their sticks in silence. The rough shelter in the corner of the garden was like a frail, blue mouth, open and gasping in the heat. Behind the fence, nothing was visible except the motionless grass and the dome of sky covered with opaque clouds. The light bent my head, drawing me into the thin column of shade under my hat, and, within this tiny, private world, I listened to Goluwaizo.

On these days I placed my fingers on the raw wounds of uncertainty that lay beneath his surface of indifference. My general perception of his character remained essentially the same, but the details became more precise. Whatever the reason for his inhibition, Goluwaizo could not conduct himself with the open transparency of other Gahuku, and his fellows could sense the dissatisfied uncertainty that is now my strongest memory of him.

In these hours spent beside him in the garden, I fought with his doubts and his ambitions. Little by little I realized that what he needed most was my support, my reassurance of success. He could vaguely see the ends I had in mind, as he could see also what they would mean to him, but his doubts demanded continual justification. I cajoled and argued, going to his garden again and again to discuss the area we would give to the vines, and the following day he would have reduced its size, always ready with excuses he expected me to counter. I became fully committed to him, neglecting other things to give him the support on which he had come to depend. What he did became immensely important to me, so that if he failed it would reflect upon my own adequacy.

But I never saw the outcome of my effort. Even before we had planted the vines, I was compelled to leave Susuroka, and Goluwaizo became an unfulfilled relationship in my life. Of course I saw him again in a very different setting, under the blue shadows of an arbor built at the edge of a spur projecting over the high valley, where Gohajaka was only a blur of trees in the middle distance, and Goluwaizo's garden no more than a memory among the grasses. He sat beside me often in the long afternoons of my convalescence, but now I did not have the will to try to breach his silence or to share his doubts. Yet even if my mind was far beyond him, I knew he was there, silent beside me in the swimming light and air, and in the end he gave me more comfort than I had given him.

CONCLUSION

▲▲▲▲▲

It is difficult to write about my last weeks in the valley and the day of my departure, when I stood at the edge of the green airstrip waiting for the plane that would take me away. This record has been unequivocally subjective. I have hoped to convey something of the quality of Gahuku life—its color, its movement, the great occasions and the everyday events, even its smells, the personalities of its participants, the motives for their actions, and the landscape that formed their setting—as it appeared through my own eyes, filtered through my own background, my likes and dislikes, qualified by my own strengths and weaknesses. These are the two dimensions that were emphasized deliberately. I believe that my professional training fosters an objectivity that has prevented me from making egregious errors in characterizing the Gahuku, and it has also helped me to see myself, to appraise my own motives more clearly. Yet this is not what I would write if my motivation had been solely the canons of professional scholarship, any more than it is all I would tell if it had been my purpose to reveal myself entirely. I have tried to steer a middle course between these two extremes.

But the middle course becomes more difficult to maintain toward the end, for my sudden illness was a major personal crisis, long in the making, which dominated every day until I watched the high, green valley disappear below its covering of clouds. Reticence lets me do no more than try to recapture the essential quality of those last weeks.

For days after my ulcer necessitated my removal from the village I lay in bed, hardly aware of the passage of time, opening my eyes only when it was necessary to respond to routine medical treatment. Outside the open window the valley passed from day to night, from the torpor of afternoon to the caressing chill of early morning, its changes leaving hardly a trace on my mind. Even thought was too much effort. I was totally unmoved by the seriousness of my condition, as though the body which I submitted regularly for examination belonged to someone else.

But I was not completely inactive. The shock of the illness forced me to pause; it was like a hand held up in warning, a command to halt. Obeying the directive, I stepped out of time, removing myself from the onward movement of the cumulative actions of the past. The intuitive self recognized that this might be the last opportunity to discover who I was or ought to be, the last chance to change direction or to choose deliberately to return to the same route, and while I lay in the suspended present the dialogue commenced, the elements of my nature debating and reviewing their respective claims to recognition. This is what I listened to behind my closed eyes, standing aside like an impersonal adjudicator and delaying the decision until all the arguments were in.

The world outside this private center impinged on me in the person of the men of Susuroka who came to visit me. I was unmoved by their solicitude, resenting their intrusion on the interior debate that called for my undivided attention. A week or ten days later Hunehune came in from Susuroka to take care of me. The arrangement had been made at his suggestion, without consulting my wishes, and his voice, waking me on the morning after his arrival, surprised me into thinking I was back in my house in the village. He was standing beside the bed with his chipped enamel basin, a towel, and a piece of soap, waiting to wash me, awakening needs I had almost forgotten. My heart opened with a sudden flood of gratitude, and all that day I waited impatiently for Makis or someone else to appear at my door, consumed by the necessity to expiate my previous neglect, afraid I would never be able to tell them what I felt.

Soon I was strong enough to be up for several hours each day, to sit in the garden house some earlier medical assistant had built on the very edge of the spur above the valley. It was no more than an open rectangle supporting a thatched roof containing two hard benches and a table, but it commanded an unsurpassed view toward the west, and its atmosphere of air, of light, of height, and of isolation perfectly matched the mood of my convalescence. Usually I took a book with me, but it lay unopened on the table while I sat with my back to the house, looking across the countryside where I had walked so recently. Now that I had to leave it, it had become immensely important to establish, once and for all, its personal meaning, so that whatever happened, whatever came of my unfinished debate, I would know its contribution to the addition of events that formed my life.

Thirty feet below the edge of the spur a single round house clung precariously to a narrow ledge that had been cleared of its covering of grass. In the morning the tiny patch of land was usually deserted, the roof dark with moisture, the surrounding grasses shadowed, the earth still chilled as when I had risen early in the village, the scents of growing things still sleeping under the pervading dampness. But every day at noon the owner of the house came to the clearing from the native hospital, where he was learning the minor skills necessary to qualify as a "doctor boy," a native medical assistant. Learning to expect him, I managed to discover him long before he reached the place below me, watching him run down the path traversing the face of the cliff, his head down, his brown body disappearing now and then as the contours of the path carried him out of my range of sight. Two strides carried him over the clearing and through the low door of the house, which faced away from me, across the valley. Exchanging his neat, hospital lap-lap for a piece of faded red cloth, he was soon outside again, where for the next hour I was privy to almost everything he did, watching him dart into the grass where he kept a few scrawny chickens in a bamboo pen, observing him on his knees in the small garden below the ledge, or smoking, his head turned to the valley below. A hundred small details of his life were shown to me, all of them acted out with unusual speed, as though the activity of a whole day had to be condensed into the single hour which he had from his hospital work. I never learned his name or spoke to him, and since I always viewed him from above, foreshortened by height, I doubt if I would have recognized him face to face, yet I felt that I knew him intimately, and as I lay awake at night his house and his person provided me with a strange comfort, a peace that was often my last conscious thought.

Gradually, everything around me appeared with extraordinary clarity, a quality I had noticed on seeing the valley for the first time, but heightened now, intensified to the point of pain by the imminence of my departure. Superficially, it was the view I had seen from Humeleveka almost two years before, a vast bowl, open to the changing sky, walled by mountains, folded into ridges where the spired groves closed above the clustered houses, laced with white streams that filled the air with the sound of their descent, veined by narrow tracks, and traversed by a few roads which carried the infrequent traffic of a new people. But now I had climbed the mountains, reaching their summit in the first light of morning, and turning to the east, toward Humeleveka, I had searched among the thousands tiny groves for the one which was known to me best. Now I had walked these tracks when the damp grasses soaked my clothes and the garden fences were etched with a tender, golden light. Following the sound of voices, I had stumbled down the folded ridges in the breathless light of afternoon. I had heard the cries of flutes beating like invisible wings against a blue sky, winding their magic thread along the paths of evening. In the torrid hours when the sun had drained the world of color, I had found the green and shadowed stillness bordering the streams, had felt the breath of moving water under a vault of leaves. I knew the sound a pig makes against a wooden door, asking for release. At night, dark figures had ringed the floor around me, faces had been turned toward me in the hissing, artificial light. I had felt the quick flash of understanding almost as often as the ache of strangeness.

Sitting in the blue shadow of the thatch, I watched the progress of the day across the valley. When the smoking veils of heat lifted, air and color returned like a promise, harbingers of the last, magic, golden hours when the circle of time closed on sounds that were a subtle variation of those that had begun the early morning. Coming to their compound along the government road, prisoners celebrated the end of work with the deeply thumping chant of strength, the stirring call to a way of life whose splendor and achievements had not been questioned until my own people had arrived. High and sweet, children's voices rose toward me from the stream where the water caught the colors of the sky and broke around the stones in an enameled foam of green, blue, and coppery gold. Bending under the products of their work, women trod the narrow tracks, stepping aside to let a man pass by, grunting a faint response to his greeting. Laughter rose from the fires in the hospital compound. A child cried for comfort, and the wind of night came down from the mountains, stirred the thin needles of the trees, traveled like a wave across the grasses, kissing them with the breath of darkness.

Day after day I steeped myself in my surroundings, anxious to fix each detail in my mind, to know how the light played on a curving leaf, to separate the colors in the shadows underneath a vine, to find the right word for the sound of distant water, for the smell of dust, for the monumental movement of the clouds, searching in these particulars for a larger meaning.

On the face of it, my personal characteristics were a questionable recommendation for the kind of fieldwork in which I had been engaged, work that seemed to ask for a considerable degree of self-reliance, to call for a more active person, for more practical skills and interests than I possessed, for a facility in establishing personal contacts quite beyond my usual ability. I accommodated easily enough to the physical conditions. But I was not completely at ease, always a little uncertain when approaching the people who were the subjects of my investigation. I could not force myself on them. I was unable to think of them simply as objects of clinical concern, as the repositories of needed information, and I could not press the ends of my work at the expense of my perception of their individuality.

Yet I have often doubted whether the traits opposed to those I possess are a more reliable measure of potential success in these situations. A nature more dependent on others for personal satisfaction, and more completely committed to a given scheme of values, could have found the isolation and the strangeness, the absence of accustomed avenues for self-expression more difficult to bear. After all, inwardness and a degree of disenchantment with one's own tradition, a touch of the romantic, are not necessarily a liability for anyone who contemplates this kind of life. They have their own reserves of strength, which may be those that are peculiarly suited to it. And for me, the warmth and depth of some of my relationships compensated amply for my personal difficulties, rewarding me more because there was so much more to transcend.

In these last few weeks, this feeling of gratitude dominated my inner debate. It was not my sole preoccupation: there were other matters requiring resolution that belonged to a much broader area of my life than the segment represented by the valley. Yet my approach to them was colored by the experience of the past two years, and my abiding feeling of indebtedness led me to decisions that might otherwise not have been made. I became consumed by a need to repay the debt, or at least to indicate that I acknowledged it. I wanted desperately to convey my recognition of the human worth of those with whom I had lived, to meet them finally in this naked condition, stripped of the extraneous clothing of color and tradition.

Day by day I waited for them to come to me, anxious when they did not appear, and elevated to a state of self-forgetfulness when I was in their presence. In the light and air of the garden house they sat beside me, Makis, Bihore, Zaho, Goluwaizo, and Namuri, others whom I had known, who had sat and slept in my room, who had called me to their fires and had seen that I did not leave their celebrations empty handed. In these last moments I wanted to embrace them, wishing them more than I or anyone could give. While the pale blue shadows deepened with the passage of the hours, I tried to keep them with me, talking of things that had happened since I left the village, reminding them of past events. The questions and replies had little to do with what I wanted to say. I could not ask them to share my state of mind in which every sense was heightened by my gradually returning strength and also by the intuition that I would not come this way again.

Each day passed with a bright perfection, a dazzling combination of light and air and moving clouds. In the mornings, I walked along the government road, cherishing everything within the landscape: the purple shades of cultivated earth, dark with dew, fading under the consuming sun; the green mounds of the vines and the lighter, emerald standards of the rows of corn testifying to human care, symbols of the larger promise men seek in everything they do. Each turn of the road opened a new vista, lifted me higher into the light like the heady ascensions of a swing, until at last, before I retraced my steps, I stood miraculously suspended at the apogee, commanding all the valley that I knew. In the middle distance, almost an illusion under the streaming shadows, was the ridge where I had lived, the grove of Gohajaka, already old, and closer to me, Susuroka, a scant two years beyond its founding, its trees searching the air above the sea of grass, no more than a faint hope penciled on the future. Looking out toward it, I felt the clutch of time, the sudden pull of the abyss, the surge of loss that sweeps across the mind in the moment when our lives change direction, and hurriedly, seeking to postpone the forward thrust, I turned once more to the road, and climbed the hillside to the garden house.

But, finally, I had to go, leaving in the last weeks of the year, when the familiar seasonal concerns and interests of Christmas magnified my feeling of final separation. I had returned once to Susuroka, a brief visit, remaining only long enough to collect my books and papers. It was the middle of the morning; the street had been quite empty, and inside the house I had hurried at my task, avoiding the signs of a life that had ended. My clothes and my work were all I took with me on my last journey to the airstrip, traveling down the road that many months ago had lifted me so lightly to the green plateau of Humeleveka. The house where I had stayed was closed, falling into disrepair under its shading casuarinas, for the pace of change that I had felt on that first morning had increased in the intervening period, and only one white official remained at Humeleveka; the others had moved to the new bungalows that dominated the already considerable township of Goroka.

The jeep set me down near a shed at the margin of the strip. It was almost eleven o'clock. Overhead, the vast array of clouds moved with slow precision, their blinding whiteness bruised with heat. Only the mountains rose above the grass, a stationary wall of blue and green, the rim of a larger world whose claims I thought I had to resist.

Several white acquaintances had come to say good-by to me, but while we talked I was waiting for the others, and my mind opened to receive them when they appeared—the villagers whom I had known best, Makis, Bihore, Hunehune, Namuri, Zaho, Goluwaizo, even Hasu and Hutorno, Guma'e, with Lusi at her hip, Toho and Gotome, their very names echoing with the rhythm of a life that had once seemed so alien, but that now fell from my tongue like the movement of my own heart. They were constrained in the presence of my white friends, withdrawing after they had greeted me, separated by the barriers of caste. I looked toward the plane, which had been refueling for the past half hour, hoping for the word to move toward its open door. I had nothing left to say to one of the groups beside me, and no words to tell the other what I wanted to say. The signal to go aboard released me. The formal, meaningless farewells were over quickly, and I turned to Makis for the last time. He met me as he had when I first set foot in his village, but now my own arms answered to the pressure of his body, accepting with it all of the past two years. I had not been able to meet his expectations, but I hoped he had found in me something else, that he felt it now in the pressure of my hands, the only gift I have, the only one I need to receive.

GLOSSARY

INDEX

GLOSSARY

▲▲▲▲▲

affines, relatives by marriage.

age mate, see aharu.

aharu, a Gahuku term of address used by age mates, people of approximately the same chronological age; *see also* pren.

bilum (pidjin English), an open-mesh, string bag. The native article is made from bark fibers.

bush kanaka (pidjin English), an unsophisticated native, someone out of touch and unfamiliar with the changes effected by contact with white culture.

cargo (pidjin English), material goods, particularly the material goods of white culture.

cargo boy (pidjin English), an unskilled laborer, one who also carries cargo for whites.

casuarina, a soft-wooded, quick-growing tree. The timber is used principally for firewood and in house construction. The majority of the trees are hand planted and are individually owned.

clan, a group of men and women who believe in their common descent from the same ancestor. Gahuku clans are *patrilineal*, that is, descent is traced through males, not females. Each clan is divided into a number of *subclans*, and a subclan contains a number of *patrilineages*. A patrilineage is a group of men and women who trace precise relationships to one another in the male line from a common, known ancestor. Members of the clan and subclan cannot trace such precise connections, but they believe they are related to one another.

crotolaria, a soft-wooded shrub with yellow flowers. It was introduced by Europeans and is used for firewood by the Gahuku.

croton, a shrub or foliage plant bearing brilliantly colored ornamental leaves.

dracaena, a shrub terminating in sword-shaped clusters of leaves. The shrub attains great age and is often used to mark the boundaries of gardens.

gene, the distinctive, long plaits worn by boys until their initiation.
grease man (pidjin English), a flatterer or sycophant.

hina, the Gahuku word for a feud.

idza nama, the greatest of Gahuku festivals. They are essentially competitive exchanges of wealth.

Kate, a vernacular used for proselytizing and teaching by Lutheran missionaries.
kunai, a tall grass, from four to six feet in height.

lap-lap (pidjin English), an introduced article of male clothing. It is a piece of cotton cloth that is wrapped around the body at the waist extending midway down the calf.
luluai (pidjin English), a headman who is appointed to the position by the white government. He acts as the official representative of his group.

nagisa, a type of arrow. The name means "anger."
nama, the sacred flutes of the Gahuku.
nuguro, the kinship term for "brother-in-law"

ozaha neta, a Gahuku fertility rite. The name may be freely translated as "the old men's object," possibly because the rite is usually performed no more than once in each generation, so that only older men are familiar with the ritual. Its aim is to promote the fertility of men and pigs and to give the clan strength to withstand the attacks of enemies.

pandanus, a large genus of tropical plants. The stems are slender and palmlike, often supported on immense prop roots, and the branches have a terminal crown of swordlike leaves, some of which furnish a useful fiber. The plant's seeds are edible.
pit-pit, a shrublike cane used by Gahuku to fence their gardens.
pren (pidjin English), friend. Also used as a term of address by age mates.

rova, warfare

taro, a domesticated plant with leaves similar to an arum lily. It has a tuberous, starchy, edible rootstock.

tul-tul (pidjin English), a government appointed official who acts as assistant and interpreter for a headman; *see also* luluai.

INDEX
▲▲▲▲▲

ABOUT THE AUTHOR

Kenneth E. Read was born in Sydney, Australia, and came to the United States in 1957. He is at present Professor and Chairman of the Department of Anthropology of the University of Washington, Seattle.

Before this, he was Senior Lecturer in Anthropology at the Australian School of Pacific Administration, Sydney, and Research Fellow of the School of Pacific Studies, the Australian National University, Canberra.

He was educated at the University of Sydney, where he received his M.A. in 1946, and at the University of London, England, where he received his Ph.D. in 1948.

An active contributor to anthropological literature, Professor Read has published a number of articles in technical and scholarly journals.